Handbook *for* Student Law *for* Higher Education Administrators

EDUCATION MANAGEMENT
Contexts, Constituents, + Communities

M. Christopher Brown II
GENERAL EDITOR

Vol. 6

PETER LANG
New York • Washington, D.C./Baltimore • Bern
Frankfurt • Berlin • Brussels • Vienna • Oxford

James Ottavio Castagnera

Handbook *for* Student Law *for* Higher Education Administrators

PETER LANG
New York • Washington, D.C./Baltimore • Bern
Frankfurt • Berlin • Brussels • Vienna • Oxford

Library of Congress Cataloging-in-Publication Data

Castagnera, James.
Handbook for student law for higher education administrators /
James Ottavio Castagnera.
p. cm. — (Education management: contexts, constituents, and communities; vol. 6)
Includes bibliographical references and index.
1. College students—Legal status, laws, etc.—United States.
2. Graduate students—Legal status, laws, etc.—United States.
3. Education, Higher—Law and legislation—United States
4. School management and organization—Law and legislation—
United States. I. Title.
KF4243.C37 344.73'079—dc22 2009035452
ISBN 978-1-4331-0742-9 (hardcover)
ISBN 978-1-4331-0741-2 (paperback)
ISSN 1947-6256

Bibliographic information published by **Die Deutsche Nationalbibliothek**.
Die Deutsche Nationalbibliothek lists this publication in the "Deutsche Nationalbibliografie"; detailed bibliographic data is available on the Internet at http://dnb.d-nb.de/.

Cover design by Claire Castagnera

The paper in this book meets the guidelines for permanence and durability of the Committee on Production Guidelines for Book Longevity of the Council of Library Resources.

29 Broadway, 18th floor, New York, NY 10006
www.peterlang.com

Printed in the United States of America

This book is dedicated to the author's wife and best friend of more than 40 years, Joanne Cain Castagnera.

CONTENTS

ACKNOWLEDGMENTS

Dr. Castagnera wishes to acknowledge the critical contributions of his daughter, Claire Castagnera, a creative writing student at Washington College, who did extensive editing of this book and designed the cover.

He also acknowledges Publisher Jeff Wendt of *The Greentree Gazette*, who has granted his permission to reprint a number of Dr. Castagnera's magazine articles in this volume.

INTRODUCTION

The Social and Legal Environment of Student Administration

Origins of the American System of Higher Education

Four distinct epochs or waves can be discerned in the history of higher education: In the 85 years between the Declaration of Independence and the Civil War, some 800 liberal arts colleges sprang up across the United States. A typical example is Franklin & Marshall College, which owes half its name to a modest amount of seed money donated by the great Benjamin Franklin in 1787. Another example is Case Western Reserve University, today a Research-One institution, which first saw the light of learning as Western Reserve Academy. "The undergraduate college took…the essential step necessary for a broad education for general citizenship….These institutions were of a size and scale that could be created by a group of private individuals—not requiring great fortunes or state support" (Cox 2000, p. 14).

The end of the Civil War until the turn of the last century was the era of the great land-grant institutions. This expansion of higher education led to the first shakeout. "By 1900, only 180 of those first 800 small colleges remained active; larger, subsidized state universities consumed market share by offering more educational services, subsidized prices, and often more pragmatic and career-oriented curricula" (Cox 2000, p. 14).

Around the turn of the last century, the third great wave broke upon the shores of higher learning. Wealthy industrialists, such as John D. Rockefeller (The University of Chicago), Andrew Carnegie (Carnegie Mellon University), Cornelius Vanderbilt (Vanderbilt University), and Leland Stanford (Stanford University) founded high-quality, private universities. The institutions were often world-class in their curricula, faculty, and architecture, importing many of these elements from their great European counterparts. Thus, with Chicago, "Cambridge inspired the architecture, while Berlin inspired the pedagogy and faculty structure" (Cox 2000, p. 14).

Fast forward yet another 50 years and we see the GI Bill and the postwar technology boom, fueled in part by the Cold War, driving the creation of the "megaversity." This term is commonly used to describe a variety of large institutions, all of which share at least the following characteristics: faculty numbering in the thousands and student bodies numbering in the tens of thousands; sprawling and/or multiple campuses containing a large number of undergraduate, graduate, and professional schools and colleges; and a large and cumbersome administrative bureaucracy overseeing these complex operations. (We have also seen the proliferation and maturation of the community college. However, this book, by and large, will focus principally upon four-year institutions, albeit some case citations will concern community colleges.)

American Higher Education Today

The fifth wave is breaking on global shores. "The age of the Internet and other new media forms is giving rise to a new wave of institution building, right before our eyes....Ours is an extraordinary moment in history" (Cox 2000, p. 17). What is it we may expect to observe and experience among the phenomena of this new era? Among the main indicia of this new wave are the following:

Some observers predict a shakeout of weaker institutions as the current expansion leads inevitably to a concomitant contraction. Others have noted the persistence of even the weakest among first-wave colleges, as the following article illustrates.

The Mice That Roar: Small, Sectarian Colleges Resist Efforts to Extinguish Them

By Jim Castagnera

The Greentree Gazette, May 2007

I first met Jim Noseworthy early in the present decade at a workshop on serving disabled students. The program was put on by the University of New Hampshire's extension division at a hotel outside Washington, D.C. Serendipity put the Doctor of Ministry, whose prominent proboscis fits his surname, at the same table as I. We lunched together and hit it off, and after that kept in sporadic contact.

In August 2003, after sharing a recent op-ed piece of mine with Jim, he wrote back to me, "I have left the United Methodist Board of Higher Education and Ministry and now serve as president of United Methodist-related Hiwassee College in Madisonville, Tennessee." His missive on Hiwassee College stationery continued, "I moved in February to a situation which is both challenging and delightful. I am glad to be back on campus and working with such marvelous individuals as we shape the future of this two-year college."

If the Southern Association of Colleges and Schools gets its way, Hiwassee College has no future.

SACS's Commission on Colleges is the accrediting body for higher education institutions in 11 southern states, including Tennessee. Senior Fellow Jon Fuller of the National Association of Colleges and Universities describes SACS as "the most rigid and bureaucratic of the six national accrediting organizations." He adds that SACS has a tough task, because, "The South has more fragile institutions as a percentage of its higher education stock than any other region of the country."

Absent the SACS imprimatur a college is cut off from federal financial aid funds. For a college like Hiwassee, whose fewer-than-500 rural students almost all rely on substantial financial aid, such a sanction is fatal. SACS, however, is finding that Hiwassee is hard to kill.

Hiwassee, which awards associate degrees, was first accredited by SACS in 1958. That accreditation was confirmed most recently in 2000. The Reaffirmation Committee noted that at the millennium Hiwassee had many "financial challenges." The committee's report cited deferred maintenance, projected-revenue shortfalls, and inter-fund borrowing among those "challenges." SACS required a follow-up report. When that document failed to meet the accreditor's criteria, Hiwassee was issued a warning and required to submit yet another 12-month status report. In December 2002, following review of this second report, SACS placed Hiwassee on probation. The beleaguered college submitted its third report in December 2003, Meanwhile, a so-called Special Committee conducted a site visit to the Monroe County campus.

The college's accreditation crisis came to a head on January 16, 2004, the date on a SACS letter which informed the Reverend Noseworthy and his staff, "With its upcoming review in December 2004, your institution will have exhausted its probationary status and its period of continued accreditation for good cause. At that time, the institution must be determined to be in compliance with all of the Principles of Accreditation or be removed from membership." Yet another Special Committee visited Hiwassee in mid-October 2004. The committee's report was damning. On December 4th Hiwassee defended itself at a Compliance Committee meeting, but the committee voted to remove accreditation. On February 24, 2005, an Appeals Committee affirmed academic capital punishment for Hiwassee.

However, reports of Hiwassee's demise proved premature. The college took its case to the federal courts. On March 22, 2005, Judge Thomas Vartan of the U.S. District Court for Eastern Tennessee issued a temporary restraining order, restoring Hiwassee's accreditation. "This is good news," Rev. Noseworthy modestly understated this early victory. The case then was transferred to the federal court for Northern Georgia, home to SACS headquarters.

On February 5, 2007, following extensive pre-trial discovery and a hearing, Senior District Judge Owen Forrester issued his ruling. In many aspects his honor's 18-page decision goes against Hiwassee. For example, he rejects the college's contention that "the entanglement between the (U.S.) Department of Education and SACS in its role as an accrediting agency under the Higher Education Act" makes SACS a "state actor" subject to the 14th Amendment's "due process" clause. On the other hand, Judge Forrester finds that SACS must be held to common-law principles of fair play.

Having so held, his honor goes on to conclude that a conflict of interest was created when Appeals Committee member Ann McNut suffered a family emergency and was replaced by Jimmy Goodson, a voting member of the Commission on Colleges. Since he had already voted to withdraw Hiwassee's accreditation, ruled Judge Forrester, "Mr. Goodson did have a conflict of interest and should not have served on the appeals panel."

Comments President Noseworthy, "We have prevailed on one of the several issues of our case." However, Judge Forrester found in favor of SACS on many another issue. More ominous is the district judge's observation that "it is significant to the court that Hiwassee has never front-on challenged the ultimate decision of SACS that Hiwassee failed to come into compliance...." This bit of dicta may prefigure the ultimate outcome of the case, which remains pending as this article is written. On March 16th, Jim Noseworthy wrote to me, "We are awaiting additional action by the judge in the case...." With characteristic aplomb, reminiscent of his 2003 letter, he added, "Hiwassee is a great place to be!"

Hiwassee College is not the only great little place under fire for financial instability. SACS has also been gunning for Edward Waters College in Jacksonville. In 2005 the historically black institution, like Hiwassee, won an injunction in federal court, staving off implementation of the accrediting agency's decision to withdraw recognition. News photos depicted some of the school's 900 students marching with signs that said, "EWC must survive!" Fuller of NAICU commented, "A new chapter is opened. It's going to require accreditors to question some of their procedures."

Elsewhere it's not accreditors but donors who are putting pressure on the Lilliputians of our industry to reform or perish. For instance recent reports out of Omaha, Nebraska, tell of Howard L. Hawks, a major donor to both Midland Lutheran College and nearby Dana College, who has advised the two tiny schools to merge duplicative academic and administrative functions or lose his support.

These developments beg the question, "Do such small-enrollment, under-endowed private colleges have a place in the highly competitive, globalized higher education arena?" I asked that question of NAICU's Jon Fuller. He explained that from Eastern Kentucky's Pikesville College to New Jersey's Bloomfield College, these small schools serve local communities "where people grow up with a limited sense of what's possible." In other words, absent the Bloomfields, Pikevilles, and Hiwassees, many of these minority and/or rural youngsters would never go to college.

Fuller adds that both federal and accreditation standards use financial stability as a place-holder for quality education, since the latter is difficult to measure. "The fed doesn't want to have to clean up if a college closes suddenly. What isn't considered is that many of these schools have been around 100 or 150 years, and I doubt they were ever any less fragile than they are today. Yet they always have a hard time meeting such standards."

I suggested to Fuller that the pluckiness of these colleges reminds me of the tiny nation in the Peter Sellers film, "The Mouse that Roared." He retorted, "They remind me of bumble bees. Measure the wingspan and the bumble bee shouldn't be able to fly. Since it does fly, there must be other factors we are failing to measure."

With regard to the Hiwassees of our world, Fuller cited "deep loyalty" from alumni and "faith communities," a willingness to sacrifice on the parts of administrators, faculty and even students, and—perhaps most significant where the likes of Jim Noseworthy and Hiwassee are concerned—"an ethic which says, attend to the needs of today and somehow tomorrow will take care of itself."

Concludes Fuller, "At a time when the Spellings Commission is concerned with degree completion and eight Asian and European nations boast higher percentages of college graduates than the U.S., it's hard to understand why anyone would want to mess with these colleges."

Source: The Greentree Gazette*, May 2007 (Reprinted with permission of* The Greentree Gazette: The Business Magazine for Higher Education.*)*

In June 2009, the U.S. Department of Education reported that 114 private, non-profit colleges had failed the department's financial-responsibility test at the close of fiscal 2008–09 (Blumenstyk). "Although not designed as such, failing the test can be an indicator that a college is in danger of not surviving" (Ibid.). When and if the shakeout is complete, higher education will not be populated exclusively by e-educators. Nor will the landscape of higher education boast only the largest and wealthiest brick-and-mortar institutions. Rather, as in the past, we should anticipate a mix of liberal arts colleges, land-grant universities, and wealthy private universities, including megaversities, coexisting in rationalized competition with the e-educators and other for-profit entrants of this 21st century wave of institution building.

A mature industry may be defined as "An industry that has passed both the emerging and the growth phases of industry growth. Earnings and sales grow slower in mature industries than in growth and emerging industries" (http://financial-dictionary.thefreedictionary.com/Mature+Industry).

American higher education is in the midst of a profound transformation. Some leaders in higher education contend that it is a mature industry, which must co-exist and compete in the global marketplace, while others argue that its primary role remains as ever a public responsibility to create good citizens.

For some, like Arthur Levine, president of Teacher's College at Columbia University, college and university education as we know it is a relic of the past, irrelevant to the economic developments and desires for individual career advancement in the global economy. The real business of the "mature industry" of higher education is to serve the marketplace of information economies. This, he claims, can best be done through on-line technology by the profit-making sector. Quaint campuses, classroom lectures, and a community of scholars are irrelevant to the business of education.

For others, higher education has a different purpose and an historical tradition that is tied to education for effective citizenship. In this view, higher education should have a central role to play in the health of our democracy, but has been deficient in rebuilding the civic life of the country. Our institutions of higher education were shaped in the era following WWII, which was not readily adaptable to meeting the need of transforming civic life. The structure, organization, administration, and academic culture of campuses embraced science and technology, emphasized a cult of objectivity and detachment, and elevated the role of the scientifically educated expert over ordinary citizens in public affairs. This ethos of professionalism and expertise that defined higher education's response to the national crisis of the Cold War now contributes to public disillusionment with institutions that represent and legitimize a system that no longer addresses the most pressing national needs. Ivy towers, inert knowledge, and credentialed students are irrelevant to the civic purpose of education (Saltmarsh).

Most colleges and universities have attempted to take a middle ground, reforming antiquated practices and encrusted procedures sufficiently to meet the more competitive market of the millennium, while retaining many vestiges of the venerable past, such as faculty tenure and academic freedom. Critics complain that reform for the most part has been thus far a case of too little, too late.

Colleges and universities provide a setting for the contemplative life. The word "school" is derived from the Greek *schole*, meaning leisure. Efficiency is not always prized on campus, and this spirit has translated to fiscal matters. Bowen (1980) captured the spendthrift philosophy of higher education in his "revenue theory of cost": "Each institution raises all the money it can" and "spends all it raises" (p. 20).

College costs have escalated for reasons rooted primarily in organizational culture and market forces. Institutions of higher education often have defined quality in terms of resources acquired rather than results achieved (Guskin,1994; Lovett, 2005). Colleges and universities have survived profligacy through monopolistic competition, achieving sufficient differentiation from other institutions by geographic location and programs (Bowen, 1980). But high technology, which supplies the capacity to deliver academic programs at a distance from the physical campus, is eroding the product differentiation so long enjoyed by traditional colleges and universities.

The pressure on institutions to control costs has likely never been greater. Tuition at four-year public institutions in the 2003–04 academic year increased at the highest rate in three decades, an average of 14 percent more than the prior year (Farelle, 2003). State appropriations to public colleges and universities fell 2.1 percent from the 2002–03 fiscal year to the 2003–04 fiscal year—the first decline in 11 years (Hebel, 2004). Colleges and universities, particularly private institutions, are only now recovering from endowment losses in 2002. The National Association of College and University Business Officers' study of endowment for that year showed that institutions of higher education lost six percent on their investments, marking the first time investments had declined for two consecutive years since 1974 (Lyons, 2003). In company with other employers, colleges and universities struggle with the escalating cost of health care for employees. Health insurance premiums rose 13.9 percent in 2003, the third consecutive year of double-digit increases (Basinger, 2003).

Institutions of higher education confront many barriers to cost control. Perhaps the most basic impediment is poor cost information. Progress toward improved costing for higher education was advanced in the 1970s by the work of the National Center for Higher Education Management Systems (NCHEMS), but the cost systems proposed by NCHEMS largely were abandoned in the affluence of the 1980s (Turk, 1992). Day (1993) noted "no general consensus on costing methodology in higher education" (p. 13). Even now internal management reports focus on salaries, travel, and research costs, and generally ignore such indirect costs as facilities and administration.

Higher education is also a labor-intensive endeavor, making gains in productivity more difficult and exposing institutions to the spiral of benefit costs. Moreover, consensus management continues to pervade academic administration and bring inefficiency to the decision-making process (Zemsky and Massy, 1990) (Adams).

Faced with these pressures, colleges and universities are:

1. Competing harder than ever for students, as well as grants and gifts;
2. Seeking to control and exploit intellectual property that, once upon a time, was left to faculty to promulgate as they saw fit;
3. Growing and expanding, often at the expense of competing institutions and for-profit providers of post-secondary education;
4. Streamlining operations where possible, such as by bringing Student Life divisions under the umbrellas of Academic Affairs; hiring more adjunct and non-tenure-track full-time faculty; offering accelerated degree programs, sometimes at the expense of traditional core requirements; and
5. Being all things to all potential students, such as by offering on-line courses, professional certifications, and remote-site alternative facilities.

Legal Implications

One significant implication of these many profound changes is that university legal staffs are growing. A 2006 survey by the National Association of College and University Attorneys (NACUA) disclosed not only that such staffs are getting bigger, but also that a major reason is an average of 33 open litigation files at any given moment in time per institution. The survey revealed that chief legal officers with budgets in excess of $2,000,000 earned on average $240,000 per year, while at schools with smaller legal-office budgets, the average hovered around $130,000. Small schools pay on average $105,000 per year (Selingo). In 1961, only about 65 schools had in-house legal counsel, and most of these employed but a single lawyer. Today, membership in NACUA totals more than 3,200. Some of the legal developments that help explain the perceived need for ever-more attorneys in higher education include civil rights and civil liberties issues with their genesis in the sixties and seventies, such as:

- "Attempts by colleges and universities, influenced by state political leaders, to suspend or expel students for protesting racial discrimination in higher education. The courts held that students are entitled to due process of law.
- "Questions involving the parameters of protest and the protection of unpopular speech and debate about social and political issues. Landmark rulings held that colleges should protect the content of student speech but that reasonable limitations on time, place, and manner of speech and protest—like restrictions that prevent the disruption of academic activities—are appropriate.
- "Cases revolving around whether students have the right to associate and form organizations that promulgate unpopular political and social topics. Some historic cases involved unsuccessful attempts by colleges to ban gay-rights organizations and political groups, like the Students for a Democratic Society, that were critical of 'Americanism.' Student religious groups also gained access to public campuses' facilities during this period.
- "The freedom of the campus press, redefining it in keeping with the fundamental protections of the First Amendment. Attempts by public colleges to withhold financial support for campus newspapers when their content was deemed distasteful or even loathsome by the administration were rebuffed by the courts.
- "Faculty rights in their most basic sense, in cases that questioned the legitimacy of restrictions on academic freedom. For example, a loyalty-oath requirement was found to violate free speech because it limited the scope of a professor's teaching and research. Faculty members sought the protections of labor laws and the right to bargain collectively.
- "Employment-discrimination laws that considered the disparate treatment of minority groups and women in hiring, pay, job assignments, promotion, and the awarding of tenure.
- "The formal breakup of racially structured systems of public higher education in Alabama, Louisiana, Tennessee and at least nine other states." (Bickel & Ruger)

Issues which today's top university attorneys predict will be on their front burners as the 21st century moves inexorably ahead include:

- Health & safety issues, including student violence
- Government investigations
- Race-conscious admissions
- Intellectual property rights
- Computer law and distance learning
- Conflicts of interest
- Individual privacy v. public accountability
- The graying of the workforce
- Employee benefits
- Consumer and educational malpractice
- Alternative income streams and for-profit ventures
- Organized labor

Obviously, these legal issues are not unique to higher education. Neither are the major branches of the law that dictate the rules by which these issues are analyzed and resolved. The sources of these legal principles and rules are:

a. Constitutions: The U.S. Constitution defines the structure and powers of the three branches of the federal government, its limitations, and the rights remaining to the states and we the people. All states also have constitutions. These mimic the federal document in many ways, but also contain provisions unique to each one of them. For example, while an individual privacy right implicit in the U.S. Constitution's Bill of Rights has been a controversial issue for decades, some states' constitutions expressly accord such a right to citizens within their boundaries.

b. Statutes: Laws are passed by legislative bodies. At the national level, this of course is the Congress. All states have legislatures as well. Most mimic the U.S. Congress in being bicameral, but a few have but one house. Federal statutes must conform to the requirements of the U.S. Constitution. On an equal footing with these federal laws are **Treaties** signed by the executive branch and ratified by the U.S. Senate. At the state level, statutes must comport not only with the state's constitution, but also with the federal constitution and any relevant federal statutes. In some areas federal law almost entirely preempts state law, such as in the fields of intellectual property and employee benefits. In other areas, such as discrimination law, the federal and state legislatures share statutory authority, and states may enact statutes so long as they do not trim back rights provided under federal law. For instance, no federal statute forbids discrimination on the basis of sexual preference, but the laws of a growing number of states do forbid such behavior by employers, landlords and public services. The New Jersey Law Against Discrimination is one such statute.

c. Rules and Regulations: If the universe of codified law can be compared to an iceberg, then the statutes enacted by federal and state lawmakers are only the tip. The vast body of the berg is comprised of a dizzying variety of rules and regulations promulgated by the agencies and offices of the vast federal bureaucracy, its counterparts in the 50 states, and the governmental entities at the county and municipal levels. From labor to discrimination to environmental protection to corporate accountability to zoning, a vast national bureaucracy—much of it staffed by lifetime appointees under civil service rules and union contracts—develops, disseminates and enforces countless rules and regulations. Not only does this bureaucracy mimic the legislatures in propagating such quasi-laws (which, of course, must comport with relevant constitutions and statutes); it also mimics the court system in conducting administrative hearings (typically subject to judicial review).

d. The Common Law: Our federal and state constitutions, and the plethora of statutes, rules and regulations, are interpreted by our courts. At the federal level, the U.S. Constitution authorizes a court system which today is comprised of U.S. District (trial) Courts scattered across the country and staffed by about 1500 federal judges and magistrates; U.S. Courts of Appeals, divided into 11 geographic regions, plus one for the District of Columbia, and several specialized, mid-level appellate venues, such as the Claims Court; and on top the U.S. Supreme Court. Most state court systems mirror the federal model. The thousands of decisions and opinions issued and published by these courts, particularly (but not exclusively) the supreme and mid-level appellate courts, are collectively called the American Common Law. Researching and interpreting this Common Law is something that lawyers spend much of their time learning as law students and doing in practice.

Once upon a time in England, and a little later the United States, Australia, Canada, and many other former colonies of Great Britain, most law was to be found in published and collected court opinions, i.e., the Common Law. Today, as much, if not more, of the body of law is located in the statute books and regulatory manuals of the federal and state bureaucracies, as well as the books of local ordinances enacted by city councils, county commissioners and the like.

The major fields of law, as generally taught by law schools and recognized in legal treatises, are:

a. Contract Law: Contracts are promises supported by mutual consideration. For example, when your university makes an offer of admission to a student-applicant and that applicant accepts your offer, a contract has been formed. Typically, the current college catalog becomes an implied part of that contract. Contract law was developed by the courts and contained in the common law, where much of it still resides. It is mainly a matter of state, rather than federal law, although the U.S. Constitution specifically insures the enforceability of contracts within U.S. boundaries, and your institution's federal grants and student financial aid are subject to complex federal contract rules. An important statutory source of contract rules is the Uniform Commercial Code, which has been adopted with minor variations by all 50 states.

b. Tort Law: From the Norman French a "tort" roughly means a force or a hurt. Tort law is personal injury law. With contract law, it may correctly be characterized as one of the two great areas of the common law on the civil (non-criminal) side. Today, as with contract law, statutes and regulations have stepped in to preempt much of what was once exclusively common (judge-made) law. The breadth of tort law is vast, including but not limited to assault and battery, auto accidents, defamation, harassment, intentional and negligent infliction of emotional distress, toxic torts, wrongful discharge and wrongful death. Statutes outlawing discrimination based on such factors as race and sex are in essence a subset of traditional tort law.

c. Criminal Law: Contract and tort law share the label "civil law." They are primarily areas of private law enforcement. Litigants institute lawsuits, seeking money damages and, sometimes, court orders to establish their respective rights and recover their losses. Criminal law by contrast is the province of the public sector, i.e., the U.S. Department of Justice, the States Attorneys General, and local prosecutors and district attorneys. These officials, in close cooperation with federal, state, and local police and other law enforcement organizations, investigate crimes and prosecute criminals. Often the statutes that establish crimes and set penalties are intimately connected with tort law on the civil side. For example, when the celebrity O.J. Simpson was accused of murdering his ex-wife and her friend, he was first tried—and acquitted—of the crime of murder, and subsequently sued by the friend's family for the tort of wrongful death. In the second trial, which applied not the test of "guilty beyond a reasonable doubt" but the diminished standard of "liable by a preponderance of the evidence," the jury awarded the survivors substantial monetary damages.

The Legal Environment of Academic Administration

Colleges and universities may be grouped into a variety of classifications. With regard to their degree-granting missions, institutions often are classed as:

1. Community and county colleges awarding two-year degrees such as Associate of Arts;
2. Four-year colleges granting baccalaureate degrees (B.A., B.S.);
3. Comprehensive universities granting baccalaureate and masters degrees;
4. Universities that grant all of the above plus Ph.D.s and/or other so-called terminal degrees such as the J.D. and M.D.

These classifications have legal significance. An institution cannot grant degrees that its accrediting organizations and/or state(s) of incorporation have not yet authorized or approved.

1. Of equal or greater legal significance is the corporate form the institution has taken. Three major forms define the bulk of American's 5,000-plus post-secondary institutions today: Public colleges and universities, organized, owned and operated by the states;
2. Private, not-for-profit colleges and universities;
3. Private, for-profit (sometimes called "proprietary") companies, often either calling themselves universities, or operating subsidiaries under such names (e.g., Apollo Group, a publicly traded corporation, parent to the University of Phoenix).

Variations on these three general classifications abound. For example, some universities are "state-affiliated," usually meaning that they receive substantial support from their state legislatures, but operate in main, or even most, respects like private universities, notably in the area of private fund raising and auxiliary enterprises.

Where your institution falls on this spectrum will often determine which law(s) apply to any particular situation. If you work at a public college or university, certain significant provisions of the United States Constitution will directly impact personnel policies, as well as student rights. The Fourteenth Amendment, which requires states to extend due process and equal protection rights to all persons and all U.S. citizens, respectively, incorporates significant elements of the Bill of Rights (the first ten amendments) such as the freedoms of speech, association and religion, and such protections as a shield against unreasonable searches and seizures.

In the field of labor relations, private universities fall under the jurisdiction of the National Labor Relations Board, which since 1980 views most faculty as managerial employees who are not protected by the National Labor Relations Act. [*See* ***NLRB v. Yeshiva University****, 444 U.S. 672 (U.S. Supreme Court, 1980)*.] Similarly, the NLRB more recently ruled that graduate assistants are primarily students, not employees, and therefore are not entitled to the federal law's rights and protections in trying to join labor unions and engage in collective bargaining with their universities. [*See* ***Brown University****, 342 NLRB No. 42 (National Labor Relations Board, 2004).*] By contrast, public (and most state-affiliated) colleges and universities look to their (often more union-friendly) state laws for guidance with regard to labor organizations. Consequently, unionized employees, including faculties, are to be found far more frequently in the public sector than in the private. (Unions are virtually unknown in the for-profit arena of higher education.)

In the realm of illegal discrimination, obligations are more likely to overlap, since federal and state laws tend to include both public and private employers under their regulatory tents. However, the Eleventh Amendment to the U.S. Constitution accords some measure of immunity to public employers with regard to some types of actions and forms of damages available against private entities. [*See* ***Fitzpatrick v. Bitzer****, 427 U.S. 445 (U.S. Supreme Court, 1976).*] Likewise with regard to intellectual property, the preemptive powers of the federal government impose a general uniformity across the public-private chasm.

Whether a public or a private institution of higher learning, the typical university is comprised of several schools and/or colleges. Likewise many colleges contain subsidiary schools. Virtually all such institutions have a governing board, typically termed trustees in the private sector, and governors or some similar term in the public realm. Serving beneath a president will usually be her/his cabinet, composed of vice presidents. A typical cabinet of senior officers looks something like this:

1. Vice President for Academic Affairs and Provost, usually the first among equals and the person who stands in when the president is incapacitated or absent on extended business travel.
2. Vice President for Finance, also often known as the chief financial officer. This officer's sphere of responsibilities can include such diverse realms as facilities, campus security, and environmental health and safety, as well such typical functions as payroll and management of the endowment.
3. Vice President for Enrollment Management, to whom admissions, financial aid, and related offices report.
4. Vice President for Institutional Advancement, formerly called "Development," and typically subsuming public relations and alumni relations, as well as fund raising.

5. Dean of Students and/or Vice President for Student Life (or Student Affairs), who deals with such student issues as food, housing, extracurricular activities, student disciplinary matters, and, increasingly, career counseling and job placement services. The trend in recent years has been for the Dean of Students to report to the Provost, thus drawing Academic Affairs and Student Affairs under a single tent.

Within the Academic Affairs Division, typically, a counsel of deans reports to and serves at the pleasure of the Provost/VP for Academic Affairs. Each dean heads a school or college of the institution. Under each dean are academic departments, usually headed by department chairs.

The role of the department chair varies vastly from one institution to another, and even sometimes within the colleges and schools of a single university. Some chairs function as highly autonomous managers with significant budgetary and governance discretion, ranging from allocation of workload among the department's faculty to promotion and tenure recommendations. At the opposite end of the spectrum, some chairs are little more than glorified secretaries, managing the day-to-day paperwork of the department. At this extreme, faculty of the department usually rotate the chair's duties among themselves. In unionized environments, the chair may be a part of the bargaining unit and in status be analogous to the "working foreman" who is so common in the construction trades. From a legal standpoint, where a particular chair falls on this spectrum will help determine whether her/his actions can bind the institution with regard to contracts and torts.

Purpose and Structure of This Book

As you can see, the campus landscape where education and the law encounter each other is a highly complex environment, populated by a multitude of challenges and threats. Academic Affairs, being at the heart of the higher-education enterprise, is also often in the eye of the legal storm. Provosts, deans and department chairs, who once devoted the bulk of their professional time to curricular concerns, today must deal with a broad spectrum of issues, both regarding the institution's students and faculty/staff, all of which are infused with legal implications, which in turn can dramatically affect the bottom line. While the enormous increase in university legal counsel, and the general expansion of support staff on "the other side of the house"—the finance, enrollment management and university advancement divisions—provide a crucial managerial/fiscal/legal platform on which much of the success of

Academic Affairs rests, no provost, dean or department chair today can afford to be ignorant of or to ignore the plethora of laws and regulations impacting higher education.

The purpose of this handbook is to help you, the academic administrator, confront these legal threats and challenges knowledgably and confidently. It is your map through the legal minefields. In some circumstances, it will be all you need. In others, it will identify the dangers, so that you can seek appropriate guidance and support from other institutional resources, such as legal counsel, human resources, or campus security.

As noted above, Student Affairs (student life) Divisions today tend to work closely with their institutions' Academic Affairs Divisions. On an increasing number of campuses, they are under the same administrative umbrella. (One final note: On July 31, 2008, five years past the sunset provision of the Higher Education Act, Congress finally reauthorized this statute, which is the core repository of federal higher education policy. The Higher Education Opportunity Act (HEOA)(H.R. 4137) was signed by then-President George W. Bush on August 18, 2008. Many of the HEOA's provisions technically went into effect immediately, albeit many of the most important pieces of this gargantuan (1,100-page) piece of legislation will require extensive rulemaking under the tutelage of the U.S. Department of Education. Where the HEOA is relevant to a chapter's topic, the final section of that chapter provides you with a summary of the statute's provisions, as well as a prediction of its likely impact upon your institution.

Sources

Adams III, O.L. (2006). Cost Control in Higher Education. University Business, June 2006.Retrieved June 25, 2006 from <http://www.universitybusiness.com/page.cfm ?p=1316>.

Bickel, R.D., and Ruger, P.H. (2004). The Ubiquitous College Lawyer. *Chronicle of Higher Education,* June 25, 2004. Retrieved June 25, 2006 from <http://chronicle.com/weekly/v50/i42/42b00101.htm>.

Blumenstyk, G. More Than 100 Colleges Fail Education Department's Test of Financial Strength, *Chronicle of Higher Education,* June 12, 2009, at A21.

Cox, G. M. 2000. Why I Left a University to Join an Internet Education Company. *Change* (November/December): 12–18.

Saltmarsh, J. (2000). *A New University with a Soul.* Retrieved June 25, 2006 from <http://ether.asu.edu/peekaboo/news/03-13-00response.html>.

Selingo, J. (2006). Survey Finds Top-Paid Higher Education Lawyers Are at Private Colleges and Research Universities. *Chronicle of Higher Education,* May 26, 2006. Retrieved June 25, 2006 from <http://chronicle.com/weekly/v52/i38/38a03403.htm>.

CHAPTER 1

Admissions

Let's begin at the beginning. Our principal enterprise, our main mission, is delivering education to our students. The relationship of a college or university to its students is complex and may be fraught at times with high emotion. These emotional attachments, if positive, often carry over into later life. Indeed, the health of the institution may depend on this and, so, we encourage it.

No matter. In the eyes of the law, at its core the relationship is contractual. The contract is formed when the institution offers the applicant admission into its hallowed halls and the applicant accepts.

So let's begin at the beginning, examining the steps in the typical admissions cycle and the legal issues that underlie our efforts at attracting prospective students.

Advertising and Marketing the Institution

Baby-boomers, such as your author, can recall an era in which colleges responded to student inquiries with a catalogue, a cover letter and an application form. Many guidance counselors performed their role "out of their back pockets," so to speak. Their "real" job was assistant principal, school disciplinarian, or classroom teacher. Students applied to a school or two, three or four at the outside, and sometimes seriously considered the armed forces, beauty or secretarial school, or a parents' (often unionized) trade as a viable alternative.

Times have changed. As outlined in the Introduction, today's higher education landscape is populated (some would say overpopulated) with a dizzying variety of public and private, large and small, non-profit and for-profit institutions. All are competing furiously for students, especially the best and the brightest. Many, perhaps most, are straining to expand... in size, in geographic locations, in comprehensive academic programming, and in state-of-the-art delivery systems. All desire diverse, talented student bodies. All want to rise in the *U.S. News & World Report* and *Princeton Review* annual rankings.

To attract star students and to rise in the rankings we must market ourselves in increasingly sophisticated ways. As we do, over-enthusiasm may open the (courtroom) doors to accusations of fraudulent misrepresentation. This exposure is all the more acute because today's students are all the more litigious than their predecessors of just a generation or two ago.

> [G]raduate and professional schools will soon enter a new era. The basic reason is that Gen Xers often hold different attitudes toward college and postgraduate education than their boomer counterparts, largely because of the economic environment in which they came of age. College was generally less of a financial burden for boomer students than Gen Xers.... Thus, more than boomers, Gen Xers viewed college as a calculated market choice... (William Strauss and Neil Howe, "Millennials as Graduate Students," The Chronicle of Higher Education, Mar. 30, 2007)

Thus, it's no surprise that university lawyers attending an annual meeting of their national association not long ago described their institutions as "legal minefields."

> The lawyers were also asked how much their colleges would be willing to spend to settle a lawsuit they considered a nuisance. For the plurality of respondents, 43 percent, the amount was $5,000 to $10,000. About 28 percent said they would spend less than $5,000, and about 9 percent said more than $21,000. (Jeffrey Selingo and Goldie Blumenstyk, "At Meeting of College Lawyers, They Talk of Costlier Settlements and Whistle-blowers," The Chronicle of Higher Education, July 7, 2006)

Fraudulent Misrepresentation

We academics dislike calling students "customers," referring to the academic enterprise as a "business," and labeling academic programs "product lines." Like it or not, as we compete with one another ever more intensely, and at a level of sophistication rivaling the most savvy corporate advertisers (indeed, oftentimes in collaboration or contractual partnership with players from the for-profit realm, such as Coke and Pepsi, Nike and Adidas), we can learn a lot from the local used-car salesman.

The law draws a crucial distinction between "puffing" and lying. A good used-car salesman feels the difference in his guts. "Puffing" may sound slangy at first blush, but it enjoys a fairly precise legal meaning.

> An expression of opinion by a seller not made as a representation of fact. Exaggeration by a salesperson concerning quality of goods (not considered a legally binding promise); usually concerns opinions rather than facts. (Black's Law Dictionary, Sixth Edition, 1991, p. 860)

In other words, advertising which merely states in broad generalities that the advertiser's product is somehow "superior" to the competition is only "puffing" and cannot lead to a successful lawsuit for fraud.

By contrast, the law defines a "lie" as:

> A falsehood uttered for the purpose of deception; an intentional statement of a non-truth designed to mislead another; ...the uttering or acting of that which is false for the purpose of deceiving.... (Black's, supra, p. 635)

Perish the thought that we scholars would proclaim such falsehoods from our ivory towers. And yet, as our institutions anoint young professionals, who might as easily have become stock brokers or real estate salespeople, with august titles such as vice president for enrollment management and appoint them to our presidents' senior cabinets; as in our mega-universities, coaches court seven-figure incomes (not counting product endorsements and speaking engagements); as our for-profit, publicly traded competitors come on strong...

Well, we might just find our institutions puffing a bit. If they do, and if we academics are marshaled to the cause, then we need to recognize the legal limits. For if we stray beyond those legal boundaries we may find ourselves in the realm of "fraudulent misrepresentation." The elements, or components, of a case of fraudulent misrepresentation include:

Checklist: Elements of Fraudulent Misrepresentation

1. A false statement
2. Of a material fact
3. With intent that the listener rely on the lie
4. Actual reliance of the listener
5. Inducing her/him to take action
6. To her/his detriment

Fraudulent misrepresentation frequently follows a breach of contract case into the courtroom. However, this form of personal injury is capable of standing on its own hind legs, as the following case confirms.

Harman v. Sullivan University System, Inc. *(2005 WL 1353752, U.S. District Court, W.D. Ky., 2005).* Spencerian, a university owned and operated by the corporate defendant, was accredited by the Accrediting Council for Independent Colleges and Schools ("ACICS"). In 2001, the ACICS approved Spencerian's Radiology Technologist ("RT") program. Melony Bryant and LaVetta Reliford were responsible for developing Spencerian's RT program and completing the accreditation process. Bryant's employment was terminated in the fall of 2001. The plaintiff enrolled in the first class of Spencerian's RT program in January 2002 and she graduated in June 2003.

False statement of material fact? Prior to enrolling in the RT program, the plaintiff attended Spencerian's Limited Medical Radiography ("LMR") program. A letter was distributed to members of the LMR program, including the plaintiff, on November 30, 2001. The letter stated that Spencerian had just been approved to start the RT program, that the RT program "addresses the competency specified by the Joint Review Committee on Education in Radiologic Technology (JRCERT)," and that graduates of Spencerian's RT program "are eligible to take the national certifying examination given by the American Registry of Radiologic Technology (ARRT)."

The handbooks, which were distributed to the RT program students, also stated that the program met the competency requirements of JRCERT and that graduates were eligible to take the national certifying exam. The school's website also contained those statements. Before she enrolled in the RT program, the plaintiff spoke with Erin Weiss, an admissions counselor. Weiss told the plaintiff that she would be eligible to take the ARRT exam upon graduation.

Listener's reliance. The plaintiff claimed that she would not have enrolled in the RT program if she had known that it was not accredited or if she had known that she would not be eligible to take the national exam.

Spencerian submitted its self-study to JRCERT in June 2003, seeking accreditation. Spencerian understood that it should submit its self-study after the first class completed the program. Students who graduated from an RT program prior to the accreditation of that program were entitled take the ARRT exam if the school is accredited by a mechanism recognized by the ARRT. Spencerian believed that it was accredited under such a mechanism; however, ARRT did not recognize the ACICS as an accrediting mechanism. Consequently, ARRT did not allow the June 2003 graduates of the Spencerian RT program to take the ARRT examination as national candidates. Spencerian made special arrangements with the Commonwealth of Kentucky Cabinet for Health and Family Services for the 2003 RT program graduates to take the ARRT examination as state candidates in the fall of 2003. The examinations for state and national candidates actually were identical. The plaintiff took the ARRT examination as a state candidate in the fall of 2003 and failed it. She took the national ARRT examination in November 2004 and failed it also.

Upon graduation from the RT program, the plaintiff began working at Floyd Memorial Hospital in Indiana as a Radiology Technologist. She worked in this position until she was demoted to technology assistant when the hospital learned that the Spencerian RT program was not accredited.

Analysis. Although the plaintiff-student was already enrolled in Spencerian, we can analyze this case as if she were a new applicant, since she applied for a new program of study. Spencerian made a number of promises to the plaintiff and her fellow applicants for the RT program. Most significantly, on the school's web site, in its publications and correspondence, and in a personal interview, she was assured that she would be enrolled in an accredited program. This was significant, since accreditation ensured the rights to take the national licensing test and seek employment in the profession anywhere in the U.S. Thus, the statements were **material.**

At the time they were made, the statements were **false.** They certainly were intended to **induce** applicants to matriculate into Spencerian's RT program. The plaintiff's testimony that she **acted in reliance** on the statements is perfectly credible. Why else would she have enrolled?

So far the plaintiff appears to be on her way to a victory in the U.S. District Court for the state of Kentucky. However, two issues pose important stumbling blocks. First, the school seems to have honestly believed at the time it told applicants it was accredited that it would accomplish this accreditation by the time they graduated. Had school officials told applicants that accreditation was only a prediction, they would have protected themselves from liability. Unfortunately, they didn't do that. Consequently, the plaintiff should be able to overcome this obstacle to winning her case against Spencerian. (Spencerian's claim that it believed its ACICS accreditation was sufficient is of little help to its defense. After all, school officials should have been easily able to clear up that point had they made a few simple phone calls. Purposefully remaining ignorant is no excuse.)

The second issue is a little higher hurdle for her. When she finally was able to take the national examination, she failed it. Unless she can also prove that the education she received at Spencerian was inadequate preparation for the exam, the burden seems to rest squarely on her shoulders going forward.

Outcome. The federal judge refused to grant a summary judgment in favor of Spencerian and its parent company, because "The plaintiff has presented sufficient evidence to establish a genuine issue of material fact as to whether the defendant negligently misrepresented that she could take the national ARRT examination upon graduation and that the RT program met the competency requirements of the JRCERT for the same reasons discussed above with regard to her fraud claim." In other words, although she eventually was able to sit for the national exam, this was not the case when she first graduated, as had been promised. Further, her failing the exam might be laid at the defendant's feet if, as she alleged, the RT program failed to meet the competency requirements that would have enabled her to pass the test.

Advice:

1. When launching a new academic program, ***don't*** present as presently true what are only your predictions for the program's future.
2. ***Do*** insure that the program's curricula comprise all the components required by all relevant accrediting and licensing agencies your students will have to satisfy in order to work in their chosen field.
3. ***Don't*** agree to the solicitation and processing of applicants for the program until you are satisfied that points one and two have been met by your faculty and staff.

The Formation and Dimensions of the Contractual Relationship

Fundamental contract law figures directly into the formation of the relationship between the applicant and the university. For the formation of a contract, the law demands an exchange of promises supported by some sort of consideration. Usually, this means that one party makes an offer, the other accepts the offer, and both sustain some change of position in support of the arrangement.

In the context of an applicant's overture to the university's office of admissions, this is usually deemed to be the solicitation of an offer of admission. In other words, even if the application arrives in response to an institution's promotional materials, no contract is as yet formed. In fact, even when your admissions office responds with a positive response to the application, no contract is formed—not quite yet.

Only when the successful applicant accepts the admission office's offer of admission is the contract consummated. After that, the university is obligated to make good on its promises to the new student. These promises are found partly in the correspondence exchanged between the parties. Consequently, if the college admissions office promises a financial aid package, the institution will have to make good on that scholarship/grant money. But there's more to the contract than that. The most significant document in the contractual mix is your current college catalogue.

McConnell v. LeMoyne College *(808 N.Y.S.2d 860, N.Y. Appellate Division, 2006)* presents a classic example of holding an institution of higher learning to what is contained in its college catalog. In this case, while still an undergraduate student, McConnell applied for admission to the Master of Science for Teachers program at LeMoyne College. By letter dated March 25,

2004, the Interim Chair of the College's Education Department for the College wrote the student to inform him of his "conditional acceptance as a student in the [Program]." The letter stated that, "[u]pon earning a grade of 'B' or higher in your first four courses, and upon completion of all admission requirements and/or course deficiencies, your status will change to full matriculation." On January 13, 2005, McConnell received a letter from Dr. Cathy Leogrande, the chair of the Education Department and Director of the Graduate Education Program. Leogrande wrote that she had reviewed the grades earned by petitioner thus far in the Program and had discussed his work with his professors. Based on her "grave concerns regarding the mismatch between [petitioner's] personal beliefs regarding teaching and learning and the [Program's] goals," Leogrande did not believe that he should continue in the Program. Therefore, he was not allowed to register for additional courses, and his registration for the spring 2005 semester was withdrawn. McConnell sued.

Analysis. On these facts, the court of appeals held as follows:

"We conclude that petitioner met all of the admission requirements set forth in the Catalog and the conditional acceptance letter. According to that letter, 'upon completion of all admission requirements and/or course deficiencies,' petitioner's status would change to full matriculation. Nothing in the letter indicated that petitioner would be subject to subsequent review, and nothing in the Catalog or the College Handbook indicated that a subsequent, subjective review of petitioner's personal goals would take place before a final decision was made.

"The Catalog lists five criteria for admission:

1. Completion of a baccalaureate degree from an accredited institution with a B average in the major field of study and a minimum grade-point average (GPA) of 3.0. If conditionally accepted, candidates with less than a 3.0 GPA must achieve at least a B in each of their courses prior to formal matriculation;
2. Graduate Record Exam General Test (GRE) score required, with no specification for a minimum score;
3. Letters of recommendation stating that the student is capable of graduate study;
4. Candidate's statement of purpose; and
5. Evaluation of transfer credit, if applicable.

"The fifth criterion was not applicable to petitioner and, although petitioner had less than a 3.0 GPA, there is no dispute that, as a conditionally accepted student, he received grades of B+ or higher in his first five classes. Petitioner therefore met the first criterion for full matriculation as stated in the Catalog and his conditional acceptance letter. The College does not contend that petitioner failed to submit a GRE score, letters of recommendation or a statement of purpose. Thus, it appears from the record before us that petitioner met all the criteria for admission as set forth in the Catalog and the conditional acceptance letter.

"Although the Catalog states that the College's programs are available to those "whose personal goals match the selected program," neither the Catalog nor the conditional acceptance letter states that personal goals are a criterion for admission. Thus, petitioner fulfilled the conditions outlined in the conditional acceptance letter and, according to the terms of that letter, petitioner's status changed automatically once those conditions were met. We thus conclude that petitioner was a fully matriculated student at the College on January 13, 2005, when Leogrande dismissed him from the Program, and he was entitled to the due process procedures set forth in the College's rules and regulations before he could properly be dismissed.

"In other words, since nothing in the college catalogue required the applicant to demonstrate acceptable "personal beliefs" that comported with program goals, the department couldn't impose that additional matriculation requirement following the formation of the student-college contract."

Outcome. The court concluded, "We therefore modify the judgment accordingly, and we direct the College to reinstate petitioner to the Program forthwith."

Advice. The obvious advice is to know what is in your catalogue, and either abide by it or change it. Here, based upon the authors' own experiences, we want to go a step farther. What we want to suggest is that you, as dean or department chair, think long and hard about the imposition of *attitudinal* admission requirements. It is not uncommon in professional programs, such as teaching and counseling, for departments and programs to impose such qualitative, normative requirements for admission and matriculation.

The problem inherent in such requirements is one of demonstrating their validity. The disappointed applicant will often assert that her/his gender, age, race, or other protected attribute was the "real" reason why admission or matriculation was denied. Absent compelling documentation—e.g., a criminal record check—you and your faculty must fall back on your own professional competency to support the "denial" decision. While your level of competency may be high and your conclusion correct, in a court of law these considerations may or may not prove to be compelling to a judge and jury.

Mistakes

The American common law recognizes two types of mistakes in the formation of contracts: mutual mistakes and unilateral mistakes.

The law makes a distinction between incorrect beliefs at the time of contracting —"mistake" and incorrect beliefs about events occurring after the agreement but before performance. Excuses for incorrect beliefs about later events are classified as performance excuses rather than formation excuses, and while they raise similar issues, we will not treat them here. "Mistake" itself covers a broad set of situations, and courts often distinguish between unilateral mistake and mutual mistake, a distinction that will be the focus of this article. A unilateral mistake is an incorrect belief of one party that is not shared by the other party. A mutual mistake is an incorrect belief shared by both parties. The conventional wisdom is that the contract is more likely to be voidable if the mistake is mutual, a distinction emphasized by courts for over a century.

Although judicial excuse for either unilateral or mutual mistake is relatively rare, courts continue to cite mutual mistake as grounds for avoidance. Law digests continue to list mutual mistake as a separate doctrine with regular new holdings, and the term appears frequently in contract cases. Informal excuse is also common. Many stores allow customers to return merchandise even when no promise to do so had earlier been made, and in transactions between businesses, purchasers are often allowed to cancel orders even though this may formally be a breach of contract.

Ayres & Rasmusen, "Mutual Mistake in Contract Law," 22 Journal of Legal Studies 309 (1993) (Copyright 1993 by The University of Chicago Press. All rights reserved.)

A recent example of mutual mistake was a high incidence of scoring errors by the Educational Testing Service in 2006:

Four thousand SAT scores out of 500,000 tests taken in October of 2006 were affected by scanning errors, resulting in scores that were either too low or too high. Although the number of tests affected by the error was not too significant, the impact of the miscalculations was marked for both the College Board and its contractor, Pearson Educational Measurement. Because of the errors in scoring, the credibility of the College Board was called into question, as increasingly inconsistent information about the scope and degree of the SAT problem surfaced.

Soon after discovering the errors in the initial set of tests, the College Board admitted that it would have to re-examine further 1,600 exams that may also have been scored incorrectly. The organization was so focused on correcting the errors encountered in the first set of tests that they overlooked the other 1,600 exams that had been put on administrative hold earlier for further review. Placing exams on administrative hold is a routine occurrence when there are concerns regarding the security of a test or test-taking session, but the executive director of SAT information services at the College Board, Brian O'Reilly, admitted that the mistake should have been caught sooner.

Students and colleges were notified of any changes in test scores, and college admissions officers were forced to re-evaluate applicants—even the smallest differences in scores can be vital when dealing with competitive college programs.

The credibility of the College Board was questioned, as well as the importance placed on standardized testing as a measurement tool in education in general. One of the biggest complaints from admissions officials and critics of the SAT was that little explanation was given for the scoring errors in the first place. Pearson Educational Measurement released a statement citing "abnormally high moisture content" due to heavy rain as one reason for the errors. The moisture caused answer sheets to expand and create inaccurate versions of the answer sheets. Another reason for the errors may have been answer sheets that were filled in too lightly or incompletely to be read by the scanner. However, other problems may have contributed and would have to be investigated further by Pearson.

Another point of contention was why the College Board waited so long to report the scoring errors. The association claimed to have been unaware of the problem until two students challenged their scores in December, but college officials and students were not informed of the problem until March. Mr. O'Reilly explained that the College Board wanted to wait until they could provide the most comprehensive information possible regarding the errors.

The College Board will grade tests an additional time, by hand, for an extra $50, but doing so often does not result in a different score. When it does result in a changed score, it is usually due to a student erasing an answer and filling in a different one on the answer sheet.

No pattern was discerned, however, to fully explain the errors in the 4,000 October tests. At least five law firms sought clients interested in suing the

College Board—with a strong case, according to Catherine Riccards at Balestriere PLLC, a New York law firm. According to her, it's difficult for admissions officials to look at applicants objectively after a mistake like this one has been made, and there is no way to change or avoid that.

Analysis. Certainly Attorney Richards makes a telling point with regard to ETS. However, with respect to the colleges and universities which relied on the incorrect SAT scores in rendering admissions decisions, this debacle would seem to be a clear case of mutual mistake. In other words, both the student-applicants and the higher education institutions assumed—mistakenly—the accuracy of the test scores. Consequently, while offers of admission already accepted by such students amounted to otherwise-binding contracts, where the SAT scores were incorrectly reported to be higher than they were, the college and university admissions offices would seem to have been within their rights in rescinding those offers of admission.

By contrast, had one of the affected universities accidentally mis-transcribed an applicant's SAT scores and admitted her on that basis, the student-applicant would have had a strong case for resisting any subsequent effort by the admitting school to withdraw its offer, providing the applicant had already made a timely acceptance of it.

Reservations of Rights

Where the college catalogue or other materials provided to applicants contains a statement, reserving to the institution the right to cancel a program or close a school subsequent to admitting such applicants, some courts have condoned such a programmatic or curricular alteration, even though its effect is to rescind or nullify the contract of admission.

An example is ***Beukas v. Board of Trustees of Fairleigh Dickinson,*** *255 N.J.Super. 420, 605 A.2d 708 (New Jersey Superior Court, Appellate Division, 1992).* In this case, Fairleigh Dickinson University maintained a private college of dental medicine in Hackensack, New Jersey. The university published an annual Graduate Studies Bulletin detailing the various graduate programs offered and an annual bulletin for the dental college. That bulletin set forth the dental programs offered, the curriculum for each of the four years of courses, and the terms upon which acceptance and admission into the dental college and continuation of the program to completion would be conditioned. The Graduate Studies Bulletin contained, among other things, a reservation of rights provision as follows:

"The University reserves the right in its sole judgment to make changes of any nature in the University's academic program, courses, schedule, or calendar whenever in its sole judgment it is deemed desirable to do so. The University also reserves the right to shift colleges, schools, institutes, programs, departments, or courses from one to another of its campuses. The foregoing changes may include, without limitation, the elimination of colleges, schools, institutes, programs, departments, or courses, the modification of the content of any of the foregoing, the rescheduling of classes, with or without extending the announced academic term, the cancellation of scheduled classes, or other academic activities. If such changes are deemed desirable, the University may require or afford alternatives for scheduled classes or other academic notification of any such change as is reasonably practical under the circumstances.... [Payment of tuition or attendance at any classes shall constitute a student's acceptance of the University's rights as set forth in this and the two preceding paragraphs.]"

Completion of the entire curriculum of courses over a period of no less than four years was required for graduation and eligibility for the degree of Doctor of Dental Medicine. The opportunity to take the New Jersey Dental Boards, a requirement to practice dentistry in the state, was conditioned upon completion of the four-year program. Fairleigh Dickinson's dental program was accredited by the Commission on Dental Accreditation, and approved by the New Jersey State Board of Dental Examiners.

Eighty-three students were accepted each year for the four-year program leading to the D.M.D. degree. In order to be accepted into the dental college, each applicant was required to take the Dental Admission Test given by the Council on Dental Education of the American Dental Association, complete a written application from the American Association of Dental Schools Application Service, submit recommendations and transcripts, and be interviewed.

After completing the application process, plaintiffs were notified by defendants that they had been accepted into the dental college for the course of studies leading to the D.M.D. degree. The plaintiffs accepted FDU's offer, rejected alternative career options, notified defendants that they accepted the offer, paid defendants the tuition for the coming semester, took appropriate steps respecting alternative career options, arranged their affairs to enable them to attend the program offered by defendants, and entered into the course of studies beginning in September 1986, 1987 or 1988. All the plaintiffs were enrolled as full time students in the four-year program, although tuition was due and payable on a semester basis. No formal written contract was ever executed.

On January 26, 1989, Fairleigh Dickinson University President Robert H. Donaldson was informed by the Chancellor of Higher Education, T. Edward Hollander, that the Governor's budget had appropriated 25% less money for the dental college for the 1989–90 school year than the college had received in 1988–89. On March 7, 1989 defendants and President Donaldson met with Governor Kean, who informed them that the dental college would receive no state aid after the 1989–90 school year because the governor had made a policy determination that it could no longer fund both the University of Medicine and Dentistry of New Jersey and the FDU dental college. State aid constituted 38.1% of the dental college's total budget for the 1988–89 school year. Due to this loss of aid, Fairleigh Dickinson University incurred a deficit of approximately $6,200,000 for the 1988–89 academic year. The university did not have funds available to make up for the loss of state aid to the dental college.

As a result, on March 28, 1989, President Donaldson recommended to the defendants that the following actions be taken: (1) that the process for consultation with faculty over closing of the dental college be initiated; (2) that the acceptance of a freshman class for the dental college for the 1989–90 school year be suspended; (3) that the search for a new dean for the dental college be suspended; (4) that the dental college be kept open so that certain students currently enrolled in their junior year at the dental college could complete their education during the 1989–90 school year; and (5) that the dental college close permanently in June 1990.

Meetings between university officials and dental college students to inform the students of the governor's actions and President Donaldson's recommendations were held on March 27, April 11 and 12, 1989. On June 14, 1989, the defendants resolved that the dental college would be closed at the end of the 1989–90 school year.

In the spring of 1989 the university appointed Dr. Blaise Curcio, a dental college professor, to coordinate and effectuate transfers of first, second and third year students. Dr. Curcio had a number of meetings with students to inform them of their transfer options and provide information concerning transfers. University officials reached agreements with the University of Medicine and Dentistry of New Jersey, Columbia University School of Dentistry, New York University School of Dentistry, Tufts University School of Dentistry, and Temple University School of Dentistry to accept Fairleigh Dickinson University dental students as transfer students during either the 1989–90 or 1990–91 school year. The dental students were offered two transfer choices: (1) they could transfer immediately for the 1989–90 school year, either to one of the five schools previously mentioned or to other accredited dental colleges; or (2) the dental college students could remain at Fairleigh Dickinson University for the 1989–90 school year and then transfer to one of the five schools listed above or to any other accredited dental college. If the students chose the second option, they would receive a tuition subsidy at the dental college of their choice. More specifically, the students would be provided money to make up the tuition difference between Fairleigh Dickinson University's dental college and the school the students transferred to for the 1990–91 school year. The source of these monies was the New Jersey Department of Health & Education.

Dental students were also offered additional clinical and academic instruction so as to facilitate their transfer to other dental schools. Finally, Fairleigh Dickinson University coordinated with the State Dental Accreditation Society to ensure that the dental college retained its accreditation for the 1989–90 academic year.

Holding. On these facts the New Jersey appeals court held, "Even if we assume, for analytical purposes, that the various University bulletins constituted an enforceable contract, that contract would include the reservation of rights reproduced above. Moreover, to the extent that the University's freedom of action under its reservation of rights was limited by an implied covenant of good faith and fair dealing, *see Onderdonk v. Presbyterian Homes of N.J., 85 N.J. 171, 182, 425 A.2d 1057 (1981),* we perceive no violation of that covenant. The University, faced with a substantial budgetary shortfall due to the State's unilateral decision to discontinue its financial aid, acted reasonably and humanely in arranging for transfers of its dental students to other dental schools and in subsidizing any differences in tuition."

Important to note in analyzing, and particularly in relying upon, this decision is that the justices accorded great weight to the fact that FDU had acted honorably with regard to its current dental students and those who were admitted, but whose admissions were cancelled. The court stated in its initial opinion (supplemented by the decision cited above):

> "Had defendants acted arbitrarily; had they refused to avail themselves of reasonably available alternative funding; had they failed to promptly disclose the withdrawal of state funding; had they lulled plaintiffs into believing the funding would be restored; or had they failed to make proper arrangements for transfer of plaintiffs to other dental schools, thus causing a delay in plaintiffs' opportunities to pursue their educational goals, the situation would be different. But no one contends that defendants did anything but act promptly and forthrightly as soon as they learned of the change in their financial circumstances. Defendants made a reasonable decision to close the dental college because it could no longer operate in a fiscally sound or

> educationally responsible way after state funding was withdrawn. An institution involved in training health care professionals, where the conferral of a degree places the school's stamp of approval upon the student as qualified to practice the profession, (citation omitted) should be free to determine its ability to meet its educational responsibility so long as it does not act arbitrarily or in bad faith. This is because it has an obligation, not only to its students, but to the public at large. If due to a lack of financial resources, a dental school cannot meet its obligations to properly train its student body, then it is required to cease its function as a professional school without the risk of incurring liability to its students unless, of course, it acts arbitrarily or in bad faith in reaching its decision and does not deal fairly with its students in the process."

Advice. While a reservation of rights may be helpful, it is no "silver bullet." The courts will inquire into the behavior of the institution invoking the reservation. Should such a reservation of right be relied upon to shield the university from liability for abusive treatment of its students or applicants, the courts may be expected to knock it aside and impose liability as if the reservation did not exist.

Impact of the Higher Education Opportunity Act (HEOA)

The HEOA contains a plethora of provisions aimed at inducing greater transparency with regard to the cost of attending evenry college and University in the U.S. These include"

- Starting on July 1, 2001, the U.S. Department of Education (DOE) will begin releasing lists, organized by institutional categories (4-year public; 4-year private; not-for-profit; 2-year public, etc.), identifying the five percent of schools in each category the highest tuition and fees; the highest "net price" (defined as the average actual cost to a first-year full-time undergraduate, after financial aid is taken into account); the largest tuition and fee increases over the previous three years; the largest percentage increases in "net price" over the same time span; and, the major areas of budgetary inflation for each of the schools on the lists.
- On August 14, 2009, DOE released its "Net Price Calculator," all institutions must participate in the system.
- Effective July 1, 2010, publishers must provide faculty members and administrators, who choose textbooks, with the prices to be charged at the campus store; the prices charged to the general public; the copyright dates of the three prior editions of each such text, plus a description of the revisions from edition to edition; alternative formats (e.g., paperback, electronic, or

looseleaf) and the alternative prices; and, supplemental materials that are bundled with any text (including whether or not these materials may be unbundled and/or purchased separately).

Analysis. Clearly, the purpose of the HEOA provisions is to enable parents and students to ascertain the actual costs inherent in attending all American higher education institutions, so that they can comparison shop before applying and/or accepting offers of admission. While these provisions do not eliminate the possibility of any fraudulent or negligent representation of the substance and/or curricular requirements of any given degree program, they certainly lift the veil on college costs, which (sad to say) sometimes resemble the pricing procedures characteristic of new and used car sales.

CHAPTER 2

Financial Aid and Tuition

Financial Aid

If the admissions process is complicated by contract considerations, financial aid is a minefield filled with legal hazards for the hapless, or reckless, administrator. No better example can be posed, as this work goes to press, than that of the University of Phoenix.

U.S. ex rel. Hendow v. University of Phoenix, *461 F.3d 1166 (U.S. Court of Appeals, 9th Circuit, 2006).* When an educational institution wishes to receive federal subsidies under Title IV of the Higher Education Act, it must enter into a Program Participation Agreement with the Department of Education (DOE), in which it agrees to abide by a panoply of statutory, regulatory, and contractual requirements. One of these requirements is a ban on incentive compensation: a ban on the institution's paying recruiters on a per-student basis. The ban prohibits schools from "provid[ing] any commission, bonus, or other incentive payment based directly or indirectly on success in securing enrollments or financial aid to any persons or entities engaged in any student recruiting or admission activities or in making decisions regarding the award of student financial assistance." This requirement is meant to curb the risk that recruiters will "sign up poorly qualified students who will derive little benefit from the subsidy and may be unable or unwilling to repay federally guaranteed loans." *United States ex rel. Main v. Oakland City Univ., 426 F.3d 914, 916 (7th Cir.2005), cert. denied,—U.S.—, 126 S.Ct. 1786, 164 L.Ed.2d 519 (2006).* The ban was enacted based on evidence of serious program abuses.

This case involves allegations under the False Claims Act that the University of Phoenix knowingly made false promises to comply with the incentive compensation ban in order to become eligible to receive Title IV funds. Mary Hendow and Julie Albertson, two former enrollment counselors at the university, alleged that the university falsely certified each year that it was in compliance with the incentive compensation ban while intentionally and knowingly violating that requirement. They alleged that these false representations, coupled with later claims for payment of Title IV funds, constitute false claims under 31 U.S.C. § 3729(a)(1) & (a)(2).

First, they alleged that the university, with full knowledge, flagrantly violated the incentive compensation ban. They claimed that the university "compensates enrollment counselors... based directly upon enrollment activities," ranking counselors according to their number of enrollments and giving the highest-ranking counselors not only higher salaries but also benefits, incentives, and gifts. They alleged that the university also "urges enrollment counselors to enroll students without reviewing their transcripts to determine their academic qualifications to attend the university," thus encouraging counselors to enroll students based on numbers alone. Albertson, in particular, alleged that she was given a specific target number of students to recruit, and that upon reaching that benchmark her salary increased by more than $50,000. Hendow specifically alleged that she won trips and home electronics as a result of enrolling large numbers of students.

Second, the two former employees alleged considerable fraud on the part of the university to mask its violation of the incentive compensation ban. They claimed that the university's head of enrollment openly bragged that "[i]t's all about the numbers. It will always be about the numbers. But we need to show the Department of Education what they want to see." To deceive the DOE, the plaintiffs alleged, the university created two separate employment files for its enrollment counselors—one "real" file containing performance reviews based on improper quantitative factors, and one "fake" file containing performance reviews based on legitimate qualitative factors. The fake file is what the DOE allegedly saw. They further alleged a series of university policy changes deliberately designed to obscure the fact that enrollment counselors were compensated on a per-student basis, such as altering pay scales to make it less obvious that they were adjusted based on the number of students enrolled.

Third and finally, the plaintiffs alleged that the university submitted false claims to the government. Claims for payment of Title IV funds can be made in a number of ways, once a school signs its Program Participation Agreement and thus becomes eligible. For instance, in the Pell Grant context, students submit funding requests directly (or with school assistance) to the DOE. In contrast, under the Federal Family Education Loan Program, which includes Stafford Loans, students and schools jointly submit an application to a private lender on behalf of the student, and a guaranty agency makes the eventual claim for payment to the United States only in the event of default. The plaintiffs alleged that the university submitted false claims in both of these ways. They claimed that the university, with full knowledge that it is ineligible for Pell Grant funds because of its violation of the incentive compensation ban, submitted requests for those funds directly to the DOE, resulting in a direct transfer of the funds into a university account. They further claimed that the university, again with knowledge that it has intentionally violated the incentive compensation ban, submitted requests to private lenders for government-insured loans.

The case was initially dismissed by a federal district court. However, in 2006, the lower court was reversed and the case reinstated by the U.S. Court of Appeals for the Ninth Circuit. According to one observer, "The U.S. Court of Appeals for the Ninth Circuit has reinstated a massive False Claims Act lawsuit against the University of Phoenix which, with 180 campuses and over 310,000 students nationwide, is now America's largest accredited university. The overwhelming majority of students at the U. of Phoenix have federally funded tuition loans and grants, and last year U.S. taxpayers paid, and the University of Phoenix obtained, $1.7 billion in federal education funds. Yet many students who enroll at the U. of Phoenix never complete their education, and many are unable to even finish the classes they signed up for" (http://www.taf.org/).

However, the University of Phoenix is far from alone as a target of governmental scrutiny of its financial aid practices. In 2007, New York State Attorney General Andrew Cuomo launched a major investigation of universities and lending organizations, charging that they are in bed together, the former providing referrals in return for inappropriate compensation from the latter. Cuomo's initiative precipitated a national scandal and wrecked the careers of a number of prominent financial aid officers. As the scandal crested, many financial aid offices moved to revise their practices, assisted by such advice as is offered in the box below.

Federal Financial Aid Rules

To understand how the University of Phoenix could find itself in its legal fix, and how the industry as a whole could be so vulnerable to A.G. Cuomo's onslaught, we need to present an overview of the federal student-financial-aid scheme.

Funding Your Education

Through the College Cost Reduction and Access Act of 2007, Congress created the Teacher Education Assistance for College and Higher Education (TEACH) Grant Program that provides grants of up to $4,000 per year to students who intend to teach in a public or private elementary or secondary school that serves students from low-income families. Click here to find out more about the TEACH Grant Program.

The Academic Competitiveness Grant and the National Science and Mathematics Access to Retain Talent Grant (National SMART Grant) were made available as of the 2006–07 school year. Click here for additional information.

We can help make your education affordable!

The Department's Federal student aid programs are the largest source of student aid in America. If you're interested in financial aid for college or a career school, you've come to the right place. These programs provide more than $100 billion a year in grants, loans, and work-study assistance. Read on to find out more and to find out how to apply for this aid.

U.S. Department of Education student aid is the largest but not the only source! You can find out here about other sources of federal aid and about scholarships. Nonfederal financial assistance programs and requirements often vary from school to school, so check with the schools you're interested in for information about state and institutional aid.

New: Financial Aid Estimator Tool—*FAFSA4caster*

The *FAFSA4caster* provides students with an early estimate of their eligibility for federal student financial assistance. Students considering furthering their education beyond high school can use this FREE tool to:

1. Calculate their eligibility for federal financial aid, including grants
2. Reduce the time it will take to complete the Free Application for Federal Student Aid (FAFSA), the qualifying form for all federal student financial aid

Federal Student Aid is excited to provide this tool to help students and their families evaluate their options for planning and paying for education beyond high school. To access *FAFSA4caster*, visit www.fafsa4caster.ed.gov.

Transfer your MyFSA profile to FAFSA4caster

If you have a MyFSA account, click here to automatically transfer data from your MyFSA profile to FAFSA4caster so you won't have to complete the information again. If you haven't created a MyFSA profile yet, we encourage you to click on the MyFSA link in the left margin of this Web site. With MyFSA, you can create a personalized "folder" to record your career and college searches, track your progress in the college planning and application process, transfer data to the FAFSA, and much more!

Applying for Financial Aid

The Free Application for Federal Student Aid (FAFSA) is the form used by virtually all two and four-year colleges, universities and career schools for the awarding of federal student aid and most state and college aid. To assist in completing the FAFSA, see Completing the FAFSA.

Tell your friends! The official FAFSA is at www.FAFSA.ed.gov—not at a .com Web site. If you go to a .com site, you will probably be asked to pay to submit the FAFSA. Remember, the first F in "FAFSA" stands for "free"—so use the official government site to submit your application.

Transfer your MyFSA profile to *FAFSA on the Web*

If you've already created a MyFSA account, click here to automatically transfer much of your MyFSA profile to FAFSA on the Web so you won't have to repeat this information when you apply. If you haven't created a MyFSA profile yet, click on the MyFSA link in the left margin of this Web site.

Student Aid Eligibility

Find out what determines eligibility for federal student aid programs.

Federal Student Aid Eligibility Status for Incarcerated Individuals

Currently incarcerated individuals have limited eligibility for federal student aid. To find out which federal student aid programs you are eligible to apply for, check out Frequently Asked Questions About Federal Student Aid for Incarcerated Individuals.

The PIN

The Federal Student Aid PIN is the personal identification number that serves as your electronic signature or access code on our Web sites.

Get a PIN

If this is your first time filling out the *Free Application for Federal Student Aid* (FAFSA), and you haven't applied for a PIN, you should do so now. Your PIN is what allows you to complete the FAFSA paper-free! You'll need your PIN to make online corrections to your FAFSA, including changing your name and address, or adding/changing the name of a school to receive your application data. The PIN is also your identifier to let you access personal information in various U.S. Department of Education systems.

Student Aid Report (SAR)

Have you already filled out the FAFSA and received your Student Aid Report (SAR)? The SAR contains the information you reported on your FAFSA. Here's a description of the SAR and how it's used. Your SAR must be complete and correct before you can receive federal student aid.

Federal Student Aid Programs

If you're eligible, the Federal Student Aid office has a variety of programs to help you pay for your education after high school. Click on Grants, campus-based aid, Stafford Loans, PLUS Loans (parent loans) and PLUS Loans for graduate and professional degree students for more information about these programs. For information on Consolidation Loans, click on "Repaying Your Loans" and go to "Loan Consolidation."

Borrowing Responsibly

If you decide to take out a federal student loan to help pay for school, you're taking on certain serious obligations. Find out what they are and how to maintain your account in good standing.

Understanding Federal Student Aid

Our booklet, *Funding Education Beyond High School: The Guide to Federal Student Aid* will answer any questions you might still have. *Funding Education Beyond High School: The Guide to Federal Student Aid* is a comprehensive source of information about the Department's federal student aid programs and includes an overview of federal student aid, as well as more detailed information on the application process and student loans, for example. Whatever your questions, you'll find the aid information you need in this publication.

Other Sources of Federal Student Aid

We encourage you to explore other federal Web sites to find out about additional aid sources. For example, veterans and their dependents, students training in various medical fields, and persons interested in earning funds in exchange for community service may link to other federal agencies for program descriptions and qualifications.

State Aid

Even if you're not eligible for federal aid, you might be eligible for financial assistance from your state. Contact your state higher education agency for more information.

Finding Scholarships

Under the Robert C. Byrd Honors Scholarship Program, ED gives money to state education agencies to provide scholarships to graduating high school seniors. Each state education agency has its own application and deadline. To find your state agency's Web site, click here.

You can find out about nonfederal scholarships and other sources of aid in several ways, including contacting the financial aid offices at the schools you plan to attend and checking information in a public library or online. But be careful. Make sure scholarship information and offers you receive are legitimate. Don't get scammed: You don't have to pay to find scholarships. Click here to check out our information on nonfederal sources of aid and how to avoid scholarship fraud.

To access our free scholarship search, click here.

Sample Award Package

Most schools will prepare an "award letter" that will inform you of the types and amount of student aid you will receive at that school. Once you've selected the types of aid you want to receive, that selection is referred to as an "award package."

Financial Aid Wizard

Explore your financial aid needs and options with a step-by-step process for calculating your cost of attendance and expected family contribution, and discovering potential scholarships and loans available to you. If you're planning on going to college in the future, we can't predict what you might be awarded then, but you can find out what you'd get if you applied this year. Use that as a guide as you prepare for the time you enter college.

Tax Break

Find out how the Hope and Lifetime Learning Tax Credits can help with education costs by reading IRS Publication 970, "Tax Benefits for Education."

Saving Money for College

Paying for college is easier when you can invest money in a Coverdell Education Savings Account (formerly an Education IRA) that will accumulate interest tax free, and when you can withdraw money from this account without penalty. Also, it's possible to put money into a state- or institution-sponsored prepaid tuition plan and not pay taxes on it until you withdraw the money.

Reducing College Costs

The typical cost of attendance includes not just tuition, but room and board, fees for special programs or activities, books, personal items, and traveling to and from college. Here are 22 tips for reducing your college costs.

Funding your Education

Transfer your MyFSA profile to FAFSA4caster

Applying for Financial Aid

Transfer your MyFSA profile to *FAFSA on the Web*

Student Aid Eligibility

Federal Student Aid Eligibility Status for Incarcerated Individuals

The PIN

Get a PIN

Student Aid Report (SAR)

Grants

Campus-Based Aid

Stafford Loans

PLUS Loans

PLUS Loans for graduate or professional students

Borrowing Responsibly

Funding Education Beyond High School: The Guide to Federal Student Aid

Other Federal Web Sites

State Higher Education Agency

Sample Award Package

Financial Aid Wizard

Tax Break

Saving Money for College

Reducing College Costs

Last updated/reviewed June 23, 2009. *Source:* U.S. Department of Education at <http://studentaid.ed.gov/PORTALSWebApp/students/english/funding.jsp>

Armed with this brief summary of the major federal student financial aid programs, we can consider some of the legal pitfalls that await colleges and university administrators involved in managing their institution's share of these substantial amounts of taxpayers' money.

The Student's Duty to Repay Federal Loans

Lockhart v. U.S., *546 U.S. 142, 126 S.Ct. 699 (U.S. Supreme Court, 2005).* Petitioner James Lockhart failed to repay federally reinsured student loans that he had incurred between 1984 and 1989 under the Guaranteed Student Loan Program. These loans were eventually reassigned to the Department of Education, which certified the debt to the Department of the Treasury through the Treasury Offset Program. In 2002, the government began withholding a portion of petitioner's Social Security payments to offset his debt, some of which was more than 10 years delinquent.

Facts. Following three years on the unemployment line, James Lockhart decided to go back to school. Lockhart relied on student loans to take courses at a total of four colleges, but he never succeeded in finding steady employment. The schooling spanned six years (1984–1990). In 1999 he endured double-bypass heart surgery that left him reliant upon half a dozen drugs. Lockhart applied for and received Social Security disability benefits until 2003, when he turned 65. The disability benefits were then replaced by a monthly retirement payment of $874.

At that point Lockhart owed Uncle Sam some $80,000 in student loan debts. Some of these obligations dated back almost two decades. In 2002 he was notified that the government would begin withholding 15% of his Social Security benefits toward repayment of the loans.

Representing himself, Lockhart filed suit in the U.S. District Court for the state of Washington. The district judge dismissed his complaint, holding that he lacked jurisdiction. The plaintiff appealed to the U.S. Court of Appeals for the Ninth Circuit, which appointed counsel to represent him.

The appeals panel noted that "a puzzle has been created by the codifiers" of the Higher Education Act and the Debt Collection Act. The court resolved the puzzle in the government's favor, holding that the government was entitled to offset Social Security payments to recover on its loans. The Supreme Court granted certiorari and a divided Court affirmed.

Analysis. The Supreme Court held, "It is clear that the Higher Education Technical Amendments remove the 10-year limit that would otherwise bar offsetting petitioner's Social Security benefits to pay off his student loan debt. Petitioner argues that Congress could not have intended in 1991 to repeal the Debt Collection Act's statute of limitations as to offsets against Social Security benefits since debt collection by Social Security offset was not authorized until five years later. Therefore, petitioner continues, the Higher Education Technical Amendments' abrogation of time limits in 1991 only applies to then-valid means of debt collection. We disagree."

In so holding the majority noted, "The fact that Congress may not have foreseen all of the consequences of a statutory enactment is not a sufficient reason for refusing to give effect to its plain meaning."

The opinion explained, "The Debt Collection Act of 1982, as amended, provides that, after pursuing the debt collection channels set out in 31 U.S.C. § 3711(a), an agency head can collect an outstanding debt 'by administrative offset.' § 3716(a). The availability of offsets against Social Security benefits is limited, as the Social Security Act, 49 Stat. 620, as amended, makes Social Security benefits, in general, not 'subject to execution, levy, attachment, garnishment, or other legal process.' 42 U.S.C. § 407(a). The Social Security Act purports to protect this anti-attachment rule with an express-reference provision: 'No other provision of law, enacted before, on, or after April 20, 1983, may be construed to limit, supersede, or otherwise modify the provisions of this section except to the extent that it does so by express reference to this section.' § 407(b)."

However, the Court continued, "The Higher Education Technical Amendments, by their terms, did not make Social Security benefits subject to offset; these were still protected by the Social Security Act's anti-attachment rule. Only in 1996 did the Debt Collection Improvement Act—in amending and recodifying the Debt Collection Act—provide that, '[n]otwithstanding any other provision of law (including [§ 407] ···),' with a limited exception not relevant here, 'all payment due an individual under ··· the Social Security Act ··· shall be subject to offset under this section.' 31 U.S.C. § 3716(c)(3)(A)(i)."

In other words, reasoned the court, the Higher Education Act trumped the protections otherwise provided Social Security Benefits by the Debt Collection Act.

Outcome. The high court concluded, "It is clear that the Higher Education Technical Amendments remove the 10-year limit that would otherwise bar offsetting petitioner's Social Security benefits to pay off his student loan debt." Of Justice Sandra Day O'Connor's opinion for the majority, Lockhart's lawyer, Director Brian Wolfman of the Public Citizen Litigation Group, complained, "It means that you can take the Social Security Benefits of someone who is 90 years old and living on a small amount of money. The losers are clearly older Social Security beneficiaries."

Advice. If *Lockhart* tells university administrators and their students anything, it is that Uncle Sam is deadly serious about collecting loan debts incurred in the course of obtaining higher education. Students may be well advised to "mortgage" their diplomas only with extreme caution... a practice that does not seem to pertain in today's high-tuition environment.

To the contrary, a recent investigation found that today's 20-something generation is straining under the weight of college loans. Two thirds of the college grads in that age group have loans to pay off. Average debt is about $16,000, but debt burdens of $150,000 or more are increasingly common. Meanwhile, the economic prospects of young college graduates are not what they once were, to wit:

1. Wages are flat. Three decades ago a male college graduate made on average the equivalent of $51,123 2004-dollars per year. In 2004 the average was $50,700.
2. Home prices are rising. In 1970 the median home price was $23,000, the equivalent of $155,770 today. But today's median price is $219,000. Consequently, the 2000 Census found that 19% of men and women aged 18–34 reported moving back home with their parents to cut costs and pay off debt.

3. Bad savings rates. Fifty-five percent of this generation are saving nothing, either in a tax-sheltered retirement account or otherwise.
4. Tuition has skyrocketed. Four-year public university tuition has climbed 268% since 1976–77. Private college tuition has leaped 248%, averaging $22,218 per year today. Student debt has surged accordingly (Fetterman). Most of this money is loaned or guaranteed by the federal government. *Lockhart* solidifies Uncle Sam's ability to get it back.

Checklist: Potential Penalties for Defaulting on Loans

- Loans may be turned over to a collection agency.
- The defaulting graduate is liable for the costs associated with collecting the loan, including court costs and attorney fees.
- S/he can be sued for the entire amount of the loan.
- Her/his wages may be garnished. (Federal regulations limit the amount that may be garnished to 10% of the borrower's take-home pay.)
- Federal and state income tax refunds may be intercepted.
- Defaulted loans will appear on credit records, making it difficult to obtain an auto loan, mortgage, or even credit cards. A bad credit record can also harm the graduate's ability to find a job.

  S/he won't receive any more federal financial aid until either repayment of the loan in full or establishment of a repayment plan, plus at least six consecutive, on-time, monthly payments.
- S/he will be ineligible for deferments.
- Federal interest benefits will be denied.
- S/he may be blocked from renewing a professional license held. (Mortgage Bankers Association)

Bankruptcy Court Relief for Defaulting Graduates

In re Gerhardt, *348 F.3d 89 (U.S. Court of Appeals, 5th Cir., 2003).* Jonathan Gerhardt was the child of two classical musicians. He studied at the prestigious New England Conservatory of Music and other high-priced schools, ultimately amassing a whopping $ 77,000 in student loans. After performing with two city orchestras, he succeeded in landing the principal-cellist's slot on the Louisiana Philharmonic Orchestra, based in New Orleans. Despite also teaching the cello at Tulane, he was clearing little more than $20,000 per year. Buckling under the burden of his student loans, Gerhardt filed for bankruptcy.

Under amendments made to the Bankruptcy Code in 1998, negotiated by the Clinton Administration in return for lowered interest rates, student loans are not readily subjected to discharge in a bankruptcy proceeding. In Gerhardt's case, the Department of Education took a tough line. Its attorneys contended that Gerhardt could cut back his modest life style, such as by canceling his gym membership and his Internet service.

Bankruptcy Judge Jerry A. Brown was sympathetic, determining that Gerhardt needed his workouts to relieve back pain induced by playing his cello and Internet access to seek additional work. He even let the hapless musician keep his cat, commenting that as a single man, living alone, he required the companionship. He discharged Gerhardt's loan debt on the basis of undue hardship.

The DOE appealed and obtained a reversal from the U.S. district judge. Gerhardt took his case to the U.S. Court of Appeals for the Fifth Circuit.

Analysis. The appeals panel was no more sympathetic than the district judge down below. Affirming the district court decision, the appellate judges defined the applicable test as follows:

"To justify discharging the debtor's student loans, the…test requires a three-part showing:

(1) that the debtor cannot maintain, based on current income and expenses, a 'minimal' standard of living for [himself] and [his] dependents if forced to repay the loans; (2) that additional circumstances exist indicating that this state of affairs is likely to persist for a significant portion of the repayment period of the student loans; and (3) that the debtor has made good faith efforts to repay the loans."

On the basis of these standards, the court reasoned that "nothing in the Bankruptcy Code suggests that a debtor may choose to work only in the field in which he was trained, obtain a low-paying job, and then claim that it would be an undue hardship to repay his student loans. *See, e.g., In re Grigas,* 252 B.R. 866, 875 (Bankr.D.N.H.) (concluding that a debtor could not satisfy the second… prong when financial distress was self-imposed)." Under the facts presented by Gerhardt, it is difficult to imagine a professional orchestra musician who would not qualify for an undue hardship discharge. Accordingly, Gerhardt "has failed to demonstrate the type of exceptional circumstances that are necessary in order to meet [his] burden under the second prong.... Finding no error, the judgment of the district court is AFFIRMED."

The judges went so far as to suggest that Gerhardt might find himself a job as a sales clerk in a music store. Gerhardt alleged that he was already working some 60 hours per week, rehearsing, practicing, performing and teaching. As a result of the court's ruling he moved in with a roommate, curtailed his trips to Columbus, Ohio, to see his 80-something-year-old mother, and began paying $200 a month to Uncle Sam, who had asked for $900.

Advice. Strapped alumni who hope to escape their loans via the federal bankruptcy court must be prepared to meet a high evidentiary standard in order to establish a sufficient hardship to justify discharge of their student loan debts. The government insists upon other sacrifices being made before the former student is permitted to off-load this burden. This is one reason why the default rate has dropped dramatically over the past two decades. The other is the pressure placed on colleges and universities to make sure their alumni come up with the cash.

The Institution's Role in the Loan-Repayment Obligation

It is long established that a university's alleged misconduct toward a student does not relieve that student of a later obligation to repay student loans. In ***U.S. v. Cawley,*** *821 F. Supp. 1219 (U.S. District Court, E.D. Mi., 1993), affirmed, 16 F.3d 1221 (U.S. Court of Appeals, 6th Cir., 1994),* Plaintiff Cawley had been a Ph.D. student at the University of Michigan. The plaintiff a decade earlier had filed a lawsuit against the U.S. Attorney General and the Director of the National Science Foundation, as well as several other parties, including the Michigan Attorney General, the University of Michigan Board of Regents, and various individuals associated with the university. The complaint was hundreds of pages long and alleged claims based on faculty absence from classes, professional malpractice purportedly violating academic freedom, fraud and negligence by the university in its administration of a scientific research grant, torts arising out of allegedly unconstitutional university residency requirements, tortious interference with an employment contract, tortious interference with academic freedom, and "psychic eavesdropping." The district court struck the original complaint, and Cawley filed an amended complaint. The court later dismissed the amended complaint without prejudice, and the Sixth Circuit affirmed the district court's decision.

On these facts, the court commented, "Cawley's defenses of misconduct prohibiting performance, frustration of purpose, and impossibility or impracticability of performance are all based on the same allegations. Cawley contends that the University and the National Science Foundation failed to hear his grievances regarding faculty absence from classes and negligent or fraudulent administration of federal grant monies. He claims that the failure to hear his grievances caused the following consequences:

"[The failure to hear his grievances] breached the NDSL loan agreement, prematurely causing the NDSL loan debt to come due, while leaving Cawley with no means of egress to complete his Ph.D. work at the U-M and enter the job market in order to pay back the loans, while saddling Cawley with (1) over a decade's lost time in administrative grievances and lawsuits, (2) a bad credit rating foreclosing other borrowing, (3) around $30,000 or more in upfront grievance litigation costs, (4) some $100,000 plus loses (sic) in 'lost wages,' and (5) a hostile U-M Ph.D. training program environment."

The court held, "Cawley may intend to argue that somehow he is not liable on his student loans due to alleged University misconduct or due to the University's failure to award him his Ph.D. However, courts have rejected this argument."

Advice. Granting that the facts suggest a mentally disturbed student-litigant, nonetheless, the case's holding, like those of the cases cited, suggests that, whether or not a disgruntled student or alumnus can pursue a cause of action for educational malpractice and/or breach of contract (see Chapter 1), such claims do nothing to relieve the litigant of his/her loan obligations.

More problematic for the institution is its obligation to aid in the collection of loan debts. The Deficit Reduction Act, signed into law by President Bush in February 2006, modified some of the parameters of the student loan programs, affecting loans that are granted on or after July 1, 2006. These loans are also affected by provisions in legislation passed in 2002 that were already scheduled to take effect in July. Under current federal law, institutions can be dropped from participation in the federal student loan program if their default rate is either more than 40 percent for one year or more than 25 percent for three consecutive years. Consequently, colleges and universities have a high incentive to help assure that their graduates do not default on their loans.

Tuition

The Issue of "Sticker Price" v. Tuition Differentials

If the Higher Education Opportunity Act is the elephant in the financial aid office's living room, in-state preferential rates for illegal aliens is the 500-pound gorilla in resident v. non-resident tuition differentials at state universities.

Can a state university system offer resident illegal aliens better tuition rates than it charges American students attending from outside the state? The Superior Court for Yolo County, California, is asked to answer this question by some 60,000 current and former students of California's extensive public-college system. More accurately, the court will be required to rule on this issue if the lawsuit, filed in mid-December, survives the defendants' demurrer (i.e., motion to dismiss).

The defendants were pretty sure they can persuade the court to toss out the action. They point to a similar suit, filed in the federal court in Kansas, which was dismissed on July 5th last year. They had better be right. If the Yolo County lawsuit survives defendants' demurrer, and if the court grants plaintiffs' motion for class certification—meaning all 60,000 allegedly aggrieved out-of-state students and alumni can participate—a verdict ultimately could climb into the hundreds of millions of dollars.

It's a matter of simple arithmetic. California's public system is three tiered. The top tier is the University of California System, which includes such crown jewels as Berkeley and UCLA, and boasts about 220,000 students. Just below that is the California State University System, featuring more campuses, easier entry criteria, and another 350,000 students. On the bottom rung are the community colleges, easier still to enter, even lower in cost, and hosting 1.5 million scholars. Costs comport with quality. The top tier universities charge out-of-state student on average about $20,000 more per year than the state's resident students shell out. The difference at the mid-level schools is about $11,000, while it's about $7,000 at California's community colleges. To gain a rough idea of the high-level stakes in play here, assume that the average out-of-stater pays the average differential, that is, around $12,600 more than the "townies." Multiply that by 60,000 potential claimants and the state's treasury could be looking at a three-quarter billion-dollar blow.

The unlikely mastermind behind this swashbuckling assault on California's gleaming ivory towers is an insurance-defense lawyer out of Redwood City, not far from San Francisco. Michael J. Brady, a partner for some 35 years at the firm of Ropers, Majeski, Kohn and Bentley and a man in his mid-sixties, says he "just got interested when I heard about the state statute in 2002." Referring to the California law that opened the state's colleges to resident illegal aliens at the substantially lower in-state tuition rates, he adds, "I was listening to a radio program. And what I heard didn't make me happy."

Brady did some research then tackled the task of convincing his firm to launch the lawsuit. The initial phalanx of plaintiffs includes San Diego City College sophomore Briana Bilbray, daughter of the once and perhaps-future 50th District U.S. Congressman, Brian Bilbray. As residents, Briana and her dad aren't directly impacted by the differential. "It's more about fundamental principles of fairness," she told the press conference where the action was announced on December 18th.

Michael Brady adamantly agrees. "California being the biggest state," he begins, "illegal aliens cost the state $15 billion a year." Education, health and welfare, and prisons are the primary state expenses to which Brady points. Taking an oblique swipe at the powerful education unions, he contends, "Certain political groups love to see more people go to school to make the education empire bigger and bigger." Claiming to count supporters on both sides of the political aisle, Brady concludes, "What upsets most people is the lack of fairness. It's not fair for an illegal alien to get this benefit, when neighboring Americans from nearby Arizona, for example, are forced to pay so much more."

So what, I ask him, ,... if opponents like Ricardo Vasquez of the state system's Office of Strategic Communications is correct when he contends, "Our policy is consistent with federal law," then isn't your suit going down the same legal drain as *Day v. Sebelius*, the ill-fated Kansas case?

First of all, Brady cautions, the Kansas case is up on appeal to the U.S. Court of Appeals for the Tenth Circuit, sitting in Denver, which might decide to reinstate it. Second, he says he was smarter in instituting his case in a California state court. "The 11th Amendment, which says a state agency usually can't be sued in a federal court, doesn't come into play here. We have no restriction on suing for damages." The Kansas plaintiffs couldn't come after damages, a fact which fatally flawed their claim in the eyes of the federal judge. District Judge Rogers ruled last July that "students and parents lacked standing" to sue, because they didn't stand to gain any money from a victory.

His Honor also held that the 1996 Illegal Immigration Reform and Responsibility Act on which the suit was grounded failed to afford a private right of action to enforce it. Brady points out that the Congressmen who sponsored the statute—former-Senator Simpson of Wyoming and Representative Lamar Smith of Texas—have filed amicus briefs with the Tenth Circuit in which, says Brady, they assert Congressional intent to allow private suits.

The crux of the matter is section 1623 of the statute, which says, "An alien who is not lawfully present in the United States shall not be eligible on the basis of residence within a state... for any post-secondary education benefit unless a citizen or national of the United States is eligible for such benefit... without regard to whether the citizen or national is such a resident."

Argues Brady, "It's price versus principle. Congress said, okay, you want to establish a principle? Fine, but you have to pay the price. If a state wants to establish the principle that illegal aliens ought to be educated at the same tuition rates as legal residents, then it has to pay the price of giving up the privilege of extraordinarily-high out-of-state tuitions."

Proponents of the California law concur with Sheldon Steinbach, general counsel for the Washington-based American Council on Education, that it makes no sense to deny the privilege of in-state tuition rates to second-generation illegal aliens who have already made it through the public K–12 system. The right of such aliens to enjoy free public school education was established by the U.S. Supreme Court two-dozen years ago in a case involving Mexican children living illegally in Texas.

California contends that its statute escapes the onus of section 1623, because eligibility is based on graduation from a California high school, and not upon mere residency in the state.

This is specious, Brady retorts, because there's no way a child can attend a California public school unless the family has first established residency in the school district. "It's a de facto residency statute."

Source: Jim Castagnera, Should This Issue Be Left to Lawyers? The Greentree Gazette, *March 2006, at 36 (Reprinted with permission of* The Greentree Gazette: The Business Magazine for Higher Education*).*

Establishing Residency

In ***Spielberg v. Board of Regents of University of Michigan,*** *601 F.Supp. 994 (U.S. District Court, E.D. Mi., 1985),* the plaintiff sought to establish his Michigan residency in order to benefit from in-state tuition rates. The federal judge hearing the case identified the following "bundle of sticks," none of which was deemed dispositive, but all of which were relevant:

1. Ongoing presence in the state while not a college student;

2. Michigan-based sources of financial support, such as parents or guardians;
3. A former domicile in the state plus continuing connections to that home while residing outside the state;
4. Current home ownership in the state;
5. A professional license of some sort, issued by the state government;
6. A long-term military-service commitment in the state, such as the National Guard or a Michigan-based unit of the Army, Navy, Marine, Air Force or Coast Guard Reserve;
7. Acceptance of an offer of "permanent" employment within the state.

In ***Smith v. Board of Regents of the University of Houston System**, 874 S.W.2d 706 (Texas Court of Appeals, 1994),* the plaintiff paid the out-of-state tuition rate for his first year in school. After that he asked to be billed as a resident. In support of that application he offered the following evidence of residency:

- Part-time employment with a Houston law firm;
- A Texas driver's license;
- Texas automobile registration papers;
- Voter registration in the Lone Star State.

The courts deemed these four factors, without more (such as a history of full-time employment in the state), insufficient to carry the day.

Advice. In the words of two leading experts, "[A] student who moves from one state to another may have a very difficult time establishing residence in the new state for college tuition purposes, unless she demonstrates connections to the state (such as full-time employment) for a substantial period of time before enrolling at (sic) the state university" (Gerstein and Gerstein at 6). In short, while the controlling statutes and common law of each particular jurisdiction will be somewhat unique, a good rule of thumb is that a successful residency application will reflect a long-term commitment to the state *prior* to commencing one's college education.

Impact of the Higher Education Opportunity Act (HEOA)

The "Information Dissemination Activities section of the HEOA (20 USC 1092[a]) is worth quoting verbatim:

"Each eligible institution participating in any program under this title shall carry out information dissemination activities for prospective and enrolled students (including those attending or planning to attend less than full time) regarding the institution and all financial assistance under this title. The information required by this section shall be produced and be made readily available upon request, through appropriate publications, mailings, and electronic media, to an enrolled student and any prospective student. Each eligible institution shall, on an annual basis, provide all enrolled students a list of the information that is required to be provided by institutions to students by this section and section 444 of the General Education Provisions Act (20 USC 1232g)(also referred to as the Family Education Rights and Privacy Act of 1974), together with a statement of the procedures required to obtain such information."

A laundry list of categories of information to be provided follows this statutory provision. Financial aid information is, of course, high on the list. (Other categories are noted in the chapters that follow.)

By February 14, 2010, the U.S. Department of Education (DOE) was required to complete consultations with its various constituencies (students, families, college and university representatives, lenders, and even high school guidance counselors) to ascertain what information, over and above that already required by the federal Truth in Lending Act, that students and parents need in making student-loan decisions. In fulfillment of this mandate, the DOE conducted so-called negotiated rulemaking in the summer and fall of 2009.

Additionally, the HEOA requires colleges and universities to provide exit counseling to graduates, who leave with "mortgages" on their diplomas. This counseling for student-borrowers must include:

- available repayment plans
- debt-management strategies
- terms and conditions of loan forgiveness or cancellation
- consequences of defaulting

Sources

Dillon, Tim, Court: Disabled Can't Escape Student Loans, USA TODAY, December 7, 2005.

Fetterman, Mindy and Barbara Hanse, Young and In Debt, USA TODAY, November 22, 2006.

Gerstein, Ralph M. and Lois Gerstein, EDUCATION LAW: AN ESSENTIAL GUIDE FOR ATTORNEYS, TEACHERS, ADMINISTRATORS, PARENTS AND STUDENTS (Tucson, AZ: Lawyers and Judges Publishing Co., Inc. 2004).

Hechinger, John, U.S. Gets Tough on Failure to Repay Student Loans, WALL STREET JOURNAL, January 6, 2004.

Lapp, Alison, On the Docket: Lockhart, James v. U.S. et al., MEDILL NEWS SERVICE, September 1, 2005 [http://docket.medill.northwestern.edu/archives/002385.php].

Mortgage Bankers Association, Student Loan Defaults [http://www.studentloanrx.com/student_loan_defaults.php]

CHAPTER 3

Student Activities

Athletic Programs

Colleges and universities in the current competitive environment are expected to present to their students a panoply of athletic opportunities. These broadly include: (1) competitive inter-institutional programs, typically under the auspices of the National Collegiate Athletic Association (NCAA), (2) inter-mural activities, and (3) fitness opportunities. The institution that lacks any one of these is likely to find itself at a severe competitive disadvantage vis a vis its peer competitors. Each of these levels of athletic activity posed its own particular challenges to university administrators. However, they share in common several legal issues: (a) student eligibility; (b) discrimination considerations; (c) liability for injuries.

Student Eligibility

At the level of inter-collegiate athletic competition, our discussion will be limited to the NCAA. The non-profit organization boasts more than 1,000 member colleges and universities. These schools are divided among Divisions I, II and III.

Division I

See chart on following page.

Division	Sports Sponsorship	Football Attendance Requirements	Scheduling Requirements: Football	Scheduling Requirements: Men's Basketball	Scheduling Requirements: Women's Basketball	Men's Swimming and Diving; Men's Indoor and Outdoor Track and Field	Scheduling Requirements: Other Sports	Financial Aid Minimums	Annual Dues
Bowl Subdivision (formerly I-A)	16 varsity including football; minimum of six male/mixed, minimum eight all female (emerging sport max: two).	15,000 average actual or paid attendance for all home football games. Institution must perform annual certified audit.	At least 60 percent against Football Bowl Subdivision members, including a minimum of four home contests against Football Bowl Subdivision opponents. One contest against a NCAA Football Championship Subdivision opponent may be counted provided the opponent has average 90 percent of the maximum grant in aid over a rolling two-year period.	All but four games against Division I teams, 1/3 of all contests in home arena.	All but four games against Division I teams.	At least 50 percent of contests against Division I opponents.	Contest used to meet minimum number of contests must be against Division I teams. Fifty percent of all additional competition must be against Division I teams.	Provide an average of at least 90 percent of football maximum grants over a rolling two-year period, and annually offer a minimum of 200 athletics grants in aid or $4 million total.	$1,800
Championship Subdivision (formerly I-AA)	Seven male/mixed and seven female, including two team sports per gender and not more than two emerging sports. (Or six male/mixed and eight female).	N/A	At least 50 percent of games schedules and played against Football Bowl Subdivision or NCAA Football Championship Subdivison.	All but four games against Division I teams, 1/3 of all contests in home arena.	All but four games against Division I teams.	At least 50 percent of contests against Division I opponents.	Contest used to meet minimum number of contests must be against Division I teams. Fifty percent of all additional competition must be against Division I teams.	Fifty percent of max grants in 14 sports; or aggregate expenditure of $964,700 ($482,350 for women) on 38 full grants (19 for women) exclusive of football and basketball; or 50 of full grants (25 for women) excluding football and basketball; or exception for institutions with exceptional reliance on federal assistance for student's needs.	$1,800

Division 1. *Source: National Collegiate Athletic Association [http://www.ncaa.org]* *©National Collegiate Athletic Association, 2009. All rights reserved.*

Division II

General Requirements for Division II Membership

	Sports Sponsorship: Number of Sports						
	All-Male or Mixed-Team Sports		**All-Female Sports**	**Minimum Number of Team Sports**	**Three-season Requirement**	**Scheduling Requirement**	**Financial Aid Requirement**
Active Division II	4		4	2-All male/mixed 2-All female	One sport, per gender, per season per Bylaw 3.2.1.4	Must meet minimum contests and participant requirement per Bylaw 20.10.3.5	NONE
Active Division II After 8/1/05	5 4	OR	5 6	2-All male/mixed 2-All female	One sport,per gender, per season per Bylaw 3.2.1.4	Must meet minimum contests and participant requirement per Bylaw 20.10.3.5	Must meet minimum financial aid requirement per Bylaw 20.10.1.2
Reclassifying Member After 8/1/02	5 4	OR	5 6	2-All male/mixed 2-All female	One sport,per gender, per season per Bylaw 3.2.1.4	Must meet minimum contests and participant requirement per Bylaw 20.10.3.5	At the end of the first year of the reclassifying period must meet minimum financial aid per Bylaw 20.10.1.2
Provisional Member After 8/1/02	5 4	OR	5 6	2-All male/mixed 2-All female	One sport,per gender, per season per Bylaw 3.2.1.5	Must meet minimum contests and participant requirement per Bylaw 20.10.3.5	At the end of the first year of the reclassifying period must meet minimum financial aid per Bylaw 20.10.1.2

Source: National Collegiate Athletic Association [http://www.ncaa.org]

Division III

NCAA Division III is the competitive level that does not grant athletic scholarships. It is typically identified with small colleges that place special emphasis on the "scholar-athlete." In the NCAA's own words, "Colleges and universities in Division III place highest priority on the overall quality of the educational experience and on the successful completion of all students' academic programs. They seek to establish and maintain an environment in which a student-athlete's athletic activities are conducted as an integral part of the student-athlete's educational experience. They also seek to establish and maintain an environment that values cultural diversity and gender equity among their student-athletes and athletics staff….

"Division III institutions have to sponsor at least five sports for men and five for women, with two team sports for each gender, and each playing season represented by each gender. There are minimum contest and participant minimums for each sport. Division III athletics features student-athletes who receive no financial aid related to their athletic ability and athletic departments are staffed and funded like any other department in the university. Division III athletics departments place special importance on the impact of athletics on the participants rather than on the spectators. The student-athlete's experience is of paramount concern. Division III athletics encourages participation by maximizing the number and variety of athletics opportunities available to students, placing primary emphasis on regional in-season and conference competition."

Just as the requirements for institutional membership are spelled out in detail, as reflected in the foregoing tables, student eligibility to participate in Divisions I and II and win scholarship money for doing so are also detailed. Minimum requirements for Division I and II eligibility include:

- Graduation from high school;
- Completion of a minimum of 14 core courses (beginning August 1, 2008, Division I participation will require completion of 16 core courses);
- A minimum grade-point average (GPA) in those 14 (or 16) core courses; and
- A qualifying test score on either the ACT or SAT test.
- Under some circumstances the NCAA will permit a waiver of one or more of these requirements.

Not surprisingly, high school students denied the opportunity to accept a scholarship and participate in competition under these requirements from time to time have taken the NCAA to court, challenging its rules.

Phillip v. Fairfield University, *118 F.3d 131 (U.S. Court of Appeals, 2d Cir, 1997).* Having determined during the spring of 1996 that Darren Phillip, then a high school senior, had failed to complete the minimum of 13 "core courses" at that time required under the NCAA's Division I eligibility standards, the NCAA notified Phillip that he was ineligible to play college basketball for, or receive financial aid from, his intended college, Fairfield University. Fairfield applied to the organization for a waiver of the eligibility requirements. The NCAA denied the request on the grounds that there were neither exceptional circumstances present nor independent evidence of Phillip's academic qualifications that warranted granting relief. Following the initial denial of the waiver, Fairfield proceeded through the NCAA's appellate process, ultimately appealing to the very highest level of the NCAA, the NCAA Council. In January of 1997, the Council upheld the denial of the waiver.

On October 21, 1996, Phillip moved for an injunction before the United States District Court for the District of Connecticut in an attempt to prevent the NCAA from further interfering with his opportunity to attend Fairfield and play basketball for its team. By this time, Phillip had begun attending his first semester at Fairfield (the tuition for which was paid by his mother, using her retirement fund), although he was prohibited from receiving aid or playing basketball. On November 22, 1996, Magistrate Judge Smith issued his recommendation that the preliminary injunction be granted, and on January 24, 1997, the district court overruled the NCAA's objections, and adopted the magistrate judge's recommendation, reasoning principally that Phillip would suffer irreparable harm if the injunction were denied and that he was likely to prevail on his argument that the NCAA breached its duty to Phillip by arbitrarily refusing to grant him a waiver of its eligibility requirements. The NCAA appealed.

Analysis. The Second Circuit appeals panel found that the district judge in granting Phillip's motion for an injunction reasoned that the NCAA had a contractual obligation to treat the student fairly, given that his ability to receive a basketball scholarship from Fairfield was dependent upon meeting the NCAA registration requirement and then meeting the eligibility requirements established by the organization. The judge then proceeded to find that the NCAA had to apply its rules in good faith to Phillip. Reasoning that a contract claim implicated state-law standards of good faith and fair dealing, the appellate judges went on to hold that His Honor had failed to do so. Rather, wrote the panel, "The district judge… seemed to be of the view that arbitrary enforcement of one's own rules alone could establish the likely merit of a breach of contract claim. Indeed, the district court opined that 'if it can be shown that the [waiver] rule has been violated for no good reason in this case, then I see no reason why this plaintiff should not get relief.'"

Outcome. The Second Circuit panel disagreed, holding, "Because the district court failed to apply principles of good faith and fair dealing as defined by Connecticut contract law, and, because of this omission, also failed to make any factual findings of bad intent, we are unable to affirm the district court's order."

Advice. While the basis of the Second Circuit's decision suggests that, had the district judge done it right, the injunction might have been affirmed, the court's rejection of his honor's reasoning implies a significant level of deference to the NCAA in the interpretation and application of its own rules, not unlike the deference accorded to colleges and universities in areas of discretionary activity such as promotion and tenure decisions, where the institution is deemed to enjoy special expertise not shared by the judiciary. Consequently, a costly court-challenge to an NCAA ruling should not be lightly undertaken.

Indeed, the NCAA has survived sophisticated legal challenges grounded in complex areas of federal law, ranging from constitutional considerations to antitrust statutes.

In ***NCAA v. Tarkanian,*** *488 U.S. 179, 109 S.Ct. 454 (U.S. Supreme Court, 1988)*, the high court held that the NCAA could not be deemed to be a "state actor," even though its recommended sanctions in a recruiting-scandal investigation were accepted and implemented by a state university. In this case, the organization conducted a lengthy investigation of alleged recruiting violations at the University of Nevada, Las Vegas. At the conclusion of the inquiry, the NCAA found 38 violations, notably 10 that it laid at the feet of UNLV's head men's basketball coach. The NCAA demanded that the coach be suspended, threatening additional sanctions against the university if the latter declined to comply with the demand. The coach took the NCAA to court and the Nevada Supreme Court ultimately held that for constitutional purposes the organization had made itself a state actor, had denied the coach due process of law, as required by the Bill of Rights and as applied to state actors by 42 U.S.C. section 1983. It affirmed dismissal of the coach's suspension and the award of his attorney fees, the U.S. Supreme Court granted certiorari and reversed, holding that because UNLV had the option of withdrawing from the NCAA, rather than implementing the organization's recommended sanctions, the NCAA had not directly taken the disciplinary actions and therefore was not a "state actor." Four years later, the U.S. District Court for Rhode Island reached a similar conclusion in the case of a wrestler who transferred from the University of Nebraska to Brown and was subsequently told by the NCAA that he couldn't compete until he repeated a failed course. See ***Collier v. NCAA****, 783 F. Supp. 1576 (U.S. District Court, D.R.I., 1992).*

In the area of antitrust law, the NCAA has long been buffeted by the slings and arrows of misfortune. As long ago as 1984, the U.S. Supreme Court affirmed lower federal court findings that NCAA efforts to control TV rights to college football games violated federal antitrust laws. See ***NCAA v. Board of Regents of the University of Oklahoma****, 468 U.S. 85, 104 S.Ct. 2948 (U.S. Supreme Court, 1984*) ("The interest in maintaining a competitive balance among amateur athletic teams that the NCAA asserts as a further justification for its television plan is not related to any neutral standard or to any readily identifiable group of competitors. The television plan is not even arguably tailored to serve such an interest. It does not regulate the amount of money that any college may spend on its football program or the way the colleges may use their football program revenues, but simply imposes a restriction on one source of revenue that is more important to some colleges than to others. There is no evidence that such restriction produces any greater measure of equality throughout the NCAA than would a restriction on alumni donations, tuition rates, or any other revenue-producing activity. Moreover, the District Court's well-supported finding that many more games would be televised in a free market than under the NCAA plan, is compelling demonstration that the plan's controls do not serve any legitimate pro-competitive purpose.")

However, the high court was cautious about articulating an overly broad ruling against the NCAA:

"The NCAA plays a critical role in the maintenance of a revered tradition of amateurism in college sports. There can be no question but that it needs ample latitude to play that role, or that the preservation of the student-athlete in higher education adds richness and diversity to intercollegiate athletics and is entirely consistent with the goals of the Sherman Act. But consistent with the Sherman Act, the role of the NCAA must be to preserve a tradition that might otherwise die; rules that restrict output are hardly consistent with this role. Today we hold only that the record supports the District Court's conclusion that by curtailing output and blunting the ability of member institutions to respond to consumer preference, the NCAA has restricted rather than enhanced the place of intercollegiate athletics in the Nation's life." They went further, also observing, "It is reasonable to assume that most of the regulatory controls of the NCAA are justifiable means of fostering competition among amateur athletic teams and therefore pro-competitive because they enhance public interest in intercollegiate athletics."

The case has been interpreted as sanctioning such NCAA rules as "those that determine the size of the field, the number of players on a team and those which regulate physical violence. NCAA points out that all sports leagues structure their postseason championships, and require their member teams to participate in the final championship games, if selected." ***Metropolitan Intercollegiate Basketball Association v. NCAA****, 339 F. Supp. 2d 545 (U.S. District Court, S.D.N.Y. 2004).*

Two new lawsuits were initiated in 2006 against NCAA scholarship rules; both were grounded upon federal antitrust law. "One of the lawsuits, filed by former walk-on football players in a federal court in Washington state, challenges an NCAA cap on the number of grants-in-aid that big-time college football programs can offer to athletes. The other suit, filed in Los Angeles by former football and basketball players, argues that the grants awarded to athletes fail to cover the full cost of attending college" (Fischer). Knowledgeable antitrust-observers gave the two actions little hope of success. In the words of one such commentator:

"I agree…that the plaintiffs are going to have a very tough time. Given the Bd. of Regents of Univ. of Oklahoma v. NCAA case, no court is going to apply a per se rule to the NCAA rules that are being challenged. Under a rule of reason analysis the NCAA is going to have a couple of strong pro-competitive justifications for those rules. First, if there were no limits on compensation, major college sports would turn into minor league sports thereby destroying the very nature of the product being offered. While tens of millions will probably watch the Final Four, not even tens of thousands will watch the championship of the Continental Basketball Association (assuming it still exists). It is true that while no limits on compensation might destroy the product of college sports, the current limits may be set needlessly low and go well beyond those necessary to preserve the 'brand identity' (no pun intended) of college athletics. While I'm somewhat sympathetic to that argument, I just can't see an antitrust court wishing to insert itself into the business of second guessing the NCAA on the how much aid should be given through athletic scholarships" (Gerla).

In summary, student eligibility to participate in inter-collegiate athletics at more than 1,200 colleges and universities, including the largest and most prestigious institutions of higher learning, is governed by the rules of the NCAA. And our federal courts have by and large upheld those rules, despite repeated challenges on the basis of constitutional and antitrust considerations.

One key exception to this broad deference accorded to the NCAA by the courts is the area of discrimination.

Discrimination Considerations: Sex

While the NCAA has an extensive set of rules regarding sex discrimination, the driving force behind the organization's efforts is Title IX of the federal Education Act Amendments of 1972. 20 USCA section 1681. Title IX, therefore, deserves our close consideration.

- **Coverage**. The act forbids sex discrimination "under any education program or activity receiving Federal financial assistance." 20 USCA sec. 1681(a) Notably, its prohibition extends to admissions only with regard to specified programs, viz., "only to institutions of vocational education, professional education, and graduate higher education, and to public institutions of undergraduate higher education." 20 USCA sec. 1681(a)(1). But with respect to athletics, the act extends to undergraduate programs at private colleges and universities as well.
- **Exemptions**. Institutions of higher education, which have traditionally been single-sex on the basis of religious tenets [20 USCA sec. 1681(a)(3)], military training [20 USCA sec. 1681 (a)(4)] or a continuous, same-sex admissions policy [20 USCA sec. 1681(a)(5)] are excluded from coverage.

The U.S. Department of Education enforces Title IX [34 CFR Part 106]. DOE's position on athletic opportunities between the sexes was most recently presented in a 2003 opinion letter, which deserves to be reproduced in full here:

THE ASSISTANT SECRETARY

July 11, 2003

Dear Colleague:

It is my pleasure to provide you with this Further Clarification of Intercollegiate Athletics Policy Guidance Regarding Title IX Compliance.

Since its enactment in 1972, Title IX has produced significant advancement in athletic opportunities for women and girls across the nation. Recognizing that more remains to be done, the Bush Administration is firmly committed to building on this legacy and continuing the progress that Title IX has brought toward true equality of opportunity for male and female student-athletes in America.

In response to numerous requests for additional guidance on the Department of Education's (Department) enforcement standards since its last written guidance on Title IX in 1996, the Department's Office for Civil Rights (OCR) began looking into whether additional guidance on Title IX requirements regarding intercollegiate athletics was needed. On June 27, 2002, Secretary of Education Rod Paige created the Secretary's Commission on Opportunities in Athletics to investigate this matter further, and to report back with recommendations on how to improve the application of the current standards for measuring equal opportunity to participate in athletics under Title IX. On February 26, 2003, the Commission presented Secretary Paige with its final report, "Open to All: Title IX at Thirty," and in addition, individual members expressed their views.

After eight months of discussion and an extensive and inclusive fact-finding process, the Commission found very broad support throughout the country for the goals and spirit of Title IX. With that in mind, OCR today issues this Further Clarification in order to strengthen Title IX's promise of non-discrimination in the athletic programs of our nation's schools.

Title IX establishes that: "No person in the United States shall, on the basis of sex, be excluded from participation in, be denied the benefits of, or be subjected to discrimination under any education program or activity receiving Federal financial assistance."

In its 1979 Policy Interpretation, the Department established a three-prong test for compliance with Title IX, which it later amplified and clarified in its 1996 Clarification. The test provides that an institution is in compliance if 1) the intercollegiate-level participation opportunities for male and female students at the institution are "substantially proportionate" to their respective full-time undergraduate enrollments, 2) the institution has a "history and continuing practice of program expansion" for the underrepresented sex, or 3) the institution is "fully and effectively" accommodating the interests and abilities of the underrepresented sex.

First, with respect to the three-prong test, which has worked well, OCR encourages schools to take advantage of its flexibility, and to consider which of the three prongs best suits their individual situations. All three prongs have been used successfully by schools to comply with Title IX, and the test offers three separate ways of assessing whether schools are providing equal opportunities to their male and female students to participate in athletics. If a school does not satisfy the "substantial proportionality" prong, it would still satisfy the three-prong test if it maintains a history and continuing practice of program expansion for the underrepresented sex, or if "the interests and abilities of the members of [the underrepresented] sex have been fully and effectively accommodated by the present program." Each of the three prongs is thus a valid, alternative way for schools to comply with Title IX.

The transmittal letter accompanying the 1996 Clarification issued by the Department described only one of these three separate prongs—substantial proportionality—as a "safe harbor" for Title IX compliance. This led many schools to believe, erroneously, that they must take measures to ensure strict proportionality between the sexes. In fact, each of the three prongs of the test is an equally sufficient means of complying with Title IX, and no one prong is favored. The Department will continue to make clear, as it did in its 1996 Clarification, that "[i]nstitutions have flexibility in providing nondiscriminatory participation opportunities to their students, and OCR does not require quotas."

In order to ensure that schools have a clear understanding of their options for compliance with Title IX, OCR will undertake an education campaign to help educational institutions appreciate the flexibility of the law, to explain that each prong of the test is a viable and separate means of compliance, to give practical examples of the ways in which schools can comply, and to provide schools with technical assistance as they try to comply with Title IX.

In the 1996 Clarification, the Department provided schools with a broad range of specific factors, as well as illustrative examples, to help schools understand the flexibility of the three-prong test. OCR reincorporates those factors, as well as those illustrative examples, into this Further Clarification, and OCR will continue to assist schools on a case-by-case basis and address any questions they have about Title IX compliance. Indeed, OCR encourages schools to request individualized assistance from OCR as they consider ways to meet the requirements of Title IX. As OCR works with schools on Title IX compliance, OCR will share information on successful approaches with the broader scholastic community.

Second, OCR hereby clarifies that nothing in Title IX requires the cutting or reduction of teams in order to demonstrate compliance with Title IX, and that the elimination of teams is a disfavored practice. Because the elimination of teams diminishes opportunities for students who are interested in participating in athletics instead of enhancing opportunities for students who have suffered from discrimination, it is contrary to the spirit of Title IX for the government to require or encourage an institution to eliminate athletic teams.

Therefore, in negotiating compliance agreements, OCR's policy will be to seek remedies that do not involve the elimination of teams.

Third, OCR hereby advises schools that it will aggressively enforce Title IX standards, including implementing sanctions for institutions that do not comply. At the same time, OCR will also work with schools to assist them in avoiding such sanctions by achieving Title IX compliance.

Fourth, private sponsorship of athletic teams will continue to be allowed. Of course, private sponsorship does not in any way change or diminish a school's obligations under Title IX.

Finally, OCR recognizes that schools will benefit from clear and consistent implementation of Title IX. Accordingly, OCR will ensure that its enforcement practices do not vary from region to region.

OCR recognizes that the question of how to comply with Title IX and to provide equal athletic opportunities for all students is a challenge for many academic institutions. But OCR believes that the three-prong test has provided, and will continue to provide, schools with the flexibility to provide greater athletic opportunities for students of both sexes.

OCR is strongly reaffirming today its commitment to equal opportunity for girls and boys, women and men. To that end, OCR is committed to continuing to work in partnership with educational institutions to ensure that the promise of Title IX becomes a reality for all students.

Thank you for your continuing interest in this subject.

Sincerely,
Gerald Reynolds
Assistant Secretary for Civil Rights

Title IX does not apply to the NCAA itself, since the umbrella organization receives no federal funds. ***NCAA v. Smith**, 525 U.S. 459, 119 S.Ct. 924 (U. S. Supreme Court, 1999)*. Nevertheless, the association provides extensive Title IX guidance to its member institutions.

Q. How is Title IX applied to athletics?

Athletics programs are considered educational programs and activities. There are three basic parts of Title IX as it applies to athletics:

Participation: Title IX requires that women and men be provided equitable opportunities to participate in sports. Title IX does not require institutions to offer identical sports but an equal opportunity to play;

Scholarships: Title IX requires that female and male student-athletes receive athletics scholarship dollars proportional to their participation; and

Other benefits: Title IX requires the equal treatment of female and male student-athletes in the provisions of: (a) equipment and supplies; (b) scheduling of games and practice times; (c) travel and daily allowance/per diem; (d) access to tutoring; (e) coaching; (f) locker rooms, practice and competitive facilities; (g) medical and training facilities and services; (h) housing and dining facilities and services; (i) publicity and promotions; (j) support services; and (k) recruitment of student-athletes.

Q. Does Title IX apply only to athletics?

Although it is the application of Title IX to athletics that has gained the greatest public visibility, the law applies to every single aspect of education, including course offerings, counseling and counseling materials, financial assistance, student health and insurance benefits and/or other services, housing, marital and parental status of students, physical education and athletics, education programs and activities, and employment.

Q. How does an institution comply with Title IX?

An institution must meet all of the following requirements in order to be in compliance with Title IX:

1. For participation requirements, institutions officials must meet one of the following three tests. An institution may:
    a. Provide participation opportunities for women and men that are substantially proportionate to their respective rates of enrollment of full-time undergraduate students;
    b. Demonstrate a history and continuing practice of program expansion for the underrepresented sex;
    c. Fully and effectively accommodate the interests and abilities of the underrepresented sex; and,
2. Female and male student-athletes must receive athletics scholarship dollars proportional to their participation; and,
3. Equal treatment of female and male student-athletes in the eleven provisions as mentioned above.

Q. Does Title IX benefit only girls and women?

Title IX benefits everyone—girls and boys, women and men. The law requires educational institutions to maintain policies, practices and programs that do not discriminate against anyone on the basis of gender. Elimination of discrimination against women and girls has received more attention because females historically have faced greater gender restrictions and barriers in education. However, Title IX also has benefited men and boys. A continued effort to achieve educational equity has benefited all students by moving toward creation of school environments where all students may learn and achieve the highest standards.

Q. Who is responsible for enforcing Title IX?

Institutions are responsible for complying with federal laws. The Office for Civil Rights (OCR) of the U.S. Department of Education enforces Title IX. OCR has the authority to develop policy on the regulations it enforces. In regard to athletics programs, OCR developed an Intercollegiate Athletics Policy Interpretation that was issued December 11, 1979. The 1979 Policy Interpretation remains current policy. On April 2, 1990, OCR issued an athletics policy document called "Title IX Athletics Investigator's Manual" that has assisted athletics departments with enforcement and compliance issues with Title IX. Anyone may file an OCR complaint, and the identity of the party who files the complaint will be kept confidential.

Q. How is Title IX compliance assessed?

Title IX compliance is assessed through a total program comparison. In other words, the entire men's program is compared to the entire women's program, not just one men's team to the women's team in the same sport. The broad comparative provision was intended to emphasize that Title IX does not require the creation of mirror image programs. Males and females can participate in different sports according to their respective interests and abilities. Thus, broad variations in the type and number of sports opportunities offered to each gender are permitted.

Q. Does Title IX require that equal dollars be spent on men's and women's sports?

No. The only provision that requires that the same dollars be spent proportional to participation is scholarships. Otherwise, male and female student-athletes must receive equitable "treatment" and "benefits."

Q. Why does Title IX not require the same amount be spent on men's and women's sports?

The Javits Amendment stated that legitimate and justifiable discrepancies for nongender related differences in sports could be taken into account (i.e., the differing costs of equipment or event management expenditures). A male football player needs protective equipment such as pads and a helmet, and a female soccer player needs shin guards. Title IX does allow for a discrepancy in the cost of the equipment as long as both the football and soccer player received the same quality of equipment. However, a female ice hockey player must receive the same protective equipment that a male ice hockey player would receive, inasmuch as the protective equipment is the same.

Q. Does Title IX require identical athletics programs for males and females?

Title IX does not require identical athletics programs for males and females. Rather, Title IX requires that the athletics programs meet the interests and abilities of each gender. Under Title IX, one team is not compared to the same team in each sport. OCR examines the total program afforded to male student-athletes and the total program afforded to female student-athletes and whether each program meets the standards of equal treatment. Title IX does not require that each team receive exactly the same services and supplies. Rather, Title IX requires that the men's and women's program receive the same level of service, facilities, supplies and etc. Variations within the men's and women's programs are allowed, as long as the variations are justified.

Q. Is any sport excluded from Title IX?

Under Title IX there are no sport exclusions or exceptions. Individual participation opportunities (number of student-athletes participating rather than number of sports) in all men's and women's sports are counted in determining whether an institution meets Title IX participation standards. The basic philosophical underpinning of Title IX is that there cannot be an economic justification for discrimination. The institution cannot maintain that there are revenue productions or other considerations that mandate that certain sports receive better treatment or participation opportunities than other sports.

Q. Does Title IX mandate that a decrease in opportunities for male athletes be made in order to provide an increase in opportunities for female athletes?

Title IX does not require reductions in opportunities for male student-athletes. One of the purposes is to create the same opportunity and quality of treatment for both female and male student-athletes. Eliminating men sports programs is not the intent of Title IX. The intent of Title IX is to bring treatment of the disadvantaged gender up to the level of the advantaged group.

Q. Is there someone at my institution who would know about Title IX?

Compliance with Title IX is a shared responsibility of an entire institution, from top-level administration to individual staff members. Title IX mandates that institutions or other recipients of federal funds designate at least one employee as a Title IX coordinator to oversee compliance efforts. Institutions also are required to investigate any complaints of gender discrimination. In addition, all students and employees must be notified of the name, office address and telephone number of the designated Title IX coordinator. A student-athlete who has questions about Title IX specific to the their institution may find the following individuals on their campus a good resource: (1) senior woman administrator; (2) director of athletics; (3) faculty athletics representative; (4) compliance coordinator; (5) the legal council; or (6) Equal Employment Opportunities office.

Q. How do I know if my institution is in compliance with Title IX?

You just need to ask. It has become easier for anyone to find out if an institution is in compliance with Title IX. In 1994, the U.S. Congress passed the Equity in Athletics Disclosure Act, which requires all colleges and universities to report each year on athletics participation numbers, scholarships, program budgets and expenditures, and coaching salaries by gender. Information may be obtained by contacting your institution's athletics department and requesting this information. The results are identified by gender, and a reader may use this information to assist in assessing an institution's compliance with Title IX.

Source: http://www.ncaa.org/

Despite such extensive guidance, litigation under Title IX, both in terms of cases coming before DOE's Office of Civil Rights and in the form of private actions in federal courts is common.

Since Title IX is interpreted as requiring gender equity in athletic opportunities, compliance can potentially entail significant institutional commitments. For example, a school that carries an 80-man football squad arguably has to maintain a number of women's sports in order to provide equal opportunities between the sexes. Rather than commit such additional financial resources, some colleges and universities have opted to drop some of their men's sports, cutting their way to gender equity. Such cuts have been challenged in a number of court cases.

In ***Miami University Wrestling Club v. Miami University of Ohio****, 302 F.3d 608 (U.S. Court of Appeals, 6th Cir., 2002)*, the university determined to dissolve three men's sports teams to achieve gender equity. These were soccer, tennis and wrestling. The plaintiffs challenged the cuts, arguing they violated both Title IX and the U.S. Constitution's Equal Protection clause. First, the court deferred to DOE's policy interpretation, which allowed for the elimination of programs in order to comply. Second, the appeals panel held that no constitutional right to participate in collegiate athletics exists under federal law.

At about the same time that the Miami University case was decided, ***Chalenor v. University of North Dakota****, 291 F.3d 1042 (U.S. Court of Appeals, 8th Cir., 2002)* reached much the same conclusion with respect to the defendant's elimination of men's wrestling. Again acknowledging the DOE's position that the "substantially proportionate" standard of Title IX can be met but cuts as well as by additions, the court approved the university's action, which was motivated both by gender-equity considerations and the need to trim $95,000 from the athletic department's budget.

Another issue of significant controversy in the federal common law has been the extent of remedies available in private actions brought pursuant to Title IX.

The case of ***Paton v. New Mexico Highlands University**, 275 F.3d 1274 (U.S. Court of Appeals, 10th Cir., 2002)* established the availability of class action status to Title IX actions. Coaches and female student athletes brought the action on behalf of a class, which they defined as present and future female student athletes, against the university, its board of regents, and various officials, alleging violations of Title IX, the Fourteenth Amendment's Equal Protection Clause, and the New Mexico Constitution. After the federal district judge decertified the class and a jury returned its verdict in favor of the named plaintiffs, they moved for declaratory and injunctive relief, and for reconsideration of class decertification order. The United States District Court for the District of New Mexico denied these motions, and the plaintiffs appealed. The Court of Appeals held that: (1) a named plaintiff was a member of the purported class, viz., the women's soccer team; (2) that named plaintiff could adequately protect the interests of the class; and therefore (3) reversal and remand of the declaratory and injunctive relief issues were required in light of erroneous class decertification.

The case of ***Mercer v. Duke University,** 50 Fed. Appx. 643 (U.S. Court of Appeals, 4th Cir., 2002)* took on the issue of availability of punitive damages to a prevailing plaintiff. Here the plaintiff was a female place kicker who was dropped by the school's football team. She alleged that the head coach discriminated against her by denying participation in the team's summer camps, games and practices, and by making offensive and demeaning remarks about her. Although the case was at first dismissed, the U.S. Court of Appeals for the Fourth Circuit reinstated it, stating that once she was allowed to try out, the defendant could not discriminate against her. Even though the DOE regulations distinguished between contact and non-contact sports made available to members of the two sexes, once the tryout took place, the distinction became irrelevant to the plaintiff's case. The case proceeded to trial, and a jury awarded her a million dollars in compensatory damages and another two million in punishment damages. The case once again went up to the Fourth Circuit, where the judges ruled that punitive damages are not available under Title IX.

Discrimination Considerations: Disabilities

As explained more fully in Chapter 8, the distinction between the K–12 environment and the campus milieu with regard to student disabilities is dramatic. The "No Child Left Behind" Act and the Individuals with Disabilities Education Act (IDEA) seek to mainstream as many disabled students into K–12 classrooms as possible. In order to achieve this goal, these two federal laws mandate a significant support network of professionals and aids in and outside the classroom. By contrast, the Americans with Disabilities Act governs disability discrimination at the university level. That statute requires only that "reasonable accommodations" be accorded to disabled students. A student who cannot participate in a program of study or an extra-curricular activity even with reasonable accommodation may be denied that college experience.

Nevertheless, an observation made by two leading authors on K–12 law applies with relatively equal aptness to athletic programs in higher education:

> Health concerns can be important when dealing with student athletes. Lawsuits have been brought when students who wanted to play were not permitted to. More often, suits charge that school officials were negligent in permitting players to play when they had medical conditions or injuries that should have kept them off the field. (Gerstein and Gerstein at 721)

This dilemma required university administrators and coaches to walk a tightrope between disability law and liability law. When does one permit a disabled student to participate in athletic activities and when does this participation pose a danger to the student and/or others?

Title III of the ADA applies to college athletics. [42 USCA section 12182 *et seq*, dealing with public accommodations; see, e.g., ***Bowers v. NCAA**, 9 F.Supp.2d 460 (U.S. District Court, D.N.J., 1998)*. NOTE: Section 504 of the federal Rehabilitation Act also may apply and was often relied upon prior to the ADA's 1992 effective date; standards are substantially the same under both acts, and the ADA will be the reference in this section of the book.] Most courts considering the question have held that the NCAA itself is a public accommodation, since the organization exercises significant control over ticket prices, souvenirs and memorabilia, concession profits, press policies, and venue access issues. [See, e.g., ***Tatum v. NCAA**, 992 F.Supp. 1114 (U.S. District Court, E.D. Mo., 1998)*.] Whether the ADA and/or state anti-discrimination laws apply to state-based intercollegiate athletic conferences have gone both ways (Gerstein and Gerstein at 77 and note 162).

NCAA guidelines deal with both physical disabilities affecting ability to compete and scholastic eligibility requirements.

Frequently Asked Questions on Students With Disabilities

Do the standards for initial eligibility change for students with disabilities?

No. All students must satisfy the same standards in order to compete in NCAA Divisions I and II athletics.

Will member institutions have access to my child's records?

No. Information submitted to NCAA Disability Services is not released to member institutions.

What are the accommodations provided to students with disabilities?

- Use courses for students with disabilities that are designated on the high-school's list of NCAA-Approved Core Courses;
- Use approved core courses taken before the student enrolls in college, including courses taken in the summer after high-school graduation;
- Use ACT and/or SAT scores achieved during nonstandard administrations.

When should a student document his or her disability with the NCAA?

The only time disability documentation needs to be sent to the NCAA is if a student with a disability would like to use core courses taken after high-school graduation to satisfy Division I initial-eligibility requirements. The student should submit his or her disability documentation to NCAA Disability Services by submitting the following information:

- A signed copy of the most recent professional evaluation report diagnosing the student's disability, including the diagnostic test results.
- A copy of the student's most recent Individual Education Plan (IEP), Section 504 Plan, or for private high schools, a statement on the high-school's letterhead describing the accommodations, if any, received by the student because of the disability.
- The signed copy of a professional diagnosis should be completed within the last three years. If the diagnosis is not within the last three years, the IEP, ITP, 504 Plan or statement of accommodations from the high school should be within the last three years.

- The student's social security number, high school graduation year, address and phone number should be included with the aforementioned documentation.
- An individual (e.g., parent or guardian) that wishes to discuss a student athlete's disability services request must be listed on the Buckley Statement form. This form should be included with the submission of the aforementioned documentation.

Source: http://www.ncaa.org/

In ***Cole v. NCAA***, *120 F. Supp. 1060 (U.S. District Court, N.D.Ga., 2000)*, the plaintiff-student took issue with the association's incoming-student eligibility requirements. The requirements were a minimum 2.5 GPA and a combined SAT Score of at least 820 or, alternatively an ACT score no lower than 58. Although the plaintiff had the 2.5 GPA, his best SAT combination was only 760 and his best ACT performance was 57. The district judge ruled that requiring the association to waive its requirements for a disabled student whose performance fell that far below the minimums went beyond what could be considered a reasonable accommodation under the ADA. Furthermore, abandoning the scholastic requirements altogether was unreasonable as a matter of law, added the court.

Knapp v. Northwestern University, *101 F.3d 473 (U.S. Court of Appeals, 7th Cir., 1996) cert. denied, 520 U.S. 1274, 117 S.Ct. 2454, 138 L.Ed.2d 212 (1997)*, involved a physical disability. The plaintiff enjoyed the requisite talent to play Division I basketball. However, he had been diagnosed with a cardiac condition that was potentially life threatening. The appeals court held that playing college basketball was not a major life activity as defined and protected by the ADA. The court reasoned that restriction from the basketball court did not prevent him from getting a college education. Furthermore, held the judges, the student could not be deemed "otherwise qualified" to participate in the sport, since even with a reasonable accommodation, the inevitable exertion posed a deadly danger to him. The fact that the student could die on the court posed a significant liability issue for school officials. As noted above, administrators and coaches often are on the horns of a dilemma, risking an ADA suit if they deny such a student a chance to compete and carry a scholarship or opening themselves to a wrongful-death action if they acquiesce and the student expires while playing for the school. In this case, school officials chose to defend the ADA action and the court agreed with this decision.

The Knapp case, posing this dilemma so squarely, serves as a nice transition to the issue of athletic injuries.

Athletic Injuries

As a leading education-law clearinghouse has observed, "Under common law, student-athletes were held to assume the risks inherent in participating in school athletics. Consequently, most lawsuits by injured individuals were unsuccessful. However, [more recently] many courts have replaced the doctrine of assumption of risk with comparative negligence principles that allow at least partial recovery of damages upon proof of [institutional] negligence" (Center for Education & Employment Law at 128).

Assumption of risk, "Asserts that the plaintiff knew that a particular activity was dangerous and thus bears all responsibility for any injury that resulted" [http://www.lectlaw.com/def/a083.htm].

Comparative negligence "comes into play when it is contended that two or more parties failed to perform at the standard of the 'ordinary reasonable person.' In a situation where each party has some degree of negligence in causing an accident, the responsibility to the other person(s) is reduced by the others' degree of negligence" [http://injury-law.freeadvice.com/injury-law/comparative_negligences.htm].

Two examples illustrate where assumption of risk ends and simple negligence begins.

In ***Geiersbach v. Frieje,*** *807 N.E.2d 114 (Indiana Court of Appeals, 2004),* the appeals panel pointed out that, while at the K–12 level schools have been held to an "ordinary negligence" standard, the Hoosier State's common law had never held higher education to that same high standard of behavior. The student argued for a "special relationship" between himself and his school. The court disagreed, holding that athletes assume the risk of foreseeable and inherent danger. It added that malicious and/or intentional conduct, or at least recklessness, ought to be present in order to hold the institution liable.

Facts. On February 5, 2000, the baseball team was practicing inside the university's gymnasium. During one of the infield drills, the coach positioned the players to resemble their positions. The pitcher and the batter each had a ball. The pitcher threw his ball to the catcher. When the catcher received the ball, he was supposed to discard it. At the same time, the batter, standing in the batter's box, would introduce his ball into play by hitting it in whichever direction he chose.

In the instance at issue, the coach positioned runners at first and third base, but the batter, also a coach, was actually conducting the drill. The pitcher threw his ball to the catcher. The catcher mistakenly believed that it was a "throw through" situation where he was to throw to second base to cut off a potential steal. At the same time, the batter hit his ball down the third base line. Second baseman Geiersbach moved to cover second base, keeping his attention on the third baseman fielding the ball just put into play by the batter. Geiersbach was prepared to receive the throw from the third baseman to render a "force out" at second base. He was struck in the left eye by the baseball thrown by the catcher. He suffered severe and permanent damage to his eye.

Geiersbach brought suit against his university, the two coaches and the catcher, alleging negligence and breach of duty.

Analysis. The court at plaintiff's behest considered significance of the Knapp case, discussed above. "Geiersbach concedes that no Indiana court has had occasion to rule in cases involving the duty of colleges and universities to their student-athletes. However, he cites ***Knapp v. Northwestern Univ.,*** *101 F.3d 473 (U.S. Court of Appeals, 7th Cir., 1996), cert. denied, 520 U.S. 1274, 117 S.Ct. 2454, 138 L.Ed.2d 212 (1997),* as a case in which the Seventh Circuit appears to recognize the imposition of a duty on colleges and universities with regard to their student-athletes. In Knapp, a student who had been barred from participating in intercollegiate basketball because of his heart defect filed an action against the university he attended. The student had been recruited on a basketball scholarship but upon learning of his heart defect, the university forbade him from playing or practicing with the team, but allowed him to retain the scholarship. The district court denied the university's motion for summary judgment and granted the student's motion for permanent injunction. Upon appeal, the Seventh Circuit reversed the district court's decision, permitting the university to deem the student ineligible to play. The court stated that the medical determinations should be left to team doctors and universities as long as they are made with reason and rationality and with full regard to possible and reasonable accommodations. Specifically, the court stated that, in cases where medical experts disagree regarding the extent of risk of serious harm or death, Congress did not intend the courts to make the final medical decision. Rather, the court held that the university must be allowed to make its own determinations of substantial risk and severity of injury provided those determinations are based on reliable evidence." The Indiana appeals panel rejected the plaintiff's contention that such cases posited a "special relationship" between student-athlete and university that raised the bar of negligence liability.

Rather, the court continued, "In respect to what dangers are inherent in a sport, we believe that the existing case law is instructive. For example, in *Kleinknecht*, the parents brought suit against the college for failure to provide medical staff at practice. The lack of medical staff is not an inherent danger of playing lacrosse, so the court properly allowed the suit to continue on a breach of duty claim. Similarly, in *King v. Univ. of Indianapolis, 2002 WL 31242233 (U.S. District Court, S.D.Ind., 2002)*, a 19-year-old football player died of heat stroke while participating in the first practice of the season. The player's family introduced evidence that the player showed signs of distress that were negligently treated by the football staff. The court determined that the player's injuries were not inherent to the game of football. While that court continued on into a discussion of incurred risk, we prefer to halt the discussion at the question of whether the danger was inherent in the sport. As it was not, the court properly held that the suit could continue.

"Likewise, in *Clark*, had the judo student merely been injured in the class, there may have been no liability on the part of the classmate or the instructor. However, because the instructor failed to act when informed of the risk, the conduct of the instructor could reasonably be found sufficiently reckless as to deny the defendants' motion for judgment on the evidence and therefore, the student could present her case to a jury even though being injured during a judo class may have been an inherent risk (*Clark,* 617 N.E.2d at 918–20).

"In ***Mark v. Moser,*** *746 N.E.2d 410 (Ind.Ct.App.2001),* a cyclist in a triathlon cut off another participant, causing severe injury to the participant. The Mark court held that a participant does not owe a duty to fellow participants to refrain from conduct which is inherent and foreseeable in the play of the game even though such conduct may be negligent and may result in injury absent evidence that the other participant *119 either intentionally caused injury or engaged in conduct so reckless as to be totally outside the range of ordinary activity involved in the sport. Id. at 420. This is the same standard of care we are following in this decision.

"More recently, in ***Gyuriak v. Millice,*** *775 N.E.2d 391 (Ind.Ct.App.2002),* trans. denied, Millice hit an errant golf ball, striking Gyuriak who was playing on a different hole. Gyuriak filed a complaint against Millice, alleging negligence and recklessness. The trial court granted Millice's motion for summary judgment and Gyuriak appealed. Gyuriak argued that Mark should be overturned because it was inconsistent with the 1985 Indiana Comparative Fault Act. This court rejected his argument, noting that only secondary assumption of risk had been incorporated into the Act's definition of 'fault.'

"This is because the primary assumption of risk occurs when an individual, by voluntarily engaging in an activity, consents to those risks that are inherent in and arise by virtue of the nature of the activity itself. In such cases, the participant is owed no duty with regard to such inherent and ordinary risks."

By contrast, in ***Hummel v. University of North Carolina,*** *576 S.E.2d 124 (North Carolina Court of Apppeals, 2003),* a state agency applied the basic common-law standard of simple negligence and the court of appeals approved this approach, on appeal affirming both the outcome and the amount of damages awarded. The plaintiff, a wrestler, was lifting weights in the university's fitness center, when a cable on the machine broke and a weight dropped on his head, seriously injuring him. Apparently recovered, the plaintiff competed for the remainder of the season, but subsequently had to give up the sport after suffering a second concussion. After graduating and going off to medical school, he continued to have medical issues relating back to the injuries. He sued the university under the North Carolina Tort Claims Act, alleging negligent maintenance of the weight machine.

Analysis. A member of the state's Industrial Commission, which takes the initial cut at cases prosecuted under the Tort Claims Act against state actors, awarded Hummel $500,000. Review by the full commission knocked the award down to $50,000. The appeals court, en banc, held, "(1) full Commission appropriately reviewed deputy commissioner's findings of fact and chose to issue its own findings of fact; (2) Commission's decision did not violate the 'law of the land' clause in state Constitution; (3) reducing award to wrestler for future loss of earnings was not reversible error; and (4) testimony of wrestler and his physician supported decision to award wrestler $50,000 in damages." In so holding the court reasoned, "Here, the Industrial Commission found that plaintiff's injury on 6 July 1996 was a 'significant causative factor' for plaintiff missing a season of wrestling, suffering headaches, and limitation of his normal physical routine for at least six months. This finding of fact was supported by plaintiff's own testimony, as well as the testimony of his physician. The evidence regarding defendant's award for pain and suffering, mental anguish, and physical impairment is credible and supports the Commission's finding. Therefore, this assignment of error is overruled."

Advice. Administrators and coaches are well advised to understand the applicable common-law principles that apply on the state(s) where their institution's athletic facilities are located. Typically, the university's liability-insurance carrier is easily able to explain these common law standards and may even provide gratis educational/training services to clients. Where, as is often the case, teams compete across state lines, conflict of law issues may arise in the event of athletic injuries.

Public colleges and universities may enjoy total or partial immunity from suit, or—as in the Hummel case—may be subject to special proceedings outside the normal trial court system of the state. Furthermore, individual coaches and administrators may enjoy qualified or absolute immunity from suit while acting in the name of the university qua state agency.

It is beyond the scope of this work to identify these differences on a state-by-state basis. The best your authors can do is alert you to the important point that these differences must be identified and considered both in terms of loss prevention programs and the defense of specific student claims.

Other Student Activities

Colleges and universities today are expected to offer their students a cornucopia of activities and organizations. A single example will suffice; following is the description of student organizations and activities at Rider University, a medium-sized institution with an enrollment of 5,500 FTE, located in central New Jersey:

Activities Outside the Classroom

University life isn't just about what you learn in the classroom. Taking those skills and using them in everyday life is essential. Discover all that Rider has to offer by getting involved and finding your passion outside the classroom.

Help people in the community with one of our many service clubs. Deejay on the radio for WRRC. Run for an office or position within the student government. Become a member of a fraternity or sorority. Choreograph and produce your own dance performance. Entertain with a comedy troupe. Lead your tennis team to victory. Play your heart out in flag football. Start your own organization. Think big!

Leadership Opportunities

Get involved!

Rider University provides students with unlimited opportunities to develop their leadership skills through participation in a variety of campus organizations. Begin now to connect your academic life with the real world: make an impact, and learn what it is to truly lead with integrity, justice, and the spirit of service.

- Office of Campus Life—Lawrenceville Campus

The Office of Campus Life complements the academic experience and strives to enrich the community experience at Rider University through our programs and services. The Office of Campus Life enhances the educational and leadership experience by providing developmental opportunities, exposure to and participation in social, cultural, spiritual, multicultural, intellectual, recreational, community service and campus governance programs. The programs and services of Campus Life are intended to instill a sense of self worth and awareness within students so they become active, responsible and civically engaged adults in today's society.

- Student Life at Westminster—Princeton Campus

The Associate Dean of Students Office on the Princeton Campus supervises and/or works closely with many offices based on both campuses, including Residence Life, Student Activities/Leadership, Career Services, Safety and Security, Counseling Services, and Multicultural Affairs/International Services. The Assistant Dean of Students for Student Life is responsible for providing leadership opportunities on the Princeton campus, as well as advising the Student Government Association on the Princeton campus.

- Student Government Association

The student government of Rider University acts as a liaison for Rider University students to faculty, staff, and administration and assists in the coordination of student activities on campus. SGA provides students with an opportunity to make a difference on campus and serve their fellow students, while learning valuable leadership skills that students will carry with them long after they graduate. There is a Student Government Association in place at both of Rider's Campuses.

- SGA Lawrenceville
- SGA Princeton

- Emerging Leaders

The Emerging Leaders program offers all new students an opportunity to become involved in campus life and begin to develop the leadership skills needed to be successful in a professional career. As a first year Emerging Leader, you will network with fellow new students while also connecting with key student leaders, alumni, staff, and faculty. You will design and implement major student social events and become recognized as a significant student leader among your peers. There are Emerging Leader classes at both of Rider's Campuses.

◦ Emerging Leaders Lawrenceville—Office of Campus Life 609-896-5327

◦ Emerging Leaders Princeton—Associate Dean of Students Office 609-921-7100 x8263

• Center for the Development of Leadership Skills

Based on the Lawrenceville Campus, the Center for the Development of Leadership Skills is designed to provide distinctive leadership education for all Rider's academic programs by identifying and promoting specific leadership skills in the curriculum, through leadership development programming across the institution, and through external experiences such as mentoring and internships.

For more information contact the center by phone at (609) 895-5776, or email at cdls@rider.edu.

Sports & Recreation

Rider University sports and recreation is comprised of a variety of activities ranging from drop-in recreation at the fitness center to varsity athletics. Rider has something for everyone. The intramural program allows students to participate in organized team competition with other students on campus. The club sport program provides specific sport competition run by student leaders, and they compete with area universities and colleges. The fitness center is another recreation outlet on campus and allows for students to drop-in when their schedule allows. A weight room facility and cardio room is available as well as open swim time in the indoor pool. Outdoor facilities allow for recreation during scheduled times on the track, basketball courts, and tennis courts. Outdoor Recreation programs are also available and provide adventure trips kayaking in the Pine Barrens, hiking along the Appalachian Trail, and a variety of other outdoor adventures. Recreation opportunities are available for all Rider University students, from the Lawrenceville campus and Princeton campus. These opportunities allow students a balanced lifestyle to add to their health and wellness at Rider and to become a success.

Although most activities are based on the Lawrenceville campus, all recreation programs are open to students from both the Lawrenceville and Princeton campuses.

Get In! Get Out! Get Active!

• Recreation Programs

Recreation Programs at Rider include intramural sports, club sports, outdoor recreation adventure trips and more! These programs are housed in the Student Recreation Center and are open to all Rider students, staff, and faculty.

• Student Recreation Center

Rider is proud to open the brand new Student Recreation Center this Fall. This exciting facility provides a variety of opportunities, starting with three indoor courts, which host basketball, volleyball, and tennis. There is a 3600 square foot fitness center with Life Fitness cardio equipment and secularized weight room machines as well as free weights. In addition, there is an elevated indoor jogging/walking track located on the second floor of the Student Recreation Center.

• Partnership with Princeton YMCA

During the 2004–05 academic year, the Associate Dean of Students Office and the Student Government Association on the Princeton campus joined resources to form a partnership with the Princeton YMCA. This partnership allows for students of Westminster Choir College to utilize the YMCA's fitness center for a low monthly cost. Students who are interested in using the YMCA's facilities simply pay the monthly membership (memberships are on a month to month basis) and show their University ID card upon arrival.

Located on Paul Robeson Place (about six blocks west on Hamilton Ave.), the Princeton Y pool offers lap and other recreational swimming. The Y also offers a wide range of other facilities and activities (weight-training, racquetball, basketball courts, adult intramural volleyball, basketball, life-saving, and scuba-diving classes). For more information, please visit the Princeton SGA at http://www.westminstersga.org/ or call (609) 497-2100 for more information on programs and membership.

Campus Activities & Traditions

Get Involved!

• Student Organization Directory

Join us! Rider University student organizations promote the well-rounded life of a college student. The social and service opportunities, academic collaboration, professional connection, leadership development, spiritual growth, and much more offered by membership in Rider student organizations is the kind of life experience that will change your life for the better.

• Campus Traditions

Make your mark! A chance to touch the past, celebrate the present, and look to the future. Rider cherishes its traditions as joyful, moving opportunities for students to come together and be part of something bigger than themselves.

• The Pub, Lawrenceville

A fun tradition for those who are 21 and older!

• Weekend Warriors

The Office of Campus Life (OCL) reaches out each semester to students who remain on campus for most weekends. Students can sign up in OCL for "Weekend Warriors" list serve. Every Wednesday OCL staff sends out a listing of events, activities and programs planned for the upcoming weekend. This is an excellent way for students to stay connected with what's going on and to link in to all of the fun things on campus. You can call the OCL (609-896-5327) for more information.

• Things to Do Around the Area

We put together a list of fun activities and entertainment in the local area. From down the street to "down town," Rider is in the perfect location so that there is always something to do!

Fraternities & Sororities

One of the best ways to take advantage of all that Rider has to offer is through the Greek Community. About 15% of the Rider community is involved in fraternity and sorority life. Many people have ideas about what it's like to be

Greek from TV or movies but remember—you should not believe everything you see or hear. Going Greek is a serious decision that requires some thought and it's worth it to check it out firsthand.

Fraternities and sororities are founded upon the common principles and core values of scholarship, leadership, community service, character and the formation of lifelong friendships; fraternities and sororities provide an exciting way to enhance your collegiate experience. Rider's Greek history dates back to 1922 and has always been an important part of the school's co-curricular activities. Currently, Rider is home to four National Panhellenic sororities, five National Inter-fraternity Conference fraternities and 5 multicultural Greek Organizations. Combined, Greek Life makes up the largest student group on the campus. Our chapters are recognized each year with various awards for excellence.

With all of the things that fraternities and sororities are involved in, it's important to remember that becoming involved will take up a good deal of your time. This means you'll have to do a really good job of managing your time. The benefits of being Greek continue long after you graduate. National studies show that fraternity and sorority members have a higher graduation rate from college, have higher satisfaction with their undergraduate experience, and give more as alumni than their non-Greek counterparts. Of North America's 50 largest corporations, 43 are headed by fraternity and sorority members and 7 out of 10 people listed in "Who's Who" are Greek. Also, 85% of Fortune 500 executives and 76% of the members of Congress are members of the Greek Community. All careers, ranging from education to business, require leadership ability, and being Greek is one of the best ways to develop and improve your leadership skills.

For more information contact the Office of Greek Life at 609-896-5327 or email the Director of Greek Life.

- Office of Greek Life

Approximately 15% of Rider undergraduate students are involved in fraternities and sororities. The Office of Greek Life is a part of the Office of Campus Life and is in place to provide programs and services for the organizations and their members. The office consists of the Director of Greek Life and the Graduate Assistant for Greek Life as well as 8 student staff.

• Greek Organizations

There are 3 governing councils that oversee the 14 traditional social fraternities and sororities on campus. There are also 3 service/professional organizations and one honors organization that are housed under the title of "Greek Life." You can get a better understanding of this by visiting the Greek Organizations page. If you are looking for academic or honorary organizations that utilize Greek Letters in their names, check out that section of the Student Organization Directory.

Rider Campus Ministry

Rider Campus Ministry includes the inter-faith activities sponsored jointly by the Board of Chaplains (various denominations at Rider). Events are open to all students regardless of their denomination and are designed to support and enhance the spiritual life of the Rider community. Particular emphasis is placed upon community service and outreach. Rev. Dr. Nancy Schluter serves as the chapel coordinator.

Religious Organizations

• Catholic Campus Ministry

In addition to Sunday Eucharist at 11 a.m. and 7 p.m., and Saturday at 4 p.m., Catholic Campus Ministry, a student organization, offers a variety of spiritual, educational, and service/learning experiences. These are published in the regular bulletin. Father Bruno Ugliano is the full-time Catholic chaplain. He resides in the Catholic Student Center (Emmaus House) located at 2116 Lawrenceville Rd., across the street from Switlik residence hall, 896-0394. Fr. Bruno is available to students on a round-the-clock basis at Emmaus House.

• Hillel Society for Jewish Students

A Jewish student organization offering social, religious and cultural programs. It participates in regional and national activities bringing Jewish students from different colleges and universities together. For weekly Shabbat services at Adath Israel Synagogue and other holiday observances, call Rabbi Daniel T. Grossman at 896-4977. Club Advisor: Jan Friedman-Krupnick, jfk@rider.edu, 609-896-5101.

• Islamic Ministry

Hajji Imam Dr. Abdul-Malik R. Ali is available for the Muslim students on campus as well as to offer information on his tradition. He can be reached at 695-8360.

• Protestant Campus Ministry

PCM (Protestant Campus Ministry) is the student organization that offers overnight retreats, opportunities for volunteer service, social events and spiritual guidance. Worship is Monday evenings at 5 p.m. in Gill Chapel where students offer a praise and worship service. Offices are also located in Gill Chapel. The Rev. Dr. Nancy H. Schluter PC (USA) is the full-time Protestant chaplain and is assisted by students from Princeton Theological Seminary at both the Lawrenceville and Westminster campuses. These interns offer weekly Bible studies on both campuses. Rev. Schluter is available for counseling, for discussions, or just to listen. Consult Campus Resources, Religious Services section for more contact information, as well as the Rider Web site, www.rider.edu, or phone 896-5180.

Religious Services

- Gill Chapel is open for meditation and prayer 8 a.m.–10 p.m. The chapel office is located in the lower level.
- The Roman Catholic community celebrates Eucharist on Saturdays at 4 p.m. and Sundays at 11 a.m. and 7 p.m., as well as Mondays and Wednesdays at 12:35 p.m. throughout the year.
- There is a weekly Protestant worship service on Mondays at 5:30 p.m. in Gill Chapel, as well as for many special religious holidays throughout the year.
- At Westminster, there is a Christian Fellowship guided by the PTS Intern; Rev. Schluter serves as advisor.
- Religious services for Jewish students are available at Adath Israel Synagogue directly across the street from the south entrance to the Lawrenceville campus.

• All times for services are subject to change.

For more information contact the center by phone at (609) 895-5776, or email at cdls@rider.edu.

Source: http://www.rider.edu/175_98.htm (Reprinted with permission of Rider University).

Clearly, this wide spectrum of activities implicates a wide range of legal issues. However, the major issues, which touch multiple points on this continuum, include:

1. Institutional liability for personal injuries;
2. Violation of students' rights, such as personal expression;
3. Illegal discrimination.

Institutional Immunity from Liability for Personal Injuries

Standards of institutional liability vary from state to state with the key competing common-law characteristics being "assumption of risk" versus "simple negligence," the latter typically tempered by "comparative negligence" considerations. Institutional immunity from suit or statutory limits on liability is also not uncommon. For example, New Jersey—Rider University's home—has enacted the following statute:

> "No nonprofit corporation, society or association organized exclusively for religious, charitable or educational purposes or its trustees, directors, officers, employees, agents, servants or volunteers shall, except as is hereinafter set forth, be liable to respond in damages to any person who shall suffer damage from the negligence of any agent or servant of such corporation, society or association, where such person is a beneficiary, to whatever degree, of the works of such nonprofit corporation, society or association; provided, however, that such immunity from liability shall not extend to any person who shall suffer damage from the negligence of such corporation, society, or association or of its agents or servants where such person is one unconcerned in and unrelated to and outside of the benefactions of such corporation, society or association."
>
> N.J.S.A. 2A:53A-7

In ***Bloom v. Seton Hall University,*** *704 A.2d 1334 (N.J. Superior Court, Appellate Division, 1998),* plaintiff Joseph Bloom, Jr. was a twenty-one year old senior at Seton Hall in 1994, when he and several friends went to the campus pub for some beers. He fell, apparently in a puddle left when a serving cart was moved. The pub, operated on Thursday nights and alternate Saturdays, was neither separately incorporated nor distinct from the University. Although not operated for profit, the pub sold beer to students of proper age and their guests, and was subsidized by the Student Government Association. Its employees were students who were obligated to keep the pub clean and to manage the equipment under the auspices of the Student Activities Department of the University.

There was testimony that the University considered the pub to be part of a student's socialization process and a factor in the development of a well-rounded person. Seton Hall's status was documented in the record as a nonprofit educational institution committed to maintaining its "essential character as a Catholic institution of higher learning," for which the Archbishop of Newark serves as Chairman of its Board of Trustees and President of the Board of Regents.

The record also revealed that some time after plaintiff's accident, a decision was made that the pub would serve only students, but no guests. Thereafter, pub losses mounted sufficiently to prompt closing of the operation. Instead, a campus coffeehouse now operates once a week.

Analysis. On these facts, the mid-level Garden State court of appeals defined the threshold issues as "whether Seton Hall lost the statutory immunity afforded to such an institution because it operated a pub catering only to students of proper age and their guests, and whether Bloom ceased to be a 'beneficiary', to whatever degree, of [its] works while patronizing the pub." In tackling this issue, the court reasoned, "Bloom was no less a Seton Hall student because he bought a beer at a University-run student pub than if he bought a sandwich in a University-run commons, and no less a beneficiary of its works. Noting that the pub has been replaced by a campus coffeehouse, we observe that the nature of the beverage sold is not critical to the immunity analysis. Rather, it is the recognition, repeated in our cases since the Legislature responded to the Collopy trilogy by adopting the charitable immunity statute (N.J.S.A. 2A:53A-7 to –11), that the focus in determining immunity is on the status of the defendant organization (as one exclusively organized for religious, charitable or educational purposes) and whether the injured plaintiff is a beneficiary of its works."

Holding. "The broad latitude afforded on both prongs, status of the defendant entity and plaintiff's receipt of its benefactions, is well illustrated in [a case where] we upheld the immunity of a church that was serving ethnic meals for a fee at its annual church festival, and held a non-member attendee to be a beneficiary of the cultural education offered at the festival. The facts under review provide a stronger case for immunity than those in [that earlier decision]."

Advice. Immunity will vary from state to state and between public and private universities within a single state. Public colleges and universities may enjoy sovereign immunity as arms of the state. Private institutions may enjoy various forms of qualified immunity, whether by statute or under applicable case law. No mater the jurisdiction, this threshold possibility must be explored in all instances of student personal injury.

Liability for Personal Injuries: Standard of Care

The Rider University student-activities site expresses pride in the opening of "the brand new Student Recreation Center this fall." The institution goes on to boast of "a 3600 square foot fitness center with Life Fitness cardio Equipment and secularized weight room machines as well as free weights." Such facilities are part of the gold standard of 21st century higher education; virtually a "must" is an institution is to be deemed by students and parents to offer a campus of the first rank. Absent such facilities, colleges and universities are at a serious competitive disadvantage. Such facilities, unfortunately, also offer ample opportunities for personal injuries. This potential is often increased by the institutional decision to sell memberships to faculty and staff, and even to alumni and other members of the public in order to keep the investment on a paying basis.

For instance, in ***Abbassi v. Regents of the University of California,*** *2003 WL 657355 (California Court of Appeals, 2003),* the plaintiff, a surgical resident, was injured on December 9, 1997, at approximately 12:40 p.m., as he was adjusting the weights on a "butterfly" weight machine at the John Wooden Center on the University of California, Los Angeles (UCLA) campus. When the plaintiff removed the pin from a stack of weights, a heavy object, apparently a "guide weight," fell on his right index finger, crushing and requiring amputation of its tip.

With respect to the university, plaintiff's complaint asserted causes of action for "premises liability" and general negligence. Both counts alleged that the university had negligently maintained the weight machine and had failed to warn of its dangerous condition. Among the defenses the university alleged in its answer was that the action was barred by a release the plaintiff had signed with respect to risks and injuries arising from "'participation and/or receipt of instruction in recreation programs.'"

The university moved for summary judgment, or alternatively for summary adjudication of each cause of action. The motion's first ground was express assumption of risk, embodied in the release, which plaintiff had signed a month and a half before the accident, as part of his application for membership to receive "recreational services." Second, the university contended that plaintiff could not establish certain elements of liability for injury caused by a dangerous condition of property, here the weight machine. The university argued that the plaintiff could not prove a dangerous condition of the machine and that there was no evidence that a university employee had placed it in the condition plaintiff claimed, or that the university had had actual or constructive knowledge of the dangerous condition. Finally, the university argued that the cause of action for general negligence was legally unfounded, because it did not have a statutory basis, as required of a tort action against a public entity.

Analysis. The court began by considering the effect of the release, which reads as follows:

> I understand that there are risks and dangers inherent in participating and/or receiving instruction in recreation programs. I also understand that in order to be allowed to participate and/or receive instruction in recreation programs, I must give up my rights to hold the [university] liable for any injury or damage that I may suffer while participating and/or receiving instruction in recreation programs. [¶] Knowing this, and in consideration of being permitted to participate and/or receive instruction in recreation programs, I hereby voluntarily release the [university] from any and all liability resulting from or arising out of my participation and/or receipt of instruction in recreation programs. I understand and agree that I am releasing not only the entities [sic] set forth in the paragraph above, but also the officers, agents, and employees of those entities. I understand and agree that this Release will have the effect of releasing, discharging, waiving and forever relinquishing any and all actions or causes of action that I may have had, whether past present or future, whether known or unknown, and whether anticipated or unanticipated by me, arising out of my participation and/or receipt of instruction in recreation programs. This Release constitutes a complete release, discharge and waiver of any and all actions or causes of actions against the [university], its officers, agents or employees. I understand and agree that this Release applies to personal injury, property damage, or wrongful death that I may suffer, even if caused by the acts or omissions of others. I understand and agree that by signing this Release, I am assuming full responsibility for any and all risk of death or personal injury or property damage suffered by me while participating and/or receiving instruction in recreation programs. I understand and agree that this Release will be binding on me, my spouse, my heirs, my personal representatives, my assigns, my children and any guardian *ad litem* for said children. I understand and agree that by signing this Release I am agreeing to release, indemnify and hold the [university] and their officers, agents, and employees harmless from any and all liability or costs, including reasonable attorneys fees, associated with or arising from my participation and/or receipt of instruction in recreation programs. I acknowledge that I have read this Release Agreement and that I understand the words and language in it. I have been advised of the potential dangers incidental to participating and/or receiving instruction in recreation programs.

Finding that the language of the release was ambiguous with regard to whether or not it reached the activity, and thus the injury, at issue in this case. The court noted, further, that resolution of such an ambiguity was a question of law for the judge to decide, unless extrinsic, conflicting evidence requires the question to go to the jury. In the instant case, the court found that the plaintiff had failed to proffer such evidence, offering merely his own conclusory opinion on the release's reach. However, the appellate court declined to resolve the ambiguity, finding that the underlying liability case was fatally flawed.

The plaintiff attempted to bear his burden of establishing the university's liability via the testimony of an expert, one Frank Smith, who claimed to have two decades of experience in the manufacture and sale of weight machines. The court found that this expert testimony fell short of making the plaintiff's case:

> On that account, defendant fulfilled its initial burdens by producing testimony of its employees that the weight machine had not been altered at the time of plaintiff's injury, and that the guide weight had not been separated and elevated by university personnel. Plaintiff responded with the declaration of Smith, who opined that the weight had been "high-pinned" in order to repair detachment of a cable from a pulley wheel, both of which the university had installed, and were not in accordance with the manufacturer's specifications. As previously noted, the university objected to Smith's opinions both with respect to his professional qualifications and the opinions' speculative basis and character. The trial court sustained defendant's objections, and also ruled that certain of Smith's opinions were conclusory and lacked a basis in personal knowledge, so that defendant's showing accordingly was uncontested. We agree that Smith's testimony failed to establish a *prima facie* case.
>
> Putting aside the question of Smith's qualifications, his opinions were not competent in a critical respect. His affirmation that the pulley wheel and cable had been changed did claim support in personal knowledge (observation of the post-accident photographs, albeit that his view was inconsistent with the manufacturer's). But Smith's further testimony, that the cable had come off, and that university personnel had high-pinned the weight to fix that condition, lacked any indication of personal knowledge, or other basis. This opinion, which constituted plaintiff's sole proof that the university created or had notice of the dangerous condition that allegedly caused plaintiff's injury was speculative, and of no weight to overcome defendant's showing in favor of summary judgment.

Advice. (1) With regard to waivers of liability, the best advice we can offer is "Why not?" While, as illustrated in the case, plaintiffs' attorneys will almost always challenge waivers, they would seem to do no harm, and under favorable circumstances may even succeed. Prior waivers, like subsequent releases, must be entered knowingly and voluntarily. They must be clear and prominently displayed. Under such circumstances, the courts of most jurisdictions are willing to enforce them, albeit often reluctantly.

(2) With regard to the underlying liability, in this case the defendant was able to proffer evidence in the form of employee testimony to the effect that the machine in question had neither been altered by the institution nor damaged by

hard use. The best the plaintiff could do—and after all the burden was on him to make his case by a preponderance of the evidence—was present an "expert" to speculate that, had the machine in fact been in proper working order, the accident could not have happened. Clearly, such speculation carried little weight with the courts as compared to the ability of the facility's employees to testify credibly, and undisputedly, that the machine was in good condition. This suggests that colleges and universities with regard to their recreation center (other employees):

Checklist: Recreation Center Practices

- Train employees (including graduate assistants and work/study students) properly;
- Instruct them to observe conditions vigilantly;
- Keep appropriate records of such things as reports of machine damage and subsequent inspection and repair;
- Ensure submission of work orders for prompt repairs, whether performed by internal maintenance employees or outside vendors;
- Maintain a procedure for closing the loop, requiring supervisory personnel to confirm that repairs have been properly accomplished.

Such sound business practices, as much as or more than waivers, can enable the college or university to prevail in such personal injury actions.

Liability for Personal Injuries: Fraternities and Sororities

You will note that Rider University's website also speaks glowingly of its Greek organizations. "One of the best ways to take advantage of all that Rider has to offer is through the Greek Community," it says. Institutional liability for injuries occurring in fraternities and sororities has been the source of substantial litigation down the decades. Following are few examples:

In ***Letsinger v. Drury College,*** *68 S.W.3d 408 (Missouri Supreme Court, 2002)*, Drury owned land in Springfield on which the fraternity house used by the Beta Iota chapter of Kappa Alpha was located. Letsinger lived there. There were female visitors earlier in the evening when the assault occurred. Some males who were not members of the fraternity began calling the house concerning the visitors. Letsinger did not know the callers. The conversations escalated. Letsinger ultimately indicated to a caller that he should either shut up or come over and fight. After this conversation, Letsinger became nervous about what was going to happen. He tried to close and lock the front door. One Daniel arrived at the house, opened the front door, pulled a gun from behind his back, crudely alleged incest, and shot Letsinger.

Letsinger pleaded that Drury had the duty to "properly maintain and repair" the house, including "the front door, and to insure that basic security of its occupants and integrity of the building were maintained." Letsinger alleged Drury breached that duty, which proximately caused his injuries. Additionally, Letsinger alleged "Beta Iota, as lessee [of Drury], had a duty to properly maintain and repair the building and insure the basic security of its occupants if Drury failed to do so." He further alleged that Beta Iota breached its duty, also a proximate cause of his injury.

The contract between Drury and Beta Iota contained a maintenance paragraph:

"9. Maintenance: [Drury] agrees to maintain the premises in a good state of repair, interior and exterior, within the limits of the reserve maintained for such purposes and within the discretion of [Drury] as to the need for repair, maintenance expenses and capital improvements, except that [Beta Iota] is required to make any repairs, including glass breakage, which may be necessary because of damage resulting from gross negligence, or willful, intentional or malicious acts."

Another paragraph provided: "[Drury] and the authorized representatives of [Drury] shall have the right to enter the leased premises at all reasonable times to examine the condition thereof, but…not…in a manner to interfere unreasonably with the occupation by [Beta Iota]."

Analysis. The state supreme court reversed dismissal of the case, finding that the key question was whether a landlord-tenant relationship existed between the plaintiff and either the fraternity and/or the college.

"The record is replete with conflicting and contradictory evidence that must be resolved to decide if a landlord-tenant relationship existed and, if so, who was the landlord. As an example, there was conflicting evidence about who collected rent from the occupants. Letsinger's affidavit recited he was to 'pay $60 to the fraternity to live in the house during the summer semester.' Contrarily, Drury employees Parker and Sweeney testified the 'fraternity' set the room rate for occupants, but Drury billed and collected the rent from each occupant. Moreover, the Drury/Beta Iota lease provided for Drury to collect rent from occupants.

"Contradictory evidence also existed about who made occupancy decisions for the house. The Drury/Beta Iota contract provides that Drury's 'policy' governs the *412 approval of occupants. Testimony that Drury would not allow non-KA students or KA freshmen to live in the house was consistent with the contract language. On the other hand, there was evidence that if Drury received too many applications from persons who wanted to live in the house, it was the "fraternity officer" and alumni advisers who decided that occupancy question. Additional confusion regarding ultimate control over occupancy arises from evidence that alumni advisers decided whether fraternity members could live in the house during summer months.

"Yet another example was the conflicting and contradictory evidence regarding what documents existed relating to the occupants. Drury employee Sweeney, who had supervisory authority over student housing, testified Drury provided two forms for students to sign regarding residency in a fraternity house. The first simply required the student to indicate where he or she wanted to live, i.e., on or off campus. The second form required those who opted for fraternity housing to designate which fraternity they chose. At one point, Sweeney referred to these forms as merely 'applications,' which were part of the student registration process, and at another time referred to a 'one page-contract' prepared by Drury that was filled out 'prior to moving in that's really a part of the registration process.' On the other hand, Sweeney had general knowledge of the fact that many fraternities on Drury's campus made their own contracts with the occupants of their houses regarding policies, fees, periods of residency, and related matters. Sweeney was unsure whether such a contract existed for these occupants.

"This and other evidence in the record show there are material issues of fact about whether a landlord-tenant relationship existed for the house occupants and, if so, who was the landlord. This Court need not address the other issues raised by the parties as to Defendants' duty, because the duty is dependent on the existence (or non-existence) of a landlord/tenant relationship, and its characteristics."

Advice. The clear implication of the case is that in the absence of evidence of a landlord-tenant relationship, the college had no duty to act reasonably with regard to Letsinger's safety. Ironically, in this case the absence of formal documentation of such a relationship seems to have worked in the institution's favor. More dispositive, perhaps, would have been a college policy or written understanding with the fraternity that clarified the college's rejection of any such relationship with its accompanying responsibilities and potential liabilities.

Where such a dispositive document does not exist, evidence that might be relevant on remand could include:

1. The location of the frat house—on the college's campus or in town?
2. Supervision of the fraternity—for instance, did campus safety patrol the premises? Did the college administer discipline for breaches of its rules occurring on the premises? Were there any college rules regarding whom could and could not reside in the house?
3. Finally, as with the Rider website, does the institution's advertising of the Greek organizations for purposes of attracting applicants raise an issue of the institution's apparent authority over the sororities and frats, such that students and their parents might reasonably expect the school to insure the safe condition of such premises?

This last question was answered in the negative by at least one state court in a relatively recent case, ***Rothbard v. Colgate University****, 652 NYS2d 146 (N.Y. Supreme Court, Appellate Division, Third Dept., 1997).*

Facts. The plaintiff in this case was intoxicated and fell from his bedroom window in the fraternity house. He was discovered the next morning unconscious and bleeding profusely onto the pavement below the open window. He contended that the university was obligated to control the behavior of frat house residents, a duty it had assumed when it said in its student handbook that roof and porticos were off limits and under-aged drinking was prohibited.

Analysis. The case is reminiscent of comments, above, concerning contributory negligence. In this case, the plaintiff had voluntarily become intoxicated and voluntarily violated yet another rule, that concerning roofs and porticos. The appeals court put it this way: colleges and universities have no legal obligation to protect students from their own dangerous activities. Additionally, since the evidence showed that the institution did not actually own the frat house, the duty fell to the owner and not the university to install any safety features that might be expected to prevent such calamities.

Advice. The notable point for our purposes here is that the appeals panel actually went beyond the usual reach of "contributory negligence" with regard to the university's liability. Colgate, they said, had no duty whatever to protect students from their own dangerous activities. (Presumably, with regard to the actual owner of the premises a more traditional contributory-negligence analysis would apply, requiring a jury to divide responsibility for plaintiff's injuries between the drunken student himself and the house owner, who, for instance, could have put bars in the windows.) The fact that the university had written rules did not reverse this legal rule. By extrapolation, presumably a university's promotional website materials, touting the educational value of its Greek system, would also not create a duty where none otherwise exists.

Liability for Denial of Free Expression and/or Campus Facilities

Beyond physical injuries, students may sue with regard to such torts as defamation. Where the college or university is a public entity, such suits may also implicate First Amendment speech and religion rights. The following cases illustrate the impact of these legal issues under varying circumstances.

The mother of "freedom of expression" cases is ***Rosenberger v. Rector and Visitors of the University of Virginia,*** *515 U.S. 819, 115 S.Ct. 2510 (U.S. Supreme Court, 1995).*

Facts. A student group that published a Christian-oriented newspaper applied for financing from the university's student-activity fund. The student council denied the application and two institutional tribunals confirmed the council's ruling. UVA is a state instrumentality. It authorizes payments from its Student Activities Fund (SAF) to outside contractors for the printing costs of a variety of publications issued by student groups called "Contracted Independent Organizations" (CIO's). The SAF receives its money from mandatory student fees and is designed to support a broad range of extracurricular student activities related to the UVA's educational purpose. CIO's must include in their dealings with third parties and in all written materials a disclaimer stating that they are independent of the university and that the university is not responsible for them. The university withheld authorization for payments to a printer on behalf of petitioners' CIO, Wide Awake Productions (WAP), solely because its student newspaper, "Wide Awake: A Christian Perspective at the University of Virginia," primarily promoted a particular belief in "a deity or an ultimate reality," as prohibited by the University's SAF Guidelines. Petitioners filed suit, alleging that the refusal to authorize payment violated their First Amendment right to freedom of speech. After the district court granted summary judgment for the university, the Fourth Circuit affirmed, holding that the UVA's invocation of viewpoint discrimination to deny third-party payment violated the Speech Clause, but concluding that the discrimination was justified by the necessity of complying with the Establishment Clause of the self-same First Amendment.

Analysis. On these facts, the high court held, "The Guideline invoked to deny SAF support, both in its terms and in its application to these petitioners, is a denial of their right of free speech." The court invoked precedents involving denial of facilities, which amounted to public forums. The justices then said,

"The University's attempt to escape the consequences... by urging that this case involves the provision of funds rather than access to facilities is unavailing. Although it may regulate the content of expression when it is the speaker or when it enlists private entities to convey its own message, the University may not discriminate based on the viewpoint of private persons whose speech it subsidizes, its argument that the scarcity of public money may justify otherwise impermissible viewpoint discrimination among private speakers is simply wrong."

As a general proposition, private colleges are not subject to the same scrutiny of the constitutionality of their funding decisions vis-à-vis student activities. However, institutions must always also consider possible restrictions imposed by their respective state constitutions. Furthermore, at least a few cases have come down on the side of finding constitutional speech rights even on a private campus.

For example, in ***State v. Schmid,*** *84 NJ 535, 423 A2d 615 (N.J. Supreme Court, 1980), app. dismissed, 455 US 100 (1982),* while distributing political literature on the campus of Princeton University, defendant Chris Schmid, a member of the United States Labor Party, was arrested and charged by the university with trespass upon private property. He was subsequently convicted under the state's penal trespass statute. On appeal he challenged the conviction on the grounds that it stems from a violation of his federal and state constitutional rights to freedom of speech and assembly.

Facts. Under the University regulations then in effect, permission was a prerequisite for the on-campus distribution of materials by off-campus organizations. No such permission was required, however, for the same activity by a university-affiliated organization or by Princeton students. The regulatory language pertaining to off-campus organizations stated in part:

> "Demonstrations and the distribution of leaflets, statements, or petitions ... are permitted on the campus unless, or until, they disrupt regular essential operations of the University or significantly infringe on the rights of others. On the same grounds, the campus is open to speakers whom students, faculty, or staff wish to hear, and to recruiters for agencies and organizations in whom students or faculty have an interest." (University Regulations as passed by the Council of the Princeton University Community, May 1975, as amended 1976.)

Analysis. The Garden State's high tribunal observed, "Notwithstanding the primary thrust of the First Amendment against state governmental interference with expressional freedoms, the guarantees of this Amendment may under appropriate conditions be invoked against nongovernmental bodies. In particular settings, private entities, including educational institutions, may so impact upon the public or share enough of the essential features of governmental bodies as to be engaged functionally in 'state action' for First Amendment purposes. The more focused inquiry therefore must be turned to those circumstances that can subject an entity of essentially nongovernmental or private character to the requirements imposed by the First Amendment." Based on this reasoning, Schmid's conviction was reversed.

Another older case, involving gay rights, also suggests that—despite the Bill of Rights applying only to state actors, i.e., public universities—private schools are not unfettered in their decisions about which student activities to permit and which to discourage by the withholding of resources. In ***Gay Rights Coalition v. Georgetown University,*** *536 A.2d 1 (District of Columbia Court of Appeals, 1987),* the Jesuit institution refused to extend full student-organization standing to two gay-student groups, which then sued. Since the Constitution was not available against a private university, the groups looked to the District of Columbia Human Rights Act, which forbad denial of "facilities and services" on the basis of (among other things) sexual orientation. The appeals court, sitting en banc (i.e., as a full court), cut the legal baby in half, holding that while the university had to make facilities and services available to the two gay-student groups on the same basis as they were available to other student organizations, Georgetown need not extend formal university recognition.

Advice. The Georgetown University case would have never been brought, or would have come out differently, in most state jurisdictions. Although all but two states have their own anti-discrimination statutes in supplementation of federal law, most do not protect gays and lesbians from discrimination.

That aside, colleges and universities—private as well as public institutions—are well advised to avoid discrimination in the recognition, funding and facilitation of student organizations. For example, a review of Rider University's website materials will readily reveal an openness to all members of the student body. Indeed, Rider refuses student-activity fee funding to organizations which are not open to all students. Thus, for example, an international-student or ethnic organization must accept American students and members of other ethnic classifications, should they care to put themselves forward for membership, or alternatively forego official funding.

Impact of the Higher Education Opportunity Act (HEOA)

Section 104 of the HEOA is a generalized "sense of the Congress" that exhorts schools to facilitate free and open exchange of ideas and discourages intimidation, harassment, discriminatory conduct and anything which might "chill" student speech or students' desire to come together in clubs and other campus organizations.

Sources

Center for Education & Employment Law, HIGHER EDUCATION LAW IN AMERICA (Malvern, PA 5th ed. 2004).

Fischer, David, The NCAA in Court, ANTITRUST REVIEW, March 28, 2006.

Gerla, Harry, Response to David Fischer, ANTITRUST REVIEW, March 29, 2006.

Gerstein, Ralph and Lois Gerstein, EDUCATION LAW: AN ESSENTIAL GUIDE FOR ATTORNEYS, TEACHERS, ADMINISTRATORS, PARENTS AND STUDENTS (Tucson, AZ: Lawyers & Judges Publishing Co. 20040.

CHAPTER 4

Academic Standing, Probation, and Dismissal

Herewith, a sample policy on this chapter's topic:

Conditional Standing and Dismissal

All students permitted to enroll at Rider University are in good standing and are qualified to be bonafide students. Decisions regarding academic conditional standing and dismissal for poor scholarship are the responsibility of the Committee on Academic Standing within each college.

Because a 2.0 cumulative average is required for graduation a student is expected to maintain a 2.0 cumulative grade point average while enrolled at Rider. Students who fail to maintain at least a 2.0 cumulative average will be reviewed by an academic standing committee and may be dismissed or placed on conditional standing. While a 2.0 cumulative grade point average may enable students to continue in their individual programs, students in teacher preparation programs must achieve a cumulative average of 2.5 before enrolling in sophomore level education classes. Before enrolling in junior level education classes, students must achieve a 2.75 grade point average. A 2.80 grade point average is required before a student can enroll in student teaching. Students not achieving a 2.75 grade point average by the time they reach their junior year may be dismissed from the program.

Students who have not done satisfactory work may be dismissed from the University for poor scholarship at the end of any semester after an appropriate review of their scholastic records by the academic standing committee of their college. There must be substantial evidence of proper motivation and a capacity for doing college level work to warrant maintaining a student in school with a record of continued conditional status. An academic standing committee may require any student who does unsatisfactory work to pursue a specific course of study during a particular academic session.

Any student who fails to pursue a course of study prescribed by an academic standing committee, or who does unsatisfactory work in the prescribed course of study, may be dismissed without right of further appeal.

Students may also be subject to academic dismissals if their cumulative grade point averages fall below the required minimum for two or more consecutive semesters, or the grade points fall below the required averages established at the freshman, sophomore, junior and senior levels. Academic dismissal at the end of the fall semester is effective prior to the beginning of the spring semester.

Readmission to Rider After Dismissal from Rider University for academic or disciplinary reasons terminates a student's relationship to the University. Although some students do apply for readmission, there is no real or implied right to such readmission. A student dismissed for academic reasons will normally not be eligible for readmission within one calendar year of the dismissal date. Any dismissed student seeking readmission must first contact the Office of the Dean of Students to obtain appropriate forms. Once the Dean of Students approves the readmission application, the application is forwarded to the dean of the college to which the student seeks reentry.

Certain restrictions or stipulations regarding attendance or privileges may apply to the readmission of students dismissed for disciplinary reasons. Students dismissed for academic reasons must also submit, with their readmission application, a personal letter to the Academic Standing Committee which will make decisions concerning their readmission.

The Source 2007–08, *Rider University (Reprinted with permission of Rider University.)*

As this sample policy suggests, both public and private institutions are closely concerned with providing appropriate procedures, so that decisions involving academic probation, suspension and dismissal are fair—this despite the fact that in general the American common law has tended to defer to academic expertise in this aspect of higher education law, both in the public and in the private sector.

Due Process Requirements of Academic Probation and Dismissal in the Public Sector

Academic disciplinary action is at least as serious, if not more so, than behavioral discipline. Academic standing goes straight to the heart of student status. Consequently, a trend developed within, particularly, the lower federal courts in the 1960s and early 1970s in the direction of according due process rights to students subjected to adverse academic actions. The courts that considered such cases and accorded such rights based their decisions primarily upon the 14th Amendment of the U.S. Constitution. Then, 30 years ago, in a seminal decision the U.S. Supreme Court stepped in and put a stop to these judicial intrusions into what the high court considered particularly the province of the faculty and academic administration of colleges and universities, albeit those in the public sector were state actors otherwise subject to the Fourteenth Amendment's "due process of law" restrictions.

This seminal case is ***Missouri v. Horowitz,*** *435 U.S. 78 (U.S. Supreme Court,1978)*. The facts are as follows:

Horowitz was admitted with advanced standing to the University of Missouri Medical School in the fall of 1971. During the final years of a student's education at the school, the student was required to pursue in "rotational units" academic and clinical studies pertaining to various medical disciplines such as obstetrics-gynecology, pediatrics, and surgery. Each student's academic performance at the school was evaluated on a periodic basis by the Council on Evaluation, a body composed of both faculty and students, which could recommend various actions including probation and dismissal. The recommendations of the Council were reviewed by the Coordinating Committee, a body composed solely of faculty members, and ultimately had to be approved by the dean. Students were not typically allowed to appear before either the Council or the Coordinating Committee on the occasion of their review of the student's academic performance.

In the spring of Horowitz's first year of study, several faculty members expressed dissatisfaction with her clinical performance during a pediatrics rotation. The faculty members noted that her "performance was below that of her peers in all clinical patient-oriented settings," that she was erratic in her attendance at clinical sessions, and that she lacked a critical concern for personal hygiene. Upon the recommendation of the Council on Evaluation, she was advanced to her second and final year on a probationary basis.

Faculty dissatisfaction with Horowitz's clinical performance continued during the following year. For example, her "docent," or faculty adviser, rated her clinical skills as "unsatisfactory." In the middle of the year, the Council again reviewed her academic progress and concluded that she should not be considered for graduation in June of that year; furthermore, the Council recommended that, absent "radical improvement," she should be dropped from the school.

Horowitz was permitted to take a set of oral and practical examinations as an "appeal" of the decision not to permit her to graduate. Pursuant to this "appeal," she spent a substantial portion of time with seven practicing physicians in the area who enjoyed a good reputation among their peers. The physicians were asked to recommend whether she should be allowed to graduate on schedule and, if not, whether she should be dropped immediately or allowed to remain on probation. Only two of the doctors recommended that she be graduated on schedule. Of the other five, two recommended that she be immediately dropped from the school. The remaining three recommended that she not be allowed to graduate in June and be continued on probation pending further reports on her clinical progress. Upon receipt of these recommendations, the Council on Evaluation reaffirmed its prior position.

The Council met again in mid-May to consider whether Horowitz should be allowed to remain in school beyond June of that year. Noting that the report on respondent's recent surgery rotation rated her performance as "low-satisfactory," the Council unanimously recommended that "barring receipt of any reports that Miss Horowitz has improved radically, [she] not be allowed to re-enroll in the … School of Medicine." The Council delayed making its recommendation official until receiving reports on other rotations; when a report on respondent's emergency-room rotation also turned out to be negative, the Council unanimously reaffirmed its recommendation that she be dropped from the school. The Coordinating Committee and the dean approved the recommendation and notified Horowitz, who appealed the decision in writing to the University's Provost for Health Sciences. The provost sustained the school's actions after reviewing the record compiled during the earlier proceedings.

The U.S. Court of Appeals continued in the *Horowitz* case a trend in the federal common law of according constitutional rights to such students. In overturning this decision, the Supreme Court slammed the door on most such efforts at judicial activism in the realm of academic discretion. The majority opinion began its analysis by observing that "To be entitled to the procedural protections of the Fourteenth Amendment, respondent must in a case such as this demonstrate that her dismissal from the school deprived her of either a 'liberty' or a 'property' interest. Respondent has never alleged that she was deprived of a property interest."

The Court then considered whether a constitutionally protected "liberty" interest was implicated in Horowitz's dismissal from medical school. Criticizing the Eighth Circuit's analysis, the opinion noted, "The opinion of the Court of Appeals… does not discuss whether a state university infringes a liberty interest when it dismisses a student without publicizing allegations harmful to the student's reputation. Three judges of the Court of Appeals for the Eighth Circuit dissented from the denial of rehearing *en banc* on the ground that 'the reasons for Horowitz's dismissal were not released to the public but were communicated to her directly by school officials.' [T]he judges concluded that '[a]bsent such public disclosure, there is no deprivation of a liberty interest.'"

The deference reflected in *Horowitz* is echoed in the much-more-recent decision, ***Wheeler v. Miller,*** *168 F.3d 241 (U.S. Court of Appeals, 5th Cir., 1999)*, which well represents of the principle as it has persisted down to the present time.

The facts are as follows: Wheeler sought a Ph.D. in school psychology as a student in Texas Woman's University's psychology department. He was originally admitted to TWU's master's program in counseling psychology in 1992. While a master's student he took a course in psychological assessment from defendant McCullough. This course was also required for the Ph.D. and included a one-hour "pre-practicum" field experience component, which involved administering tests to subjects. McCullough attested that she observed tapes of Wheeler's field tests and described his administration of the Wechsler Intelligence Scales as one of the worst she had ever observed. Wheeler received a C in the pre-practicum. McCullough attested that Wheeler fell asleep in class, to the point of snoring on one occasion, and that he frequently turned in his assignments late. She also attested that the rules of the course, as stated in the syllabus, prohibited the students from testing a family member, which was an ethical violation. Wheeler chose to test his brother, and later chose to use his brother when it was his turn to lead a "case staffing" in class, saying that the client was a friend.

McCullough added that if a student's testing protocol had too many errors, the student was supposed to administer and score a new test of a subject. Her graduate assistant had informed her that Wheeler had not followed this requirement but had picked up his protocol and returned it fifteen minutes later with corrections and changes. The grad assistant expressed concern that an unusually high number of responses supposedly gathered from the test subject were word for word from the sample answers in the back of the testing manual.

Wheeler applied to the Ph.D. program in counseling psychology in 1994 and was turned down. He then successfully applied to the school psychology Ph.D. program. Defendants McCullough and Miller were on the school psychology program committee (SPPC) that admitted Wheeler to the program. The other SPPC members were Drs. Hamilton, Jolly, and Vitro. McCullough voted against Wheeler's admission, expressing concerns about his performance in her class. McCullough agreed that at this meeting she expressed concern about Wheeler's commitment to the field of school psychology as well as his "compliance with ethical and professional practice standards." Miller supported his admission, saying that everyone deserved a second chance, and offered to serve as his advisor. The committee voted to admit Wheeler, conditioned on his completion of his master's degree, retaking the psychological assessment pre-practicum, and registering for the introduction to school psychology course. Wheeler took the introduction to school psychology course from McCullough and received an A.

Wheeler offered evidence that another professor in addition to McCullough was concerned that Wheeler had fabricated test results, and that these concerns were discussed among faculty members. Dr. Jolly testified that McCullough's comments to her regarding Wheeler's "ethical problems" were an attempt to influence her opinion. Jolly testified that McCullough also expressed her concerns to Dr. Vitro, and Dr. Miller testified that Vitro was aware that accusations of academic dishonesty had been made against Wheeler, but Vitro himself testified that he was unaware of any rumors of academic dishonesty. Miller testified that discussions linking Wheeler to academic dishonesty occurred "at various stages." In a transcript of a conversation between Wheeler and Miller, Miller stated that "apparently, there was an accusation ... brought against you that you were going out creating your own protocols, not seeing children, just making up protocols and apparently you were caught doing that and you had a big confrontation with Dr. Jackson about that." McCullough similarly testified that at a meeting Dr. Vitro had discussed "that there had been a problem with Dr. Jackson being concerned that Brent had done the same thing that I thought he had done, that is, that he had copied the answers from the test manual, that there were too many word-for-word responses ... you just don't get that many that are word for word the same when you give it to an actual client...." Wheeler testified that Drs. Miller and Jolly had told him of rumors concerning his academic dishonesty.

The school psychology graduate student handbook provided that any student who received a C must undergo some form of remediation, and any student who earned two C's might be expelled. After admission to the Ph.D. program, Wheeler took a course from defendant Miller. He received an A in the lecture portion and a B in the connected pre-practicum. In the fall 1994 semester Wheeler received a second graduate level C in a pre-practicum to a course by Dr. Vitro, the department chair. Vitro attested that the C was primarily a result of the inferiority of Wheeler's written logs. Although the student handbook provides for dismissal after a second C, the SPPC decided to place Wheeler in a remediation plan. The SPPC met with Wheeler and explained the plan, and also provided a written copy of the plan, which required the completion of certain course work, a comprehensive paper, and an oral exam, to be completed by certain dates. Wheeler was told that he would not be eligible to participate in an internship until the fall of 1996 at the earliest. Dr. Hamilton, a member of the SPPC, attested that this first remediation plan was based on Wheeler's grades and involved no discussion of cheating or unethical behavior.

On April 28, 1995, Wheeler took an oral comprehensive examination before Miller, McCullough, and Vitro. All three failed him. Miller described Wheeler's performance as the worst he had ever seen. Vitro attested that he exercised professional judgment and acted in good faith, as did Miller and McCullough as far as he could tell.

In the spring of 1995 Vitro gave Wheeler a C in a course due to a poor written exam, his third C in the graduate program. The SPPC met in June of 1995 to discuss Wheeler's status in the program. The committee decided to dismiss Wheeler from the program. McCullough attested that the basis of the decision was Wheeler's academic performance. The committee met with Wheeler a week later and informed him of its decision. However, the school administration advised the committee to reinstate Wheeler. As Miller and Vitro understood the administration's position, the original remediation plan was still in effect and technically did not address the possibility of other academic deficiencies (an additional C and failing the comprehensive exam) occurring after the plan was instituted.

After he was readmitted, Wheeler submitted a degree plan, which required the submission of a transcript from the University of North Texas. Wheeler had been allowed to take courses at North Texas as a transfer student. He had received a fourth C in a graduate statistics course. In March of 1996 Wheeler took a second oral comprehensive exam before Drs. Palomares, Rubin, and Hampton. The orals committee was appointed by Dr. Sally Stabb; Wheeler offered the trial court no evidence that Stabb was aware of charges of academic dishonesty or was otherwise biased against Wheeler. All committee members failed Wheeler, and agreed his performance was the worst they had ever seen. Further, all three swore that they evaluated Wheeler in good faith and were unaware of any allegations of cheating or unethical conduct. The next day Wheeler signed a document accepting a doctoral internship with the Lewisville I.S.D. On April 2, 1996, Miller wrote the school district, explaining that Wheeler "has not met all of his program requirements to be considered for placement as an intern during the 1996–1997 school year."

After Wheeler failed his second set of orals, Miller drafted a second remediation plan, attesting "that it was based solely on Wheeler's poor academic performance" and that "[t]he SPPC did not consider any allegations of unethical conduct in making their determination of the appropriate scope of remediation." TWU's graduate school catalog provided that "[s]tudents who fail any portion of the comprehensive exam process will be provided with remediation programs and subsequent measures for reevaluation of student progress. A student may be dismissed from a program if remediation is not completed in a satisfactory manner." The remediation plan required certain course work and applying to retake comprehensive exams by certain dates. On March 29, 1996, Wheeler met with the SPPC. By this time Dr. Palomares had replaced Dr. McCullough on the committee. According to Miller, Wheeler "was given the opportunity to address any concerns he had about his matriculation through the program at the March 29, 1996 meeting. The remediation plan was read to him and the rationale behind each activity was explained."

TWU did not dispute that the second remediation plan was unusually demanding. Wheeler appealed this plan to the dean of the graduate school. An *ad hoc* committee was appointed which unanimously affirmed the SPPC. Wheeler appealed to the vice president of academic affairs, who also affirmed. After Wheeler failed to enroll in a course specified in the second remediation plan, the SPPC formally dismissed him from the graduate program. Miller, Hamilton, and Vitro all attested that the dismissal was based on Wheeler's failure to comply with the academic requirements of the second remediation plan.

On these facts, the appeals panel looked to *Horowitz* for guidance and concluded, "In cases involving academic decisions, Texas courts interpreting the Due Course Clause of the Texas Constitution have looked to federal case law interpreting federal due process rights. The federal procedural due process rights afforded students in an academic setting were explored in ***Board of Curators of University of Missouri v. Horowitz.*** In *Horowitz,* the plaintiff, a medical student, was dismissed by school officials for failing to meet academic standards. Students at the medical school participated in rotations focusing on various medical specialties. Academic performance was evaluated by a faculty-student evaluation council. Recommendations of this council were reviewed by a faculty coordinating committee. Students typically were not allowed to appear before the evaluation council and coordinating committee.

"In her first year of study, several faculty members expressed dissatisfaction with the plaintiff's performance on one rotation. On the recommendation of the evaluation council, the student advanced to her second year on a probationary basis. Faculty dissatisfaction continued. The council concluded that the student not be considered for graduation in June and recommended that, absent radical improvement, the student be dropped from the school. The student was allowed to take a set of oral and practical examinations as an appeal of the decision not to permit her to graduate. As part of this procedure, the student spent time with several practicing physicians. After receipt of recommendations from these physicians, the council reaffirmed its prior position. After later reviewing reports of her rotations, the council recommended that the student be dropped from the school. The coordinating committee and the dean approved the recommendation. Following the school's procedures, the student appealed the decision to the provost, who sustained the action.

"The Court, assuming (as do we) that the student had a property or liberty interest subject to procedural due process protection, held that constitutional due process requirements had been met. Noting that the school had fully informed the student of the faculty's dissatisfaction with her clinical progress and that '[t]he ultimate decision to dismiss respondent was careful and deliberate,' the Court found the procedures not only sufficient, but beyond the constitutional requirements of procedural due process. By this minimal standard, TWU afforded Wheeler procedural due process. As detailed above, the school's decision to terminate him from the doctoral program was careful and deliberate, following a protracted series of steps to rate Wheeler's academic performance, identify and inform him of his weak performance, and, as in *Horowitz,* provide Wheeler with a specially tailored remedial program in light of his poor performance. The procedures were at least as careful and deliberate as those deemed more than sufficient in *Horowitz.*"

Advice. In the public sector, the constitutional requirement of "due process of law" can be satisfied by a wide variety of procedures and processes. No particular policy needs to be enacted and followed. Regardless of the particulars of your school's policy, the following "due process" elements ought to be considered.

Checklist: Elements of "Due Process"

1. Clear, published expectations
2. Provided to the student upon inception of the program of study
3. And uniformly applied to all students in the program.
4. Periodic, including interim, evaluations (ideally written) of the student's performance and progress.
5. Notice to the student of any formal action being taken.
6. Opportunity for the student to be heard and to challenge those asserting her/his shortcomings.

7. A written decision, including the decision-maker's reasoning.
8. An opportunity for appeal.

Due Process Requirements of Academic Probation and Dismissal in the Private Sector

In the strict sense, private colleges and universities are not subject to the "due process" prohibitions and prescriptions of the U.S. Constitution. The same may be said of state constitutions. With rare exceptions, these documents proscribe and prescribe only as to state and municipal governments (including, of course, public institutions of higher learning). This having been said, the fact is that student-plaintiffs and their legal counsels have been quite creative in articulating causes of action against institutions following academic suspensions and dismissals.

Sometimes such actions are grounded upon breach of contract, contending that the administration and faculty failed to follow their own academic rules and standards, as published in the college catalog, student handbook and/or other documents alleged to be a part of the implied contract between the student and the institution. In other cases, the plaintiff has been able to articulate a credible claim of discriminatory treatment in the application of academic standards and procedures to him/her. In yet other cases, the legal theory has been that the school was so closely aligned to federal or state governmental interests as to make that institution and its relevant employees "state actors."

Here we will look at a recent case by way of illustrating the "shotgun" style by which disappointed students sometimes challenge adverse academic decisions and how the American common law tends to respond to such claims.

In ***Jackson v. Texas Southern University-Thurgood Marshall,**—S.W.3d —, 2007 WL 1672094 (Texas Court of Appeals—Houston [14 Dist.], 2007),*

Jackson, a former police officer, began law school at TSU in the fall of 2003. One of his courses that fall was "The Lawyering Process I," taught by Professor J. Faith Jackson. The class was broken into several components. The final paper in the course, worth 49 percent of the total grade, was a "closed memo," meaning that the students must prepare the memo without the aid of anyone else.

One of the defendants, Jong Kim, was a classmate of Jackson's who asked for a draft of Jackson's paper on two occasions, ostensibly to use as a guideline. Jackson acquiesced by printing out a copy of his paper and giving it to Kim.

After noting the striking similarities between the papers, Professor Jackson assigned both Jackson and Kim a zero. When plaintiff Jackson saw his final grade for the course, a score of 67 percent, he went to see Professor Jackson. During their initial conversation, plaintiff Jackson admitted to giving Kim a copy of his paper. A second meeting was then arranged between Professor Jackson, Jackson, and Kim. At this meeting, Professor Jackson pointed out the similarities in the papers and allowed each person to explain to her his version of events. Concluding that, at the very least, the students had collaborated on a closed memo, Professor Jackson assigned them both a grade of zero for the memo. Plaintiff Jackson took no further steps at that time to have his grade changed.

However, during his spring semester the plaintiff pursued an honor court complaint against Kim, even though such a complaint could do nothing to change his own grade. Jackson also asked the Academic Standards Committee to extend the deadline for filing a request for a grade change, because he wanted to resolve the Kim honor court matter before he appeared before the Academic Standards Committee. After the spring semester ended, Jackson was notified by letter of his academic dismissal, pursuant to school policy. Jackson replied by letter stating that he had been waiting for the resolution of Kim's honor court proceeding before appealing his grade. He then formally filed his appeal with the Academic Standards Committee despite not having the Kim issue resolved.

The Academic Standards Committee met with Jackson and his attorney twice in the month of August. The first meeting was spent discussing Jackson's frustration with the honor court's failure to act in a timely manner on his complaint against Kim. The second meeting was approximately a week later, and Jackson and his attorney each had a chance to speak, with the committee asking questions. The committee was not concerned with whether Jackson cheated, but only with whether Jackson had been treated differently from other similarly situated students. The committee ultimately denied Jackson's petition, and his dismissal was affirmed.

Jackson sued TSU, Professor Jackson, Dean Carrington, Academic Dean Vergie Mouton, Associate Dean Fernando Colon-Navarro, and Jong Kim. He alleged defamation, breach of contract, fraud and violation of due process pursuant to a post–Civil War federal statute that has been sometimes applied to private entities. Kim was eventually non-suited. The remaining defendants moved for summary judgment on all causes of action. The summary judgment was granted without specifying which arguments in the motion the court found meritorious. Jackson appealed only the grant of summary judgment as to the due process claims. The state appellate panel held,

"In his appeal, Jackson raises a very specific complaint regarding his claim of procedural due process. He alleges a property interest in TSU's rules and regulations themselves. He states, '[w]hen TSU codified its Rules and Regulations, it conferred a right, or entitlement, to the student body that is protected by the Fourteenth Amendment.' He also cites to *Sylvester v. Texas Southern University,* 957 F.Supp. 944 (S.D.Tex.1997), for the proposition that 'TSU's Rules and Regulations conferred a benefit on the student body sufficient to merit due process protection.' In his concluding remarks in one section of his brief, he states, 'In summary, Appellant contends the success of his appeal rests upon whether the Court holds that appellant had a due process right to procedures established by TSU's Rules and Regulations.'

"However, the United States Supreme Court has made it clear that an individual does not acquire a substantive interest in specific procedures developed by the State. The Court explained,

"Process is not an end in itself. Its constitutional purpose is to protect a substantive interest to which the individual has a legitimate claim of entitlement.... The State may choose to require procedures for reasons other than protection against deprivation of substantive rights, of course, but in making that choice the State does not create an independent substantive right.... We conclude that Jackson has failed to state a cognizable due process claim because he has no substantive interest in specific rules."

The Court went on the write, "Reading his brief very generously, Jackson's brief also raises a substantive due process claim. Specifically, he claims he has the right to have his writing assignment fairly graded. He argues that the defendants' judicial admissions preclude the notion that the zero was given as a disciplinary measure for cheating; he claims the admissions prove instead that the zero was a purely subjective academic evaluation of Jackson's work. This would aid Jackson because his grade of zero is more likely to be found arbitrary and unreasonable if this Court is precluded from considering the fact that the zero was given as punishment for cheating.

"Jackson's judicial admission argument falls flat. First, the admission stating that Jackson's dismissal was academic rather than disciplinary states a conclusion of law, not subject to judicial admission (citations omitted). Second, the alleged judicial admission stating that Jackson was never accused of cheating is taken out of context. The sentence he cites in the motion for summary judgment clearly means to say only that the administration never formally charged him with cheating, since the following sentence in the motion discusses the fact that Professor Jackson gave him a zero for not working independently on a paper requiring independent work. Finally, any admissions that formal charges were not filed, or that the school itself never took any actions against Jackson, do not preclude the fact that the zero was given by the professor as a disciplinary measure. Therefore, we do not accept Jackson's judicial admission argument, nor the proposition that the zero was a reflection of the academic merit of his paper rather than a disciplinary measure.

"Since the zero was given as a disciplinary measure, the substantive due process question is simply whether the… action was arbitrary and capricious to the point of irrationality. Giving a student a zero for cheating on course work is not irrational. It is a logical punishment, often handed down by teachers, for turning in work that is not one's own, or for helping another person turn in work that is not their own. It is rational in that it gives no credit to a student who may not have done any work himself, and it is rational in that it serves as a deterrent to keep students from engaging in or repeating academic dishonesty. Jackson was not denied substantive due process in his receipt of a zero for cheating."

Thus, while allowing the plaintiff the benefit of the doubt as to whether or not this private university could be deemed a "state actor" for the limited purpose of applying Fourteenth Amendment due-process requirements, the Court still went on to rule against him, consistent with the deference typically accorded higher education actors, both public and private, where academic standards are concerned.

Advice. Thus, harking back to the sample policy presented at the start of this chapter, we can emphasize that, where an institution of higher education has a procedure in place and where its faculty and administrators apply the policy consistently, the odds of prevailing in a court challenge of an academic adverse academic decision strongly favor the institution over the disappointed student.

Impact of the Higher Education Opportunity Act (HEOA)

Colleges and universities are required to publish data on their completion and graduation rates. This data must be disaggregated by:

- Gender
- Major racial and ethnic subgroups
- Recipients of Pell Grants
- Recipients of federal aid (other than Pell Grants)

If the number of students leaving prior to graduation for military and other federal service and church mission service exceeds 20 percent of the student body, these departures can be excluded from the calculation of completion and graduation rates.

CHAPTER 5

Academic Integrity, Plagiarism, and Cheating

Plagiarism and Cheating

The satiric singer-songwriter and sometime Harvard professor Tom Lehrer once wrote the following logic: "Plagiarize, plagiarize. Let no one else's work evade your eyes." As this suggests, plagiarism and other forms of cheating are by no means confined to the student body. This point is emphasized further by the following article.

Dan Brown's *The Da Vinci Code* is the biggest bestseller of all time, boasting more than 60 million copies in 44 languages. Brown's net worth is reported to be about a quarter billion and climbing. But if another author, Lewis Purdue, were to be believed, most universities, if they played by their own rules, would fire Brown from their faculties.

Perdue, author of 1983's *The Da Vinci Legacy* and 2000's *Daughter of God,* possesses an expert opinion from Director John Olsson of Britain's Forensic Linguistics Institute, who has publicly called Brown's book, "the most blatant example of in-your-face plagiarism I've ever seen." Unfortunately for Perdue, when Brown and Random House hauled him into the federal court in Manhattan, seeking a declaration that *Code* did not violate Perdue's copyrights, the judge disallowed the expert report.

Although Perdue is pursuing the case into the U.S. Supreme Court on a motion for *certiorari,* the two lower courts ruling against him may be dead right. Current U.S. copyright law protects only the actual expression of an author's ideas, not the underlying ideas themselves. Copyright infringement is not synonymous with plagiarism.

Perhaps it should be. So suggests an article by Harvard Law Professor Arthur Miller in the January issue of his law school's journal. In the article, entitled "Common Law Protection for Products of the Mind," Miller, citing Perdue's case among many others, contends that the law should look at how the plaintiff's idea enriched the defendant... not at whether the defendant ripped off an exact copy of the plaintiff's work. This approach matches what most universities tell their students about plagiarism.

The academic penalties for plagiarism can be severe. The career-busting equivalent of capital punishment is often invoked. For example, in mid-September the University of Cincinnati announced initiation of steps to terminate its director of German-American studies on the grounds of numerous plagiarized passages in a 2000 tome, *The German-American Experience*. Charges were first made on the website H-Net, which claimed in 2003 that roughly half of the first 180 pages were lifted from a 1962 book, *The Germans in America*. A more ancient volume, 1909's *The German Element in the United States*, also allegedly was looted by the Cincinnati faculty-member/librarian for his own book.

If the University of Cincinnati imposes workplace capital punishment, the author of *The German-American Experience* will join a long line of academic plagiarizers who were marched up the steps to that same guillotine. Some casualties, however, have refused to lie down and play dead. Chris Dussold, a former Southern Illinois at Edwardsville faculty member, for instance, is fighting a multi-front campaign against his former employers. Fired in 2004 for allegedly lifting a two-page teaching statement, Dussold has since sued. Dussold apparently doesn't deny that he borrowed the statement, which he considered mere boilerplate, from a colleague. He says, simply, that plagiarism never crossed his mind. He adds that a false rumor—that he was sleeping with a student—is the real reason he was fired.

Not satisfied with suing, Dussold launched a "glass houses" campaign, pointing out for example that the school's chancellor copied several passages of a speech from a web site. The chancellor owned up and apologized. Earlier this year the chancellor of Southern Illinois's Carbondale campus admitted that portions of his 2005 state-of-the-university address came verbatim from a 1986 book he hadn't written. Both chancellors blamed staffers, but Dussold contends that since he was fired, so too should they be.

Dussold's counterattack calls into question how hypocritical plagiarism rules really are. Earlier this year, President Scott D. Miller of Delaware's Wesley College survived a plagiarism investigation and a faculty no-confidence referendum that came out even. A panel chaired by former Penn President Judith Rodin blamed public relations staffers under tremendous pressure to provide their boss with an outstanding speech. Miller promised to put safeguards in place. Professor Dussold presumably would say that this is another case of too little, too late.

Superstar profs, such as the late best-selling historian Stephen Ambrose, often likewise successfully weather accusations of plagiarism, shrugging them off as fair-use or inadvertence. Author Dan Brown and his publisher have thus far weathered two trials, one the Perdue hearing, the other a courtroom drama played out last year in London, where British authors unsuccessfully challenged Brown's right to borrow from their non-fiction *Holy Blood, Holy Grail.* In a classic example of the superstar shrug, Brown told *Today*'s Matt Lauer, "When *DaVinci Code* debuted at No. 1, I actually got a lot of calls from best-selling authors… saying, 'Well, get ready, because there are going to be people that you never heard of come out of the woodwork sort of wanting to ride your coattails'."

In recent correspondence and conversation, Perdue conceded to me "mistakes and misjudgments" which landed him in a federal court across the country from his California home, grappling with a mass media Goliath, like some David who'd forgotten to pack his sling. Even today, as he awaits rulings on whether he might actually owe Random House its attorney fees and whether the Supremes might stoop to review his case, Perdue admits, "I also realize I am too close to this issue to be as cool and rational as needed." Still he persists, as does Illinois's Professor Dussold. As Dussold uses the Internet to further his "glass houses" attack against Illinois's chancellors, Perdue employs extensive web sites and blogs to sustain his counteroffensive against nemesis Dan Brown.

Source: *Jim Castagnera, Would Your University Fire Dan Brown?* The Greentree Gazette, *November 2006, pages 36 and 56. (Published with permission of* The Greentree Gazette: The Business Magazine for Higher Education.*)*

As the foregoing article indicates, plagiarism plagues not only the academy but the more pedestrian world of mass-market entertainment. That latter realm, while it is well-armed with regard to copyright and trademark infringement, is ill-equipped to deal with plagiarism.

Nor are our students attuned to what constitutes plagiarism. Just as they have a difficult time distinguishing between legitimate scholarship and pseudo-scholarship on the Internet, many also harbor the mistaken notion that cutting and pasting materials from web sites constitutes legitimate research. The fact that their faculty, as exemplified in the article, sometimes either don't recognize their own acts of plagiarism, or in worst-case scenarios knowingly engage in plagiarism, does nothing to help students understand and respect academia's anti-plagiarism rules.

This is true even though universities generally go to great lengths to define plagiarism. Following is a typical policy:

"1.1 Ghostwriting—Written work submitted by an individual student (or group of students working together as approved in advance by the instructor) is expected to be the work of that student (or approved group)....

"1.2 Word for Word Plagiarism—Copying, word for word, from any source (book, magazine, newspaper, Internet source, unpublished paper or thesis) without proper acknowledgment by quotation and citation within the text of the paper....

"1.3 Patchwork Plagiarism—The submission of work which has been constructed by piecing together phrases and/or sentences quoted verbatim (word for word) or paraphrased from a variety of unacknowledged sources is an act of academic dishonesty....

"1.4 Unacknowledged Paraphrases—Submission of another author's facts or ideas in one's own words without acknowledgment by proper citation is an act of academic dishonesty."

Source: The Source: Student Handbook of Rider University *(2006).*
(Reprinted with permission of Rider University.)

Most institutions, wisely, provide ample measures of due process for students accused of cheating. Turning again to Rider University (the home institution of your author), the following procedures are mandated for academic-dishonesty cases:

Procedure to Be Followed in Academic Cases of Dishonesty

Step One

When a faculty member has reason to believe that an act of academic dishonesty has been committed by a student enrolled either in a current course or in one completed within the previous four months, the faculty member shall notify the student in writing of the alleged violation and require that the student meet with the faculty member at a mutually satisfactory time within five (5) working days after the faculty member's notification. The faculty member shall have the authority to extend the time within which the meeting takes place to ten (10) working days at his or her discretion. If the meeting does not occur within this time, the faculty member may proceed with the imposition of any of the sanctions described below.

At this meeting with the student, the faculty member and the student shall discuss the alleged act of dishonesty. The faculty member and the student shall seek to resolve the matter during this meeting. If the faculty member concludes that an act of academic dishonesty has not occurred, no further action shall be taken and the student shall be permitted to complete the course, if it is still in session, as if the faculty member's allegation had not been made.

If, as a result of information obtained in this meeting and shortly thereafter, the faculty member concludes that an act of academic dishonesty has occurred, he/she must notify the student of this determination in writing within seven (7) working days of the meeting and must indicate which one of the following sanctions will be invoked. The options are listed below in ascending order of seriousness. The faculty member may:

1. Direct the student to resubmit any work necessary to complete the course requirements;
2. Direct the registrar to change the grade given to the student to the notation "Incomplete" and direct the student to resubmit any work necessary to complete the course requirements;
3. Lower the grade appropriately on the assignment in which the academic dishonesty took place in light of the gravity and implications of the act of dishonesty, and recalculate the final course grade and direct the registrar to change the final course grade accordingly;
4. Direct the registrar to enter the grade of "F" for the course on the student's permanent academic record (this "F" supersedes all other grades, including the "W" notation);
5. Initiate charges against the student with the Academic Integrity Committee for the purpose of causing the student to be suspended or dismissed from the University.

Academic Integrity Committee. Following the first set of staggered appointments, the bargaining unit faculty members and administrators shall serve two-year terms, beginning with the date of appointment, and may be reappointed. The student member shall serve a one-year term. The committee shall select from among its members with faculty rank a chairperson and a vice-chairperson, and immediately notify the president, the vice president for academic affairs and provost, the chairperson of the University Academic Policy Committee, the president of the Student Government Association, and the Dean of Students of the names of the designees. The chairperson or vice-chairperson shall serve as the hearing coordinator. Any three (3) members of the committee with faculty rank (including the hearing coordinator) shall constitute a quorum. The failure or inability of any appointing body to fulfill its responsibility to appoint any member(s) to the Academic Integrity Committee shall not prevent the committee from organizing and exercising its prescribed duties. Whenever there is no chairperson or vice-chairperson of the committee, the vice president for academic affairs and provost shall appoint a convener. Ordinarily, the chairperson (or vice-chairperson, in his/her absence) shall preside over the meetings of the committee. The hearing coordinator shall have the following duties and responsibilities: 1. To assure that all procedures have been followed; 2. To inform the members of the committee that a charge of alleged academic misconduct against a student has been brought by a faculty member or that a student or faculty member has appealed a decision; 3. To see that all members of the committee receive the appropriate materials necessary for the hearing of the charge and appeal; 4. To keep a permanent record of the committee's proceedings; and 5. To see that all decisions made by the committee are prepared and distributed to the relevant parties.

Within ten (10) working days after receipt of a charge brought by a faculty member, or an appeal brought by either party, a date for a hearing shall be set and the faculty member and the student shall be notified of that date. If the hearing has not occurred within those ten (10) days, it shall be scheduled to take place as soon as possible thereafter. The committee chairperson shall have authority to extend any deadlines when it is evident that both parties have made good faith, though unsuccessful, efforts to meet the stated deadlines. Parties at the hearing shall be limited to members of the Rider University community with information pertinent to the given case. The student may choose to have a University advisor present with him/her. This advisor may be a university administrator, faculty member, or current student. If the requested sanction is dismissal from the university, the student shall have the right to be accompanied by an attorney. If the committee indicates in advance that dismissal will not be considered by the committee, no attorney shall attend. However, if the student wishes to be accompanied by an attorney, the hearing coordinator must be so notified at least seven (7) days before the scheduled hearing so that the university may also have counsel present. The committee shall establish the operating procedures by which it reviews cases. Standard operating steps include: Any letters placed in a student's academic file and student personnel file in the office of the Dean of Students according to any of the provisions in this policy will be available to individual members of the faculty and the committee when determining sanctions in subsequent incidents of academic dishonesty for that student. These letters will also be made available to the members of Academic Standing Committees for making subsequent decisions regarding conditional academic standing.

Source: The Source: Student Handbook of Rider University *(2009).*
(Reprinted with permission of Rider University.)

All this "due process" notwithstanding, disciplining of plagiarism has all-too-often led to litigation by disgruntled students and their parents. The reported decisions generally fall into four broad categories with regard to causes of action: (1) Denial of due process per the Fifth and Fourteenth Amendments of the U.S. Constitution; (2) illegal discrimination, e.g., race discrimination; (3) breach of conduct and/or fiduciary duty; and (4) common law tort liability, notably negligence.

Denial of Due Process of Law

Whenever a public institution of higher education is the target of a student lawsuit involving disciplinary action or the denial by that institution of some perceived student right or privilege, we can anticipate the plaintiff(s) will invoke the Fifth and Fourteenth Amendments of the U.S. Constitution, as well as analogous provisions of relevant state constitutions. The Fourteenth Amendment, adopted shortly after the Civil War, states in pertinent part that no state shall "deprive any person of life, liberty, or property, without due process of law; nor deny to any person within its jurisdiction the equal protection of the laws." As instruments of the state, public colleges and universities are subject to this restriction on their discretionary administration of disciplinary actions for plagiarism and other student teaching.

What quality and quantity of internal proceedings amounts to sufficient "due process?" ***Viriyapanthu v. Regents of the University of California,*** *2003 WL 22120968 (California Court of Appeals, 2003)* stands for the proposition that a full-fledged formal hearing is not necessary to satisfy the Fourteenth Amendment mandate.

Facts. Plaintiff, a UCLA law student, was accused by a professor of plagiarizing substantial portions of a major term paper from a book. The offense was what the Rider University policy, p. 116, labels "1.4 Unacknowledged Paraphrases—Submission of another author's facts or ideas in one's own words without acknowledgment by proper citation is an act of academic dishonesty." The school accorded the student the following procedures:

1. The assistant dean and the head librarian reviewed the paper and ended up agreeing with the profession that plagiarism had occurred;
2. An informal meeting was then held with the student, wherein he admitted "playing fast and loose" but adamantly denied any intent to commit plagiarism;
3. A more formal disciplinary meeting was held at which the student was allowed to bring an attorney;
4. The law school dean then reviewed the case and suspended the student;
5. The student appealed the decision and the dean confirmed his prior decision.

The student served out his suspension, then returned to school and subsequently graduated. Only after graduation did he sue the school, seeking to expunge his record on the ground that he had been denied due process of law since no adversarial hearing had ever been held.

Analysis. Although the school's Student Conduct Code called for a possible hearing before the Student Conduct Committee, the court concluded that in this case the plaintiff had been fully informed of the charges against him and was given an adequate opportunity to reply. That reply, following provision of the definition of the type of plagiarism at issue, was an admission of guilt, albeit accompanied by a denial of evil intent. Indeed, said the judges, the plaintiff had been given multiple opportunities to tell his side of the story throughout the several steps of the procedures leading to his suspension. On these facts, the court held that the absence of the formal hearing in front of the Student Conduct Committee did not fatally offend the Fourteenth Amendment's "due process" clause.

Even when the proper quantity of procedure is accorded the accused, the quality of the proceedings must also pass constitutional muster. In ***Basile v. Albany College of Pharmacy of Union University,*** *719 NYS2d 199 (New York Court of Appeals, 2001),* several professors accused a trio of students of cheating over a two-year period. The Student Honor Code Committee concurred and two of the students were expelled.

Facts. The plaintiffs, all of whom were fourth year students at the Albany College of Pharmacy, were found guilty of cheating despite the absence of any evidence as to the specific means by which they allegedly cheated. The evidence in support of the charges consisted of (1) compilations by the various professors showing that the plaintiffs gave the same incorrect answers in multiple choice examinations, (2) two anonymous notes, one of which claimed that two of the plainitffs requested information concerning the contents of exams and the second questioning whether the same two plaintiffs were cheating, and (3) similar answers to questions which required calculations, with each plaintiff utilizing different calculations uncorrelated to the answer arrived at.

Analysis. The appeals panel focused its analysis on three points:

"First, the Committee's determinations were based solely on the statistical compilation. While these may give rise to a suspicion of cheating, suspicion alone will not suffice. *An affidavit from an expert statistician, unrebutted by the College, establishes that the statistical case propounded by the professors is based upon false assumptions and therefore does not provide a rational basis to conclude that petitioners* (plaintiffs) *cheated. Specifically, the expert's opinion points out that the statistics are valid only if the persons taking the examination had no knowledge of the* subject matter ("randomness") and had not studied together ("independence")(emphasis in original opinion).

"Second, petitioners Carl A. Basile and Daniel R. Papelino were charged with cheating in nine courses and petitioner Michael Yu in seven courses. Basile was found guilty of cheating in six of the nine, Papelino in three of the nine and Yu in one of the seven. Since the same statistical methodology was used in every instance, there is no rational explanation that would support a finding of guilt in some courses but not in others.

"Third, respondents claim that in addition to these statistics, there is evidence in the record of cheating by petitioners. A careful review of these allegations reveals that they are either hearsay anonymous notes or based on sheer speculation, neither of which will rationally support the determinations of the Committee. *Moreover, it was irrational of the Committee to determine that it could rely solely on the inference of cheating raised by the statistical compilation, particularly when faced with proof that petitioners took these examinations in separate rooms and under the watchful eye of a proctor, who discerned no evidence of cheating."* (Emphasis in original opinion)

The court concluded that, despite the quantity of due process accorded to the plaintiffs, the quality of the proceedings did not measure up to constitutional requirements. Rather, "we do not find that the Committee's determinations that petitioners cheated on various examinations have a rational basis and we therefore reverse."

Advice. The good news is that courts' due-process analysis tends to look at the totality of the procedures accorded to the accused student. Where those procedures provided the student with notice of the accusation; a clear statement of the standards allegedly violated (preferably standards which were readily available to the student prior to the alleged offense); the student is offered ample opportunity to reply; and there is some level of appellate review, courts are inclined to sanction the school's imposition of discipline. A formal hearing is perhaps advisable, but is certainly not mandatory in order to meet the courts' criteria. (See Checklist: Elements of Due Process, p. 107).

The bad news is that, even when a formal adversarial hearing is included in the school's internal proceedings, if the decision makers act irrationally, no amount of procedural form will excuse this lack of substantive due process. Thus, a forum, regardless of how formalistic it is, that acts irrationally or arbitrarily in finding fault and meting out discipline will not be rubber-stamped in a judicial challenge.

Illegal Discriminatory Treatment

Where a student convicted of plagiarism or cheating believes that students of a different race, sex, religion or national origin were treated less harshly, s/he may choose to turn to an appropriate state anti-discrimination statute as the ground for at least one count in a complaint seeking to overturn the institution's decision and/or recover damages from the defendant college or university.

For example, in ***Ntreh v. University of Texas at Dallas,*** *936 SW2d 649 (Texas Court of Appeals, 1996),* the plaintiff, a Ghanaian national, based one count of his complaint—following expulsion for plagiarism—Texas Civil Practice Code sec. 106.002(b), which makes it unlawful for an employee of the state or a political subdivision, acting or purporting to act in official capacity, to impose an unreasonable burden on any person because of race, religion, color, sex, or national origin.

Facts. The decision cited above determined that UT-Dallas could not escape liability on the basis of sovereign immunity. In a subsequent, related proceeding *[2000 WL 1093233],* the appeals court provided the following statement of the relevant facts:

"In 1991, Ntreh, a Ghanaian national, was a legal resident alien and a student at UTD. During his senior year, Ntreh and his brother Joseph Ntreh ('Joseph') enrolled in the Nature of Theatrical Experience class taught by Ms. Coral Shafer ('Shafer'). To receive credit for the course, each student had to complete a final project consisting of either a research paper or a creative project. Options for the creative project included doing a performance of either already scripted material, or material written by the student, writing a script, or doing a design for a costume or a set. If the student chose to do a creative project, they were also required to write a two to three page paper placing the project within the context of the class. According to Shafer, Ntreh chose to do a creative project and write a script.

"For his final project, Ntreh turned in a play entitled 'A Return to Live' and the author of the play was designated as Abe Evan Nee, a name by which Ntreh is often referred. A two-page cover sheet was attached explaining the nature of the play. The language used in the cover sheet indicated that Ntreh wrote the play. Ntreh initially received a 'B' grade for his project. Feeling that he should have received an 'A' instead of a 'B,' Ntreh spoke with Dr. Linda Williamson ('Williamson'), the College Master for the College of Arts and Sciences at UTD, about the discriminatory manner in which 'A' and 'B' grades were assigned.

"After reviewing Ntreh's play, Shafer questioned the play's authenticity. Williamson and Priscilla Ann Beadle, the Vice President for Administration and Student Affairs, testified at trial that when they questioned Ntreh about his play, he told them the play was his original work. Williamson and Shafer decided to conduct research to determine if Ntreh had plagiarized an existing work. Shafer conducted research at the Dallas Public Library where she discovered a play entitled 'Resurrection' by Richard Rive. Except for some minor details, Shafer discovered that Rive's 'Resurrection' and Ntreh's 'A Return to Live,' were verbatim. UTD initiated a disciplinary proceeding against Ntreh for alleged plagiarism. As a result of the proceeding, Ntreh was given an 'F' in the class and expelled from the University....

"There is evidence in the record that as his final project in the class, Ntreh turned in a play entitled 'A Return to Live'; he designated the author of the play as Abe Evan Nee, a moniker by which he was known. In a two-page cover sheet attached to his play, Ntreh described in detail how he had been inspired to write the play because of a personal experience he had had at a friend's aunt's funeral, how he developed the characters and dialogue, and how he envisioned the theatrical setting, scenery, lighting, and sound. The concluding paragraph in his cover sheet stated that, '[m]ost of the things we studied in class helped me considerably to explore the components of *my story* in relation to the components of *my play.* Things we studied also helped me in considering what was essential in *my story* to meet *my objective* in the play.' (Emphasis added by the court.) Beadle testified that Ntreh represented to her that he had written all of the two-page cover sheet and play he turned in as his final project.

Ms. Veronica Davis ('Davis'), a former attorney with the Department of Education, also testified that Ntreh wrote the two-page cover sheet. There is also evidence and testimony in the record that Ntreh represented to Shafer, Beadle, and Williamson that the play was his own work.

"Williamson testified that both she and Shafer questioned whether Ntreh's play was his original work because of the professional quality of the play, a quality that is not customary for student works. Williamson testified that she and Shafer both conducted research in various libraries to determine if a play existed that Ntreh could have plagiarized. Williamson further stated that based on the language used in the play, Shafer narrowed her search to Afro American anthologies, which eventually led to Shafer's discovery of a previously published play entitled 'Resurrection' by Richard Rives. Except for a few minor changes, Ntreh's play was the verbatim script of 'Resurrection.

"In her testimony, Williamson explained the search for the 'Resurrection':

Q. How long did it take [Shafer] to locate this Rive play? How many hours did she put into it?

A. I don't know the total number of hours, I know that she went solely for the—she went to the library looking for the play.

Q. Looking for that particular play?

A. Looking for any play that looked like it might be like—

Q. How many plays are in the library?

A. I don't know.

Q. Probably thousands. Is that accurate?

A. I would not think so.

Q. You would think there is less than a thousand plays in the UTD library?

A. She wasn't at the UTD library, she was at the Dallas County-Dallas Public Library.

Q. So it's your view that there is probably less than a thousand plays at the Dallas library?

A. Plays of this nature. I mean, when you are a professional you can read a play and get a sense of language, a sense of place and a sense of what the action is, and you even have a category to go to. Obviously, having his work, you wouldn't be looking under comedies you would be looking under—you would be looking for a *needle in a haystack.*

Q. Well, I mean, that's kind of what I am thinking.

A. Uh-huh.

Q. And I am trying to figure out how this needle was located in just a few hours, what—whether you had some kind of—

A. I had an idea—
Q. —informant who told you what the play was, or maybe Mr. Ntreh told you what the play was.
A. The—I am not aware of any of this other than the fact that the play was found.
Q. Did you think it was at all unusual that the play got found like that?
A. Yes. But I would have, and did do some searching on my own.
Q. And you found it as well, independently?
A. No.
(Emphasis added by the court.)

"Ntreh argues that Williamson's testimony that finding the 'Resurrection' was like looking for a 'needle in a haystack,' supports his argument that Shafer's expediency in finding this 'needle in a haystack' is implausible without having prior knowledge of the play's existence. Ntreh argues that this is further supported by Joseph's testimony that Ntreh had informed Shafer that he was staging an *existing work.* Ntreh contends that, because the evidence demonstrates that he represented to Shafer that he was using an existing work for his project, the evidence does not support a finding of plagiarism.

"UTD argues that the phrase 'a needle in a haystack' meant that 'conducting a search for the play in a library would have been like looking for a needle in a haystack without narrowing the search to a particular category of plays.'"

Analysis. Finding at the threshold that Ntreh had been accorded appropriate due process per our discussion above, the court tackled his claim of discriminatory treatment in terms of the severer penalty of expulsion. "UTD offered evidence of the number, race, and sex of students at UTD who had been found guilty of scholastic dishonesty or plagiarism between 1989 and 1992 and the penalty assessed against the students. Beadle's testimony concerning this list revealed that of the fifty-three students found guilty of scholastic dishonesty or plagiarism, all but three of the students decided to admit the facts alleged against them and accept the penalty offered by UTD. None of the students who acknowledged the charges against them were expelled. Of the three students who did not admit the charges, two were expelled, one of which was Ntreh. The other student who was expelled was white." Based on this evidence, the court found that the plaintiff's charge of disparate treatment based on his race and/or national origin was unfounded.

Advice. The testimony quoted above is interesting. The "B" initially given to the plaintiff by the professor is curious. If the play was professional quality, why didn't she award an "A"? If the answer is, as later stated, she was suspicious of plagiarism, why didn't she confront the student in the first instance, instead of giving him a "B"? Did his race cause her to seek to avoid a confrontation, while her suspicions led her to award less than top marks for the work? And why, if he had cheated, did the student challenge the "B" grade? Would we not have expected him to grab such a good grade and run? Unfortunately for him, the courts apparently declined to pursue the "needle in a haystack" observation to its logical conclusion, i.e., that the professor knew from the start that the plaintiff was using a pre-existing work for his project, and that, therefore, the plagiarism charge was in the nature of retaliation for having the temerity to challenge his grade. We can never know if this was what really happened. Certainly, it's where the student's attorney was trying to take the case. That the courts declined to follow is a strong indication of the level of deference they are inclined to accord academia, where due process has been adequately accorded and no "smoking gun" is aimed at discriminatory intent.

In another relatively recent case, the appeals court accorded no more credibility to a plaintiff's proffered statistical evidence than it did to the defendant-institution's reliance on statistics in ***Albany College of Pharmacy*** above. In ***Cobb v. Rector and Visitors of the University of Virginia,*** *84 F.Supp.2d 740 (U.S. District Court, Western District of Virginia, 2000),* the plaintiff—found guilty of cheating by a student jury under the institution's honor code proceedings—attempted to show race discrimination via statistics intended to demonstrate honor-code prosecution of a proportionately higher percentage of non-white than white students. The federal judge rejected the statistical evidence in favor of the actual facts in the case at hand.

Facts. The facts relied upon by the trial judge in rejecting the plaintiff's race discrimination claim were "Three other students were charged with honor violations on Michener's exam. Of the three other students, one was African American and two were Caucasian. The Honor Committee dropped its case against the African American student at the investigation stage after concluding that there was insufficient evidence to proceed to trial. The case against one of the Caucasian students was prosecuted to trial, resulting in a not guilty verdict. The other Caucasian student left the University after he was formally accused of the charge and his whereabouts are unknown; thus, prosecution against him is pending and he will be tried if he ever returns to the University (though his readmission to the University is currently blocked)."

Advice. The appropriate advice here should be obvious: uniform application of the procedures and penalties in plagiarism, cheating, and indeed all other disciplinary matters make up the best defense an institution can have, if faced with an accusation of illegal disparate treatment based upon the student-plaintiff's protected classification. As reflected in *Cobb*, it is particularly important that all students caught within the school's net in a single cheating case be treated even-handedly on the basis of the evidence.

Breach of Contract and/or Fiduciary Duty

Morris v. Brandeis University, *804 NE2d 961 (Massachusetts Court of Appeals, 2004),* may be an example of a creative plaintiff's attorney—unable to sue a private university under the Fourteenth Amendment's due-process clause—finding an alternative cause of action. Morris was accused of "verbatim plagiarism," correctly defined by the Rider code, above, as "Word for Word Plagiarism—Copying, word for word, from any source (book, magazine, newspaper, Internet source, unpublished paper or thesis) without proper acknowledgment by quotation and citation within the text of the paper…."

Facts. The court presented the relevant facts as follows: "On May 7, 1997, Morris, a second-semester senior at Brandeis, submitted his final paper in a history course taught by Associate Professor Alice Kelikian. On May 12, 1997, Professor Kelikian submitted a student judicial system referral report to the office of campus life, charging Morris with verbatim plagiarism from four secondary sources on his final paper. After notice to Morris, an investigation, and a hearing in accordance with procedures as set forth in Brandeis's student handbook (handbook), Brandeis's board on student conduct (board) unanimously found against him. Morris pursued an administrative appeal of the decision on the basis of 'procedural irregularities and new evidence.' On May 30, 1997, Morris was notified that Brandeis's appeals board on student conduct had denied his request for a new hearing. Morris then brought this action in Superior Court against Brandeis for breach of contract, breach of the covenant of good faith and fair dealing, negligent misrepresentation, and breach of fiduciary duty."

Analysis. On these facts, the court reasoned, "*Basic fairness.* After reviewing the record, we conclude that there was nothing fundamentally unfair about the process received by Morris. From the date of the charge through the appellate process, Brandeis adhered strictly to its procedural rules, see §§ 18–23 of the handbook, and Morris received more process than was required, in the form of a post-hearing meeting with the dean of student affairs.

"To the extent that Morris questions the fairness of the sanction, § 5 of the handbook expressly warns students that violation of university policies on academic honesty can lead to 'serious penalties,' including failure in the course and other sanctions. See § 5 of the handbook. The sanction in this case fell within the range of permissible actions allowed by the handbook. See § 21 of the handbook.

"Morris's failure to acknowledge responsibility for his actions, and his blaming Brandeis for not teaching him appropriate methods of citation, was an invalid defense under § 5.4 of the handbook.

"Finally, Morris has failed to place into legitimate dispute the fact that the sanction ultimately imposed upon him was consistent with those imposed upon other upper class students under similar circumstances. There was no arbitrary, capricious or unfair conduct by Brandeis."

Advice. Although the plaintiff's cause of action was couched in terms of the common law of contract, the court clearly applied a standard analogous to the one we identified under "due process" above. The court characterized this standard quite correctly as one of "basic fairness." Just as failure of the institution to accord the student a full-fledged adversarial hearing did not offend Fourteenth Amendment due-process standards, likewise the court in this case did not demand that Brandeis follow the language in its student handbook with complete precision, provided the university did treat Morris with "basic fairness." So long as that was the case, no breach of contract claim would be deemed to lie against the school.

Common Law Tort Liability

A plaintiff challenging disciplinary action based upon institutional-adjudication of plagiarism or cheating may be tempted to add one or more counts sounding in common law tort and based upon such legal theories as negligent handling of the adjudication procedures or defamatory communication of the accusation and/or the disciplinary outcome. Such was the case in ***Imtiaz v. Board of Regents of the University of Michigan,*** *2006 WL 510057 (Michigan Court of Appeals, 2006).*

Facts. The plaintiff, a woman of Pakistani descent, enrolled in the University of Michigan School of Dentistry. Upon enrollment, each student signed an acknowledgment to abide by the Honor Code. Violations of the Honor Code were reported to the Honor Council, a body comprised of eleven elected students from the School of Dentistry.

The plaintiff was accused of violating the Honor Code in a class taught by Professors/Defendants Jaarda and Stoffers. Upon notification of the charges, she waived her right to an Honor Council hearing and opted to have her case heard by a three-member *ad hoc* faculty committee. Following the hearing, the *ad hoc*–committee members unanimously agreed that the plaintiff committed the violations as alleged in the complaint. Imtiaz appealed the *ad hoc* committee's recommendation for expulsion to the Executive Committee.

Within days of the Executive Committee hearing, the plaintiff admitted that she committed the alleged violation. The Executive Committee notified her of its decision not to adopt the Honor Council's recommendation for expulsion, and to suspend her until the fall semester of 2001, place her on probation for the duration of her studies at the university, record the offense on her transcript until five years after her graduation, rescind any scholarship support, and require that she attend counseling and an ethics course. To explain her absence from the university, the plaintiff sent a class-wide email stating she was returning home to care for an ill parent.

During the plaintiff's absence, an anonymous letter disclosing the fact that the plaintiff was suspended for cheating was placed in each dentistry student's mailbox. The letter was also posted for at least two days on a centrally located bulletin board in the dental school. Generally, only faculty were permitted to post letters on the bulletin board. The individual defendants denied knowing the identity of the author of the letter and to date, no investigation has occurred, although defendants concede the letter breached the confidentiality of the proceedings.

Following her return, Imtiaz was accused of a second Honor Code violation. Following an exam, a classmate submitted a complaint against the plaintiff to the Honor Council alleging "inappropriate test taking behavior." The Honor Council conducted a hearing and determined that the plaintiff acted inappropriately or acted suspiciously, but did not find sufficient evidence to support a determination that the plaintiff actually cheated. The Honor Council refrained from recommending "definitive severe sanctions" and instead imposed minor penalties. The plaintiff appealed, and a hearing was scheduled before the Executive Committee.

In the interim, a third complaint against the plaintiff was submitted to the Honor Council. Professors Jaarda and Stoffers alleged that she misappropriated another student's property, a "PVS impression." The plaintiff was notified of the charges by a letter, and the Honor Council held a hearing on the allegations of the third incident. The Honor Council concluded that the plaintiff was guilty of taking the PVS impression and presenting false information by denying guilt, and recommended her expulsion from the Dental School.

The plaintiff sued, challenging the university's actions on due-process grounds and raising a panoply of other counts, among them defamation.

Analysis. With regard to the plaintiff's defamation claim, the appeals court stated, "Plaintiff cites as defamatory, the portion of the anonymous letter which reads, '[w]ho knows how many times [plaintiff] cheated her way through school and others? Is it any wonder that she ranked high in the class?' Plaintiff contends the statements destroyed her reputation. Defendants assert substantial truth as a defense.

"To establish a defamation claim, a plaintiff must show: (1) a false and defamatory statement about the plaintiff, (2) an unprivileged communication to a third party, (3) fault by the publisher, which amounts to at least negligence, and (4) either actionability of the statement regardless of special harm or the existence of special harm because of the publication. 'A communication is defamatory if it tends to lower an individual's reputation in the community or deters third persons from associating or dealing with that individual.' The defense requires looking 'to the sting of the article to determine its effect on the reader; if the literal truth produced the same effect, minor differences were deemed immaterial.'

"In this case, even viewing the evidence in a light most favorable to plaintiff, plaintiff's claim fails because the statements in the anonymous letter are substantially true. The record evidence shows that plaintiff admitted to and accepted responsibility for switching grade sheets to receive a higher grade that she did not earn. Thus, albeit in a breach of confidentiality, the letter correctly characterized her as an admitted cheater, and the fact that a reader of the letter may ponder about her past conduct does not make the statements actionable. 'Absent evidence that the defamation defendant intended the defamatory implication,' he 'is not responsible for every defamatory implication a reader might draw from his report of true facts.'

"Moreover, the statements to which plaintiff takes offense are not actionable as defamation because they cannot be proved as false and can be properly characterized as rhetorical hyperbole."

University Honor Codes

An honor code can at once significantly enhance the institution's level of responsibility and provide a shield against adverse litigation. Obviously, the increased responsibility involves enforcement of the code. This requires much more than promulgation. The campus culture quite literally must change to accommodate and accept the code. Otherwise it will fail.

On the other hand, the institution's enforcement burden should be lightened over time as the students themselves self-police the policy. Furthermore, a student subjected to the disciplinary constraints of the code is less likely to sue, since s/he has self-selected into the institution, thus accepting the code and the consequences of its violation. Additionally, witnesses against the offending individual are more likely to be credible than in ordinary circumstances.

An excellent example of a comprehensive honor code is the following:

FLORIDA STATE UNIVERSITY ACADEMIC HONOR POLICY

Introduction

The statement on Values and Moral Standards at FSU says: "The moral norm which guides conduct and informs policy at Florida State University is responsible freedom. Freedom is an important experience that the University, one of the freest of institutions, provides for all of its citizens—faculty, students, administrators, and staff. Freedom is responsibly exercised when it is directed by ethical standards" (Values and [M]oral [S]tandards at FSU retrieved from the current General Bulletin located at http://registrar.fsu.edu/).

The statement also addresses academic integrity: "The University aspires to excellence in its core activities of teaching, research, creative expression, and public service and is committed to the integrity of the academic process. The [Academic Honor Policy] is a specific manifestation of this commitment. Truthfulness in one's claims and representations and honesty in one's activities are essential in life and vocation, and the realization of truthfulness and honesty is an intrinsic part of the educational process" (Values and [M]oral [S]tandards at FSU retrieved from the current General Bulletin located at http://registrar.fsu.edu/).

Guided by these principles, this Academic Honor Policy outlines the University's expectations for students' academic work, the procedures for resolving alleged violations of those expectations, and the rights and responsibilities of students and faculty throughout the process.

FSU Academic Honor Pledge

I affirm my commitment to the concept of responsible freedom. I will be honest and truthful and will strive for personal and institutional integrity at Florida State University. I will abide by the Academic Honor Policy at all times.

Academic Honor Violations

Note: Instructors are responsible for reinforcing the importance of the Academic Honor Policy in their courses and for clarifying their expectations regarding collaboration and multiple submission of academic work. Examples have been provided for the purpose of illustration and are not intended to be all-inclusive.

1. PLAGIARISM. Intentionally presenting the work of another as one's own (i.e., without proper acknowledgment of the source).

Typical Examples Include: Using another's work from print, web, or other sources without acknowledging the source; quoting from a source without citation; using facts, figures, graphs, charts or information without acknowledgment of the source.

2. CHEATING. Improper application of any information or material that is used in evaluating academic work.

Typical Examples Include: Copying from another student's paper or receiving unauthorized assistance during a quiz, test or examination; using books, notes or other devices (e.g., calculators, cell phones, or computers) when these are not authorized; procuring without authorization a copy of or information about an examination before the scheduled exercise; unauthorized collaboration on exams.

3. UNAUTHORIZED GROUP WORK. Unauthorized collaborating with others.

Typical Examples Include: Working with another person or persons on any activity that is intended to be individual work, where such collaboration has not been specifically authorized by the instructor.

4. FABRICATION, FALSIFICATION, AND MISREPRESENTATION. Intentional and unauthorized altering or inventing of any information or citation that is used in assessing academic work.

Typical Examples Include: Inventing or counterfeiting data or information; falsely citing the source of information; altering the record of or reporting false information about practicum or clinical experiences; altering grade reports or other academic records; submitting a false excuse for absence or tardiness in a scheduled academic exercise; lying to an instructor to increase a grade.

5. MULTIPLE SUBMISSION. Submitting the same academic work (including oral presentations) for credit more than once without instructor permission. It is each instructor's responsibility to make expectations regarding incorporation of existing academic work into new assignments clear to the student in writing by the time assignments are given.

Typical Examples Include: Submitting the same paper for credit in two courses without instructor permission; making minor revisions in a credited paper or report (including oral presentations) and submitting it again as if it were new work.

6. ABUSE OF ACADEMIC MATERIALS. Intentionally damaging, destroying, stealing, or making inaccessible library or other academic resource material.

Typical Examples Include: Stealing or destroying library or reference materials needed for common academic purposes; hiding resource materials so others may not use them; destroying computer programs or files needed in academic work; stealing, altering, or intentionally damaging another student's notes or laboratory experiments. (This refers only to abuse as related to an academic issue.)

7. COMPLICITY IN ACADEMIC DISHONESTY. Intentionally helping another to commit an act of academic dishonesty.

Typical Examples Include: Knowingly allowing another to copy from one's paper during an examination or test; distributing test questions or substantive information about the material to be tested before a scheduled exercise; deliberately furnishing false information.

8. ATTEMPTING to commit any offense as outlined above.

Student Rights

Students have the following important due process rights, which may have an impact on the appellate process:

1. To be informed of all alleged violation(s), receive the complaint in writing (except in a Step 1 agreement, described in the Procedures section, where

the signed agreement serves as notice) and be given access to all relevant materials pertaining to the case.

2. To receive an impartial hearing in a timely manner where they will be given a full opportunity to present information pertaining to the case.

Students are also accorded the following prerogatives:

1. When possible, to discuss the allegations with the instructor.
2. Privacy, confidentiality, and personal security.
3. To be assisted by an advisor who may accompany the student throughout the process but may not speak on the student's behalf.
4. To choose not to answer any question that might be incriminating.
5. To contest the sanctions of a first-level agreement and to appeal both the decision and sanctions of an Academic Honor Hearing.

The student has the right to continue in the course in question during the entire process. Once a student has received notice that he/she is being charged with an alleged violation of the Academic Honor Policy, the student is not permitted to withdraw or drop the course unless the final outcome of the process dictates that no academic penalty will be imposed. Should no final determination be made before the end of the term, the grade of "Incomplete" will be assigned until a decision is made.

Students should contact the Dean of Students Department for further information regarding their rights.

Procedures for Resolving Cases

Step 1. Throughout the Step 1 process, the instructor has the responsibility to address academic honor allegations in a timely manner, and the student has the responsibility to respond to those allegations in a timely manner. For assistance with the Academic Honor Policy, students should consult the Dean of Students Department and instructors should consult the Office of the Dean of the Faculties.

If a student observes a violation of the Academic Honor Policy, he or she should report the incident to the instructor of the course. When an instructor believes that a student has violated the Academic Honor Policy in one of the instructor's classes, the instructor must first contact the Office of the Dean of the Faculties to report the alleged violation to determine whether to proceed with a Step 1 agreement. The instructor must also inform the department chair or dean. (Teaching assistants must seek guidance from their supervising faculty member.) However, faculty members or others who do not have administrative authority for enforcing the Academic Integrity Policy should not be informed of the allegation, unless they have established a legitimate need to know. If pursuing a Step 1 agreement is determined to be possible, the instructor shall discuss the evidence of academic dishonesty with the student and explore the possibility of a Step 1 agreement. Four possible outcomes of this discussion may occur:

1. If the charge appears unsubstantiated, the instructor will drop the charge, and all documents created in investigating the allegation will be destroyed. The instructor should make this decision using the "preponderance of the evidence" standard and should inform the Office of the Dean of the Faculties.
2. The student may accept responsibility for the violation and accept the academic sanction proposed by the instructor. In this case, any agreement involving an academic penalty must be put in writing and signed by both parties on the "Academic Honor Policy Step 1 Agreement" form, which must then be sent to the Dean of Students Department. This agreement becomes a confidential student record of academic dishonesty and will be removed from the student's file five years from the date of the final decision in the case.
3. The student may accept the responsibility for the violation, but contest the proposed academic sanction. In this circumstance, the student must submit the "Academic Honor Policy Referral to Contest Sanction" form along with supporting documentation to the Office of the Dean of the Faculties. The Dean of the Faculties (or designee) will review the submitted documentation to determine whether the instructor has imposed a sanction that is disproportionate to the offense. The Dean of the Faculties may affirm or modify the sanction as appropriate. The decision that results from this review is final.
4. The student may deny responsibility. In this circumstance, the instructor submits the "Academic Honor Policy Hearing Referral" form along with supporting documentation to the Dean of the Faculties Office for an Academic Honor Policy Hearing. The student is issued a letter detailing the charges within ten class days of the receipt of the referral, and the schedule for the hearing will be set as soon as possible and within 90 days from the date of the letter. These timelines may be modified in unusual

circumstances. Unless all parties agree, the hearing will not be held any sooner than 7 class days from the student's receipt of the charge letter. The process then proceeds to Step 2.

If the student is found to have a prior record of academic dishonesty or the serious nature of the allegations merits a formal hearing, the instructor must refer the matter to Step 2 for an Academic Honor Policy Hearing by submitting the "Academic Honor Policy Hearing Referral" form to the Office of the Dean of the Faculties.

Step 2. Academic Honor Policy Hearing. A panel consisting of five members shall hear the case. The panel shall include: one faculty member appointed by the dean from the unit in which the course is taught; one faculty member appointed by the Dean of the Faculties who is not from that unit; and two students appointed through procedures established by the Dean of Students Department. The panel shall be chaired by the Dean of the Faculties (or designee), who is a non-voting member of the committee.

The hearing will be conducted in a non-adversarial manner with a clear focus on finding the facts within the academic context of the course. The student is presumed innocent going into the proceeding. After hearing all available and relevant information, the panel determines whether or not to find the student responsible for the alleged violation using the "preponderance of the evidence" standard. If the student is found responsible for the violation, the panel is informed about any prior record of academic honor policy violations and determines an academic sanction (and disciplinary sanction, if appropriate). In some cases, a Step 1 sanction may have been appropriately proposed prior to the convening of an Academic Honor Hearing. If the student is found responsible in these cases, the panel typically will impose a sanction no more severe than that which was proposed by the faculty member. The panel is required to provide a clear written justification for imposing a sanction more severe than the sanction proposed in Step 1.

The chair of the Academic Honor Policy hearing panel will report the decision to the student, the instructor, and the Dean of Students Department. The Dean of Students Department will report the decision to the University Registrar, if appropriate. If the student is found "responsible," this outcome will be recorded with the Dean of Students Department and becomes a confidential student record of an Academic Honor Policy violation. Records in which suspension or a less severe sanction (including all academic sanctions) is imposed will be removed five years from the date of the final decision in the case. Records involving dismissal and expulsion will be retained permanently, except in cases where a dismissed student is readmitted. Those records will be removed five years from the date of the student's readmission.

Sanctions

Step 1. This Step 1 procedure is implemented with first-offense allegations that do not involve egregious violations. The decision regarding whether an allegation is egregious is made by the Dean of the Faculties (or designee) and the instructor. The criteria used by the instructor to determine the proposed academic penalty should include the seriousness and the frequency of the alleged violation. The following sanctions are available in the Step 1 procedure.

1. additional academic work
2. a reduced grade (including "0" or "F") for the assignment
3. a reduced grade (including "F") for the course

Step 2. An Academic Honor Policy Hearing is held for all second offenses, for all first offenses that involve egregious violations of the Academic Honor Policy, for all offenses that involve simultaneous violations of the Student Conduct Code, and in all cases where the student denies responsibility for the alleged violation. The decision regarding whether an allegation is egregious is made by the Dean of the Faculties (or designee) and the instructor. In some cases, a Step 1 sanction may have been appropriately proposed prior to the convening of an Academic Honor Policy Hearing. If the student is found responsible in these cases, the panel typically will impose a sanction no more severe than that which was proposed by the faculty member. The panel is required to provide a clear written justification for imposing a sanction more severe than the sanction proposed in Step 1. Students will not be penalized solely for exercising their right to request a Step 2 hearing. The following sanctions are available in Step 2 (see the Procedures section, p. 134) and may be imposed singly or in combination:

1. additional academic work
2. a reduced grade (including "0" or "F") for the assignment
3. a reduced grade (including "F") for the course
4. Reprimand (written or verbal)
5. Educational Activities—attendance at educational programs, interviews with appropriate officials, planning and implementing educational programs, or other educational activities. Fees may be charged to cover

the cost of educational activities.

6. Restitution
7. Conduct Probation—a period of time during which any further violation of the Academic Honor Policy may result in more serious sanctions being imposed. Some of the restrictions that may be placed on the student during the probationary period include, but are not limited to: participation in student activities or representation of the University on athletic teams or in other leadership positions.
8. Disciplinary Probation—a period of time during which any further violation of the Academic Honor Policy puts the student's status with the University in jeopardy. If the student is found "responsible" for another violation during the period of Disciplinary Probation, serious consideration will be given to imposing a sanction of Suspension, Dismissal, or Expulsion. The restrictions that may be placed on the student during this time period are the same as those under Conduct Probation.
9. Suspension—Separation from the University for a specified period, not to exceed two years.
10. Dismissal—Separation from the University for an indefinite period of time. Readmission is possible but not guaranteed and will only be considered after two years from the effective date of the dismissal, based on meeting all admission criteria and obtaining clearance from the Dean of Students or designee.
11. Expulsion—Separation from the University without the possibility of readmission.
12. Withholding of diplomas, transcripts, or other records for a specified period of time.
13. Revocation of degree, in cases where an egregious offense is discovered after graduation.

Appeals

Decisions of the Academic Honor Policy Hearing Panel may be appealed to the Academic Honor Policy Appeal Committee, a standing four-member committee composed of two faculty appointed by the President and two students appointed by the Vice President for Student Affairs. The chair will be appointed annually by the President, and members will serve two-year renewable terms. In case of a tie vote regarding a case, the committee will submit a written report to the Provost, who will then make the final determination.

On appeal, the burden of proof shifts to the student to prove that an error has occurred. The only recognized grounds for appeal are:

1. Due process errors involving violations of a student's rights that substantially affected the outcome of the initial hearing.
2. Demonstrated prejudice against the charged student by any panel member. Such prejudice must be evidenced by a conflict of interest, bias, pressure, or influence that precluded a fair and impartial hearing.
3. New information that was not available at the time of the original hearing.
4. A sanction that is extraordinarily disproportionate to the offense committed.
5. The preponderance of the evidence presented at the hearing does not support a finding of responsible. Appeals based on this consideration will be limited to a review of the record of the initial hearing.

The procedures followed during the appeals process are:

1. The student should file a written letter of appeal to the Office of the Dean of the Faculties within 10 class days after being notified of the Academic Honor Policy Hearing Panel decision. This letter should outline the grounds for the appeal (see 1–5 above) and should provide supporting facts and relevant documentation.
2. The Academic Honor Policy Appeal Committee will review this letter of appeal and will hear the student and any witnesses called by the student, except in appeals based on consideration #5 above. The committee may also gather any additional information it deems necessary to make a determination in the case.
3. The Appeals Committee may affirm, modify, or reverse the initial panel decision, or it may order a new hearing to be held. This decision becomes final agency action when it is approved by the Provost. In cases where the student is found responsible, the decision becomes a confidential student record of academic dishonesty.
4. Appellate decisions are communicated in writing to the student, the instructor, the Office of the Dean of the Faculties, and the Dean of Students Department within 30 class days of the appellate hearing.

Academic Honor Policy Committee

An Academic Honor Policy Committee shall be appointed by the University President. The Committee will include: three faculty members, selected from a list of six names provided by the Faculty Senate Steering Committee and three students, selected from a list of six names provided by the Student Senate. The Dean of the Faculties or designee and the Dean of Students or designee shall serve ex officio. Faculty members will serve three-year staggered terms, and students will serve one-year terms. The committee will meet at least once a semester. It will monitor the operation and effectiveness of the Academic Honor Policy, work with the Faculty Senate and the Student Senate to educate all members of the community regarding academic integrity, and make recommendations for changes to the policy.

Amendment Procedures

Amendments to the Academic Honor Policy may be initiated by the Academic Honor Policy Committee, the Faculty Senate, the Student Senate, and/or the Vice President for Academic Affairs. Amendments to the policy must be approved by both the Faculty Senate and the Student Senate.

Source: The Florida State University (reprinted with permission).

An honor code, however, is no "silver bullet" against lawsuits by disciplined students. This is particularly true if the institution has failed to educate its students adequately as to honor code requirements or if discipline is applied arbitrarily or unfairly.

In ***Atria v. Vanderbilt University,*** *142 Fed. Appx. 246 (U.S. Court of Appeals, 6th Cir., 2005),* Nicklaus Atria was a pre-med student, when the events that precipitated his suit occurred. During the spring semester of 2002, Atria was enrolled in an Organic Chemistry class taught by Professor B.A. Hess. On January 29, 2002, Professor Hess gave an examination that required students to record their answers on a sheet. Professor Hess's system for returning the graded tests was somewhat unusual. After grading the tests, Professor Hess placed the answer sheets in a stack on a table outside of the classroom. Before the next class, students could thumb through the stack and locate their answer sheets, which were conspicuously marked with their names and social security numbers. Professor Hess testified that he did not know the names of most students and had no way of knowing whether students were picking up their own tests. After class, Professor Hess gathered those tests that had not been retrieved from the table and distributed them directly to the students during the next class period. Atria was absent from class on Friday, February 1, 2002, the day that the graded answer sheets were put out for general retrieval. He therefore, received his graded test on the following Monday.

Professor Hess allowed any student who believed that an answer was incorrectly marked wrong to resubmit the answer sheet for a "re-grade." To prevent students from seeking a re-grade after altering incorrect answers, Professor Hess retained photocopies of all of the answer sheets. Atria, who had taken another chemistry class from Professor Hess in the fall of 2001, testified that he was aware of Professor Hess's practice of photocopying the original answer sheets. According to Atria, when he picked up his answer sheet on Monday, the answer he had recorded for question number six was "b>c>a," which was the correct answer. Because question six was marked wrong, Atria returned his test to Professor Hess for a re-grade. According to the photocopy retained by Professor Hess, however, Atria's original answer to question number six was "b>a>a." It appeared to Professor Hess that an "a" in question number six had been changed to a "c." Professor Hess reported this irregularity to Vanderbilt's Honor Council and accused Atria of fraudulently modifying his answer sheet to get credit for question number six. Atria was not the first student whom Professor Hess had reported to the Honor Council. While most of Vanderbilt's professors never reported an Honor Code violation, Professor Hess submitted approximately five to ten violations per semester; a Vanderbilt administrator stated that Hess was putting "a heavy load on the Honor Council's docket."

Vanderbilt's Student Handbook contained a detailed description of the university's honor system, including its Honor Code, the applicability of the code, procedures for the adjudication of asserted violations, and appeals from a finding of guilt. When a violation of the Honor Code was reported, the Honor Council appointed two investigators who met with the accused and presented him with a written statement of the charges. The Student Handbook provided that "[a]n accused may obtain professional legal representation, advice, and counsel. However, an attorney may not participate in or be present during an Honor Council hearing. The Honor Council was a student tribunal untrained in the law." An Honor Council hearing was conducted by a twelve-member panel consisting of the President of the Honor Council and eleven members of the Council appointed by the President. Proof of a student's guilt had to be "clear and convincing" and ten of the twelve members must vote "guilty" to convict.

A student found guilty by the Honor Council was entitled to appeal the decision to the Appellate Review Board (ARB) by filing a petition with the Honor Council's faculty advisor. Before the petition could be heard on the merits, it had to be determined that the petition presented sufficient grounds for an appeal. Exactly who performed this gate-keeping function was not entirely clear to the court, because the provisions in Vanderbilt's Student Handbook and "Procedures of the Appellate Review Board" regarding the procedure were apparently inconsistent. The grounds for review of an appeal from conviction by the Honor Council were:

1. Insufficient evidence to support the decision;
2. Harshness of sanction sufficient to show an abuse of discretion by the original hearing authority;
3. Procedural irregularity sufficient to affect the decision; and
4. New evidence that was not reasonably available to be presented to the original hearing authority, the introduction of which may reasonably be expected to affect the decision.

If the ARB heard the student's case on the merits, it could, by majority vote, affirm, modify, or reverse the decision of the original hearing authority. On March 19, 2002, Vanderbilt's Honor Council conducted a hearing in Atria's case. Professor Hess, who did not appear personally, submitted a written accusation with copies of the altered original and the unaltered photocopied answer sheets attached. During the hearing, Atria testified that he was not guilty of the charges and that his answer sheet could have been smudged while in his book bag. At the conclusion of the hearing, the Council advised Atria that he had been found guilty as charged and imposed a sentence of failure in Organic Chemistry and a suspension from the University during the summer session.

Several days later, Atria paid for and took a polygraph test conducted by a local polygraph examiner. According to the examiner's analysis of the results, Atria's statements that he did not alter the answer to question six were "truthful."

In April of 2002, Atria's attorney signed and filed a petition for appeal on Atria's behalf with Mark Bandas, the advisor to the Honor Council. Attached to the petition was a copy of the polygraph results. Bandas contacted Atria's attorney to advise him that the University would not accept a petition signed by an attorney and, in any event, would not consider the results of a polygraph test. Atria subsequently filed a complaint in the Circuit Court for Davidson County Tennessee, seeking a preliminary injunction requiring Vanderbilt to accept the appeal and consider the results of the polygraph examination. The court denied relief.

After the ARB refused to accept the original petition, Atria submitted a second petition which he signed personally and which omitted any mention of the polygraph evidence. In this petition, Atria argued that another student, who was angry that Atria was given more time than other students to complete written examinations (due to a disability) and fearful that Atria might surpass him in

Professor Hess's curve, had framed Atria by tampering with his test. In a letter dated May 29, 2002, Francis Wells, the chairman of the Appellate Review Board, notified Atria that his appeal was meritless and that a hearing was unnecessary. This letter indicated that Wells personally reviewed the petition and did not submit it to the other members of the ARB for consideration. Wells in fact testified that, as chairman, he had the power to reject a petition as presenting insufficient grounds for appeal without allowing the full panel to hear it.

The case on appeal. The appeals court panel found that "The facts in this case are in dispute as to whether the manner in which Professor Hess distributed graded answer sheets posed an unreasonable risk of harm. A jury could certainly conclude that the burden on Professor Hess to engage in alternative conduct that would have prevented the harm is at most *de minimis*: instead of handing back the students' original answer sheets he could have retained the originals and handed back the photocopies, which could not be altered. A jury could find that the harm caused by Professor Hess's conduct was foreseeable. Bandas testified that he met with Professor Hess in the fall of 2002 because '[Professor Hess] had been submitting a number of cases to the honor council based on students altering, you know, score sheets for a re-grade. He was actually submitting a sufficient number of them, and that it was putting a heavy load on the honor council's docket.' In a prior Honor Council proceeding, a student accused by Professor Hess asserted, as a defense, that another student tampered with her test before it was returned to Hess for a re-grade. Though this student subsequently admitted to altering her own answer sheet, a jury could easily find that this incident should have alerted Professor Hess to the possibility that one student might tamper with another's answer sheet. Indeed, the record supports the inference that Professor Hess was actually well aware of the risk posed by his redistribution system, inasmuch as he made photocopies of the answer sheets in an effort to combat dishonesty on the part of students seeking a re-grade."

Advice. Both students *and faculty/staff* must be trained to apply and enforce the honor code. In the Vanderbilt case, above, not only was the professor returning the tests in a reckless manner, but the honors program was on notice that something might be amiss about the professor's practices, since the frequency of honor code complaints by him was an anomaly among the faculty. Florida State University, whose honor code is reproduced on pages 131–140, does extensive training with regard to compliance with the its code.

An example of student training is the English Department's anti-plagiarism training, which includes the following:

ENGLISH DEPARTMENTAL STATEMENT

Plagiarism is grounds for suspension from the University as well as for failure in this course. It will not be tolerated. Any instance of plagiarism must (by departmental mandate) be reported to the Director of First-Year Composition and the Director of Undergraduate Studies. Plagiarism is a counterproductive, non-writing behavior that is unacceptable in a course intended to aid the growth of individual writers. Plagiarism is included among the violations defined in the Academic Honor Code, section (b), paragraph 2, as follows: "Regarding academic assignments, violations of the Academic Honor Code shall include representing another's work or any part thereof, be it published or unpublished, as one's own."

A plagiarism education assignment that further explains this issue will be administered in all first-year writing courses during the second week of class. Each student will be responsible for completing the assignment and asking questions regarding any parts they do not fully understand.

What Is Plagiarism?

In *The Curious Researcher* (Longman 2004), Bruce Ballenger defines *plagiarism* as "using others' ideas or words as if they were your own" (130). Plagiarism can range in scope from accidentally forgetting to place quotation marks around a borrowed sentence, to careless paraphrasing, to deliberately trying to pass off someone else's paper as your own. Plagiarism is always a serious violation of the Florida State University Academic Honor Code and the English Department policy. As a university student you have many educational opportunities and obligations. Plagiarism should never be an option. When you plagiarize, you deny yourself the opportunity to express your own ideas in an academic forum and exhibit your own learning. You are also failing in your obligations to be an active member of an educational community.

SAMPLES OF STUDENT TEXTS CREATED FROM ORIGINAL SOURCES

A student in a second-semester first-year writing course is writing a researched essay on social trends in the last ten years that have influenced the popularity of tattoos. Among the sources she uses in her paper are one from the Internet, one from a book, and one from a journal. Below you will find both the original source material and passages from the student's paper in which she uses the original source material. Study each example and rewrite if she has plagiarized.

EXAMPLE OF MATERIAL FROM INTERNET SOURCE

Source: "Tattoos and the World's 100 Sexiest Women" by Vince Hemingson http://www.vanishingtattoo.com/top100_women_tattoos. htm (2003)

This is the original source:

How many of the world's top 100 sexiest women have tattoos? *FMH* Magazine published their annual list of the 100 Sexiest Women in the World 2002 as voted on by their readers. The poll offers a fascinating insight into the popularity of tattoos among female celebrities. A quick look at the Top 100 list reveals that one of the things that many of the women picked have in common is body art, i.e., tattoos!

This is the student's paper:

Many of the world's top 100 sexiest women have tattoos. Two years ago *FMH* Magazine published their annual list of the 100 Sexiest Women in the World as voted on by their readers. The poll offers a fascinating insight into the popularity of tattoos among female celebrities. A quick look at the Top 100 list reveals that one of the things that many of the women picked have in common is body art, i.e., tattoos!

Did this student plagiarize? If so, rewrite the student text so that it is not plagiarized and be ready to provide examples to substantiate your position.

EXAMPLE OF MATERIAL FROM A BOOK

Source: Addonizio, Kim and Cheryl Dumesnil. Introduction. *Dorothy Parker's Elbow: Tattoos on Writers, Writers on Tattoos*. New York: Warner Books, 2002. xiii–xvi.

From the source:

Clearly, tattooing has emerged from the underbelly to the surface of the American landscape. And as the popularity of tattoos has expanded, so has the art itself. No longer restricted to Bettie Page look-alikes,' muddy blue anchors, and ribbon-wrapped hearts reading *Mom*, today's tattoo images make bold statements of personality, as individualized and varied as any art form (xiii).

From the student's paper:

It's a fact that tattoos have arisen from the underbelly to the top of the American landscape. Tattooing has experienced a growing popularity, and so has the art itself. It is no longer limited to sailor-style ships and blue anchors, or biker-type hearts reading "Mom." Today's images include bold statements of individualized personality as diverse as any art form (Addonizio and Dumesnil xii).

Did this student avoid plagiarism in her attempt to summarize material from her source? Why or why not? If it is plagiarized, rewrite the student text so that it is not plagiarized and be ready to provide examples to substantiate your position.

EXAMPLE OF MATERIAL FROM A JOURNAL

Source: *Clinical Nursing* 10 (2001): 424–41.

From the source:

Participants queried represented a wide age range—between 19 and 55. Results showed that participants perceived few health risks involving piercing and tattooing and desired additional piercings and/or tattoos. Individual expression was an important body alteration motivation for both piercing and tattooing. These findings underscore the importance of health care professionals' maintaining nonjudgmental attitudes about those who alter their bodies, thereby facilitating important health education concerning related health risks.

From the student's paper:

According to the journal *Clinical Nursing*, individuals who wanted to have tattoos or piercings do not consider the health risks involved. This makes it clear that for health care professionals, an open-minded attitude towards patients with tattoos or piercings facilitates the optimal environment for important health education concerning related health risks.

Did the student avoid plagiarism in her attempt to paraphrase the source material? Why or why not? If it is plagiarized, rewrite the student text so that it is not plagiarized and be ready to provide examples to substantiate your position.

TIPS TO AVOID PLAGIARISM:

- Use quotations around anything borrowed word for word.

- Cite your quotations and factual information and provide a corresponding Works Cited page. In English classes, MLA is the appropriate model for citations.
- Introducing your sources within the text of your paper helps you to avoid plagiarism.
- When paraphrasing, be sure to give credit to the source you are paraphrasing from.
- Do not turn in a single paper for more than one class.
- Do not turn in a paper that you did not write.
- While researching, make sure to take careful notes and write down all the information needed for citing your work as you find material you want to use. If you cannot find the source that you got your data from, do not use it.

You must give credit for the following:

- Direct quotations from your source.
- Facts, data, and information based on other people's research.
- Paraphrases of another's work.
- Ideas, opinions, and interpretations that are not your own or that you got from another source.
- Charts, graphs, pictures, images, and raw data that you did not put together yourself.
- Comments from lectures, conversations, and interviews.

What you do not have to cite:

- Research and raw data that you have compiled yourself.
- Widely known facts/common knowledge. "Common knowledge": This refers to information so widely known (or accepted to be valid) that no supporting facts or cited research is needed to back it up, such as the following: *World War II ended in August of 1945*. Almost no one will dispute this statement, and it is commonly accepted without debate. "Common knowledge" statements can be passages like this: *Television ratings for the Super Bowl are traditionally so high that advertisers spend millions of dollars to advertise their clients' products during the broadcast*. Again, this claim refers to topics so extensively researched/documented that it is not necessary to provide an authoritative source to support it. But be aware: what is common knowledge to you may not necessarily be common knowledge to another reader, so cite any information you feel might be unknown to those outside what-

ever specific topic you're writing on.
- Your own opinions, conclusions, and feelings about your topic.

Florida State University
Department of English
Plagiarism Education Assignment

Student Name:____
Student Social Security Number:___________________________
Course Number and Section:______________________________

I understand that plagiarism in any form is a violation of the Florida State University Honor Code and the policies of the Department of English, and I am aware that it can result in a variety of academic penalties. I realize that helping or knowingly allowing others to plagiarize involves me in plagiarism. Furthermore, I understand that any instance of plagiarism needs to be officially reported to the English Department.

I have completed a plagiarism education exercise. My instructor has stressed the importance of avoiding plagiarism and satisfactorily answered my questions about what it is and what the consequences of it can be.

Signature____
Date: ____

Source: The Florida State University (Reprinted with permission.)

Checklist: Essential Elements of an Honor Code

1. A detailed, written code
2. Promulgated across the campus community
3. Accompanied by initial and ongoing training of students, faculty and staff
4. Written acknowledgment by students of receipt of policies and of training
5. Adjudicative and appeal processes that are representative of all campus constituencies
6. Supplementary policies and procedures, such as the English Department's plagiarism policy, which are subject to the same promulgation, orientation and acknowledgment procedures as the honor code itself
7. Periodic review by the office of the president, provost or general counsel to ensure compliance with policies and procedures and uniform application of policies and sanctions across the institution and over a significant span of time.

CHAPTER 6

Alcohol and Drugs

In his book, *This Side of Paradise*, F. Scott Fitzgerald described Princeton University in the 1920s as "the pleasantest country club in America"—basically a wild, self-indulgent institution where sex, alcohol, and social climbing were acceptable—even significant—elements of college life. In the story, Fitzgerald's hero, Amory Blaine, is a conceited, fun-seeking individual, intelligent but lazy about his work at Princeton, and he spends his years of "higher education" partying, drinking, and living in lethargic affluence.

Fitzgerald's story of a hedonistic college student is somewhat autobiographical, based on many of his own experiences at Princeton up until the time he wrote it. *This Side of Paradise* struck a chord with the rebellious youth of the Jazz Age, disillusioned by World War I, and of course, terrified the older generation intent on maintaining an image of decorum and respectability.

Since the 1920s, though, little has changed within the college scene. College administrators are still focused on maintaining clean, reliable reputations for institutions of higher learning, while students are often more focused on maintaining enjoyable, if frequently illegal, social lives. In the past, colleges have all too often observed a "hands-off" policy about alcohol and drugs—i.e., if it goes on behind closed doors, it's not the college's responsibility to seek out illegal drug use or underage drinking, and if anything happens to students participating in such activities, it is not the college's fault. However, that approach today is both ineffective and dangerous, due to a great increase in the number of court cases blaming colleges for accidents, deaths, and rapes related to underage drinking on campuses. Colleges are now being forced to reevaluate the ways in which they deal with underage drinking and drug use in order to protect both their students and their institutions.

Indicted Forever

August 27, 2007
The Times of Trenton
By Richard Lavinthal

In 1987, a Bronx, N.Y., trial jury found Raymond Donovan, President Ronald Reagan's secretary of labor, innocent of larceny and fraud charges. After the verdict was read, Donovan, a Bayonne native, shouted angrily to prosecutor Stephen Bookin, "Give me back my reputation."

Twenty years later, two unfairly disgraced local university administrators in New Jersey transitioned from three-plus weeks of hell into a lifetime of embarrassment. On Tuesday, their indictment on aggravated hazing charges was simply dismissed. They fared even worse than Donovan. At least his innocence was confirmed with an acquittal.

The university's director of Greek life and dean of students were now, according to the Mercer County prosecutor, victims of a runaway grand jury. Joseph L. Bocchini Jr. didn't say they were innocent, didn't offer an apology, and somehow managed to spin this "law and disorder" event past the media.

How soon will it be before the two administrators hire new attorneys to sue Bocchini and Mercer County for the thousands they've probably paid in legal fees, for the damage to their reputations, and as icing on the cake, a complete public exoneration and apology that also would be posted on the prosecutor's Web site forever.

Why forever? Because the Internet can keep reputations damaged forever, even when persons are acquitted. When Ray Donovan was acquitted, "practical obscurity" still existed. In 1987, there were fewer than 30,000 IP addresses in the world. The first browser would not even be invented until 1990. Today, nearly 30 billion Web pages exist, according to boutell.com (www.boutell.com/newfaq/misc/sizeofweb.html).

The two administrators' indictments cannot fade quietly into practical obscurity. They'll be out there in cyberspace's 30 billion Web pages 24/7 into perpetuity for anyone who Googles either of their names.

Mr. Bocchini trumpeted the indictment of the administrators and three others in news events on Aug. 3, telling the Associated Press, "The ramifications of this for colleges and universities in New Jersey, and across the country, is that it will send some kind of message that the standards of college life, when it relates to alcohol, need to be policed carefully."

By Aug. 28, he was asking a New Jersey Superior Court judge to dismiss the charges against the two of them. According to the *Newark Star-Ledger*, Bocchini and his staff reviewed the evidence and grand jury transcripts and, "he and his staff concluded they did not have proof that either official had 'facilitated' the fraternity party."

How could justice be so ill served? Why did they waste taxpayer dollars to indict the two in the media? The prosecutor told the *Star-Ledger* that he can see how "the grand jury, who are lay persons, after reviewing the evidence and having the benefit of listening to recorded statements, could have reached the conclusion there was probable cause."

We know grand juries are supposed to be secret, but was this one so secret that even the prosecutor, who baby-sits it, didn't know it was a runaway grand jury? Are we to believe that Bocchini just realized that justice was being miscarried?

I checked the coverage since Aug. 3, and can't find an instance were Bocchini even alluded (or said off the record to someone) to an inexperienced grand jury that may have hijacked the process. Only on the day of the dismissal did this excuse appear.

Prosecutors direct grand juries. We know the old chestnut about indicting the "ham sandwich," and the prosecutor is usually the short-order cook.

If the grand jury had been warned but still refused to listen to admonitions that there was not enough evidence to convict yet returned a true bill anyway, Bocchini should have sought to seal the indictment—while no one knew about it and the runaway grand jury's indictment could have been addressed in silence and probably solved.

But the prosecutor didn't worry; instead, he held a news conference.

If concerns about proof existed on Aug. 3, the prosecutor could have issued a bare-bones news release or none at all. He should not have added fuel to a fire that will continue to burn the two victims in Internet hell forever. (The prosecutor's news release dated Aug. 3 is still posted on the office's Web site. It's 1 p.m. on Thursday and no news release or explanation regarding the dropping of charges has been posted, two days after the dismissals.)

The lure of today's 24/7/365 news media is hard to resist. The prosecutor got a national platform, 15 minutes of fame. Print and electronic press across the globe reported the first charges of its kind against college administrators.

It's now time for the media to take a tough, journalistic look at what happened. The same for whoever supervises county prosecutors in the Garden State.

How soon will these administrators file their lawsuits? I suggest that they get one of the attorneys now representing one of the unfortunate Duke lacrosse players in their actions against former prosecutor Mike Nifong.

Richard Lavinthal (http://www.Lavinthal.com) is a former N.J. Statehouse wire service and daily newspaper reporter, who developed the first legal news Web site of its kind for a prosecutor's office. After creating the U.S. Department of Justice's Public Affairs Office in New Jersey, he managed it for a decade, serving as chief spokesman for former U.S. Attorneys Samuel A. Alito Jr., Michael Chertoff, and Faith S. Hochberg. A former Director of Communications for the N.J. (State) Division of Criminal Justice and Director of Criminal Justice Programs for APBnews.com in New York City, today Lavinthal is Managing Director of PRforLAW, LLC, (http://www.PRforLAW.com), providing legal media relations strategy for major case milestones, specializing in criminal and civil matters under seal, under investigation, or not-yet-public. A media relations lecturer, Lavinthal also blogs at prPROpinon.com.

Richard Lavinthal, "Indicted Forever," The Trenton Times, *August 27, 2007*
(© Richard Lavinthal. Reprinted with permissionl.)

Substance Abuse on College Campuses: An Overview

The following article sheds light on the state of substance abuse and legal liability as it still stands today:

Campus Crackdown: P.C. College Administrators Get Something Right—Political Correctness

National Review, April 5, 1999, by Naomi Schaefer

Campus Crackdown: Is the party over?

"Alcohol can irritate the lining of your stomach enough to produce nausea or vomiting." So says Positive Norm, a talking blue cartoon lava lamp that hosts Alcohol 101, a CD-ROM game passed out to 25,000 college freshmen last year. The game, which is supposed to instruct students in alcohol and its dangers, is another indication that college administrations are returning to a bygone age—when they treated students as something less than mature adults.

Not so long ago, administrators acted in *loco parentis*, trying to protect the welfare of their students by setting down rules of conduct, ethics, even dress. But in the aftermath of the '60s rebellion, all that changed. Students demanded to be treated as autonomous adults, and administrators obliged: "If it's behind closed doors," the new code seemed to say, "there's nothing we can do about it."

It was fun while it lasted. But now colleges increasingly find themselves in court defending the sometimes dangerous environment they provide for students. With legal liability rising, colleges have been forced to reclaim their parental authority even if it flies in the face of student demands. The current crackdown on student freedoms is meant to protect students' safety rather than their moral well-being, and it often comes in laughable forms (witness Positive Norm). Still, it's better than the alternative.

Yet the turn away from campus permissiveness has sparked the opposition, oddly enough, of conservatives. Dartmouth president James Wright recently announced that the college would end the Greek system "as we know it," first forcing the houses to go co-ed and ultimately eliminating them altogether. In response, an article in the (conservative) *Dartmouth Review* railed that "Dartmouth's paternalists are at it again." The article even quoted approvingly the executive director of the New Hampshire Civil Liberties Union: "The young people who attend Dartmouth College are adults. Their choices—and their right to make choices—should be respected. They should not be subjected to the dictates of administrators." (Legal questions aside, there is something to be said for Mom's old policy: "We'll treat you like an adult when you act like one.")

Conservatives have reason to be suspicious. The Dartmouth administration, like others around the country, sells its new policy in typically mushy terms. "The Trustees are giving students the opportunity to re-imagine social life and residential life at the College," Wright told the school's mainstream paper, *The Dartmouth*. Then there is the hypocrisy of liberal administrators, who disapprove of Budweiser but happily hand out condoms. But opposing the new campus paternalism means ignoring the consequences of the excessive drinking on college campuses, something administrations can no longer do because of an explosion of lawsuits.

MIT freshman Scott Krueger had been participating in "Animal House" night at his fraternity in September 1997, during which "pledges" were required to drink preposterous amounts of beer and hard liquor. He lost consciousness and was abandoned on a couch to die. An autopsy revealed that his blood-alcohol level was five times the legal limit. A grand jury concluded that "the cause of Scott Krueger's death—in real terms—was the wanton and reckless conduct on the part of the Phi Gamma Delta fraternity" (alone). No doubt. But the family has filed a civil suit against the larger university anyway.

Similar cases abound. By 10:30 one night in August 1997, more than $2,000 worth of alcohol had been served to Benjamin Wynne and his fraternity brothers in a bar near Louisiana State University. More than 24 of those drinks were served to Wynne before he passed out and was pronounced dead the next morning at his LSU fraternity. Matthew Garofalo, when a sophomore at the University of Iowa in 1995, died under similar circumstances at the Lambda

Chi Alpha fraternity house. Like Scott Krueger's parents, the Garofalos and the Wynnes are suing.

Then there are cases involving drunken sex. Boston University student Jessica Smithers alleges that a university fraternity served her alcohol at a party and that, feeling intoxicated and without money for cab fare, she went to sleep in a spare fraternity room, awaking to find one of the fraternity brothers having sex with her. She claims that she was too drunk to fend off her attacker. She is suing BU because its fraternity served her alcohol despite the fact that she was only 17. At MIT, Angela Colt has filed suit not only against Matthew Keller, her alleged rapist, but also against MIT, the Delta Upsilon fraternity, and its national corporation for allowing underage drinking to occur.

All of these suits tend to deflect responsibility from where it truly belongs, but they have at least forced colleges to take a second look at their policies. Limiting access to dorm rooms of members of the opposite sex, for example, has resulted in fewer complaints about "unwanted guests" in dorms at Boston University. Beginning with the class of 2002, MIT freshmen will be required to live on campus. Cornell University, a school dominated by fraternity life, is also changing its campus housing policies, and building more dorms, as part of an effort to require freshmen and sophomores to live on campus. Princeton too has been drafting a new alcohol policy designed to monitor more closely its students' activities.

Although recent studies have shown that the number of students who drink and binge drink has stayed about the same since 1993, according to the National Center on Addiction and Substance Abuse at Columbia University in New York City, the intensity of drinking and the amount of drug abuse in colleges have made a sharp increase.

In *Wasting the Best and the Brightest: Substance Abuse at America's Colleges and Universities*, a four-year study that examined the habits of students' alcohol and drug use, researchers discovered that 22.9 percent of college students met the criteria for substance abuse and dependence. This statistic shows that the proportion of alcohol and drug abuse in colleges is three times higher than that of the general population, producing grave results for students and their colleges. Despite efforts to educate students and prevent alcohol and drug abuse on campuses, the occurrence of binge drinking has continued to increase greatly. Similarly, extreme increases have been observed regarding the abuse of various prescription drugs such as Vicodin, OxyContin, Ritalin, and Valium, and the abuse of illegal drugs such as marijuana, cocaine, and heroine.

The increase in substance abuse on campuses has led to costly results. Some of these include poor academic performance, anxiety, depression, suicide, property damage, vandalism, injuries both to intoxicated and non-intoxicated students, and sexual assault. According to a CASA report 1,177 deaths resulted from unintentional alcohol-related injuries, a 6 percent increase from 1998; and 97,000 students were victims of alcohol-related rape or sexual assaults in 2001.

In today's world, college acceptance of substance abuse is both indefensible and extremely risky for all parties involved. Colleges cannot afford to accept rampant substance abuse as the status quo. The Drug-Free Schools and Communities Act requires that institutions of higher learning take a serious approach to dealing with drinking on campus. In the past, many institutions have evaded the duty to create an AOD prevention program, out of doubt for its effectiveness or because of a sense of invulnerability. However, the law is more relevant today than ever before, and it is vital that it be taken seriously, particularly due to the number of recent cases imposing liability on colleges for failing to provide safe environments for students.

Alcohol Abuse and Institutional Liability

Many colleges and universities distinguish between underaged drinking and drug abuse, reasoning that with regard to the former only the behavior is illegal, while with respect to the latter, the substance itself is prohibited, irrespective of the user's age. The upshot is that most schools are more lenient with regard to underaged alcohol use than they are where illicit substances are involved. This excerpt from Rider University's "The Source" student handbook is illustrative:

Rider University Substance Abuse Policy

Rider University believes that individual responsibility is extremely important in social choices. Substance abuse is prevalent on college campuses today and often hinders community members' ability to lead lives of productive work, enlightened living and community involvement. The University policy regarding alcohol and other drugs provides penalties for abuses but places major responsibility on the student for responsible decision-making.

The policies and Code of Conduct governing the use of alcohol and other drugs apply to all Rider students and their guests. The primary responsibility for knowing and abiding by the provisions of the University's policies rests with the individual student.

Drug Policy

Rider does not tolerate the use or possession of any illegal substance on its campus.

Alcohol Policy

Alcohol Policy Violation/Misuse of Alcoholic Beverages

Possession, use, purchase, or knowingly being in the presence of beer, wine or other liquor by persons under 21 years of age is prohibited. In addition, please refer to the Alcohol Policy on page 94 for further guidelines regarding alcohol on Rider's campus. (Consequences may range from levels 1 to 5. Further, within any two-year period, the first violation of this policy may result in parental notification; the second violation will result, minimally, in parental notification; the third violation will result, minimally, in removal from residency and parental notification.)

IMPORTANT NOTE: The University recognizes the right of law enforcement agencies to enforce their regulations on the Rider campus in the same manner as they do in the community beyond the campus (i.e., to execute search and arrest warrants, etc.). Students are urged to become aware of the laws regarding the illegal use of alcohol and drugs and to consider carefully the ramifications of violating these laws. For example, the legal age for possession/consumption of alcohol in New Jersey is 21 years of age. Even the most minor drug and alcohol criminal offenses typically carry a six-month minimum driver's license suspension, $500 fine and 100 hours of community service. A more complete listing of New Jersey drug and alcohol laws is available on the Rider University Web site, www.rider.edu.

The Source: Student Handbook of Rider University *(2007)*
(Reprinted with permission of Rider University.)

When student underaged drinking results in injury or death, potential targets of a lawsuit include the university, its administrators and campus police, as well as student organizations, such as fraternities and sororities. However, this does not mean that aggrieved plaintiffs will always be successful.

In ***Bland v. Scott****, 279 Kan. 962, 112 P3d 941 (Kansas Supreme Court, 2005)*, Sean Scott was 16 years old when on September 16, 2000, he drove from the family home in Shawnee to the Phi Gamma Delta fraternity house in Lawrence to visit his 19-year-old brother, Mike Scott. The Scott brothers went to The Wheel, a local bar, and met Dana and Lawrence Rieke, the Scott brothers' mother and stepfather, where the Riekes supplied the brothers and other minors with alcoholic beverages. The Scott brothers then walked back to the fraternity house, where fraternity brothers provided Sean with excessive amounts of alcohol, pressuring him to drink and mocking him if he did not. Eventually Sean left the fraternity in his car and ultimately crashed into a vehicle driven by Lisa Bland on K-10 highway. Sean's blood alcohol level tested at .15 and he was consequently convicted of involuntary manslaughter in Johnson County.

Uncertainty to Be Avoided

The high court of Kansas pondered the pros and cons of imposing liability on those who provided the alcohol. "The imposition of a common law duty of care would create a situation rife with uncertainty and difficulty. If the commercial vendor is liable for negligence, does the host at a social gathering owe a duty to prospective victims of guests? The difficulties of recognizing intoxication and predicting conduct of an intoxicated patron without imposing some duty of inquiry are evident. Problems could also arise in the apportionment or sorting out of liability among the owners of various bars visited on 'bar hopping' excursions. The correct standard of care to be used also presents a problem, as does the determination of whether all acts of the patron, including intentional torts, should be included within the liability of the tavern owner or operator."

No Negligence Per Se

The plaintiffs contended that providing liquor or cereal malt beverages to a minor is a crime under K.S.A. 41-727, K.S.A. 21-3205, K.S.A. 21-3610, and K.S.A. 41-715. Consequently, the actions were negligence *per se* and thus gave rise to a cause of action separate from a dram shop law. The same argument was broached in an earlier case, where the court "decline[d] to find negligence per se in this case since to do so would subvert the apparent legislative intention.... Clearly, the legislature would have [re-created a civil cause of action in favor of those injured as a result of a violation of the liquor laws] had it intended for there to be a civil cause of action." Additionally, the common-law rule stated that any injuries resulting from the actions of intoxicated tortfeasors were the result of the act of drinking, not the act of supplying, and therefore prohibited civil liability for suppliers. The plaintiffs also attempted to establish the case based on the fact that the fraternity members knowingly served alcoholic beverages to a minor, but "there is nothing in [the controlling precedent] or its progeny to support such a distinction being made."

No Constitutional Claim

The plaintiffs then raised two constitutional arguments. They first claimed that the "'Kansas Liquor Control Act is unconstitutional to the extent that it abrogates a common law remedy of persons injured by violations of the act.' When the legislature statutorily supplants a remedy provided by common law, subsequent restriction or abrogation of that protected remedy must be given an adequate substitute, or *quid pro quo*. Such changes are constitutional if the changes are 'reasonably necessary in the public interest to promote the general welfare of the people of that state, and the legislature provides an adequate substitute remedy…'."

The plaintiffs then argued that the Kansas Liquor Control Act violated Section 18 of the Bill of Rights of the Kansas Constitution, which states: "All persons, for injuries suffered in person, reputation or property, shall have remedy by due course of law, and justice administered without delay."

However, the constitutional arguments were without merit, concluded the court, as "Kansas did not recognize a common-law duty owed by suppliers of alcohol to third parties injured by an intoxicated person." Regarding the Bill of Rights argument, "The plaintiffs are not without a remedy under the law to recover for the injuries. They have a cause of action against Sean, the tortfeasor."

Conclusion. In this case, the plaintiffs' arguments were rejected. However, the decision was made largely due to the unusual circumstances surrounding the case and the specific law of the state. Thus, one should be cautious, since such lenient rulings will not always be the probable outcome.

Another example of a university avoiding liability exists in ***Robertson v. State ex. rel Department of Planning and Control**, 747 So.2d 1276 (Louisiana Court of Appeals, 1999)*, where Louisiana Tech University was found not liable for an intoxicated student, 23-year-old Trey Robertson, falling off a roof on college grounds. The roof was built in 1984 and stood at about 56 feet tall at its apex. Several incidents occurred of students climbing the roof while intoxicated and consequently falling and sustaining various injuries, prompting university officials to discuss whether something needed to be done about the roof. However, since all the students injured had been intoxicated, the university decided not to take any action. On April 5, 1991, Trey Robertson climbed the roof after drinking (with a blood alcohol level of .073) and sustained head injuries causing his death a week later.

Unreasonable Risk of Harm

The plaintiffs argued that the roof posed "an unreasonable risk of harm to others," and that under *La. C.C. arts. 2322*, "The owner of a building is answerable for the damage occasioned by its ruin, when this is caused by neglect to repair it, or when it is the result of a vice of original construction." However, this article does not apply to a building without an original vice or poor condition and that functions properly. Thus, the structure was found not to pose an unreasonable risk of harm, as it properly functioned as a roof.

Negligence: University/student Relationship

Plaintiffs then argued that Tech was responsible for dissuading its students from climbing the roof, either by planting shrubbery or building a fence around the roof, due to the three previous incidents that occurred in regard to intoxicated students being injured from climbing the roof. In this case, it was found that Tech's actions did not constitute negligence, as it was not Tech's responsibility to protect Trey from "his deliberate act of recklessness in climbing the roof," since "any prudent person would recognize the action of climbing the roof both as an unreasonable danger to himself and as an unlawful physical invasion of property. Any damage caused to such an off-limits structure would amount to the intentional tort of trespass."

Furthermore, "the plaintiffs' argument that the three prior instances gave rise to affirmative duty to act is a miscalculated statistical focus." This is because the area where the roof was located was passed by thousands of students and campus security officials each day, whose presence acted as an "appropriate deterrent to such a blatant act, tantamount to an act of defacement of the property." Thus, the prior incidents were not enough to prove negligence.

Conclusion. The court found that Tech had no duty to guard against the risk of falling off the roof and the university was found not negligent under the circumstances.

Dissenting opinion. In a dissenting opinion, Justice Malone stated, "Under the particular circumstances of this case, the risk and the duty are easily associated. The risk was serious, the harm great, the likelihood of recurrence obvious and the cost or sacrifice to avoid further incidents small. There is no policy reason to limit the scope of the protection of the rule of conduct under these specific facts." His Honor believed that Tech had a clear duty to avoid foreseeable injury to its students, and considering the circumstances of the case, the roof posed a foreseeable risk. All the previous injuries occurred around midnight and involved intoxicated students, but no action was taken to avoid the problem until Tech was ordered by the Office of Risk Management to build a fence surrounding the roof, after several injuries and one death had already taken place.

Drugs on the College Campus

As Rider's drug and alcohol policy (above) implies, most colleges and universities treat drug abuse differently than underage alcohol consumption. While consumption of alcohol by a student under 21 is illegal (typically a minor crime, called a misdemeanor), the mere possession of illicit drugs is a crime (often a serious crime, known as a felony, particularly where the quantity possessed suggests dealing in the drug). Consequently, while the underaged drinker may be accorded multiple "second-chances" before serious penalties—such as loss of residency rights or even suspension—are imposed by the institution, drug possession often results in arrest and expulsion, even on the first offense.

Such severity of enforcement, where it exists in higher education, does not derive exclusively, or even primarily, from internal institutional responsibility. Rather, external legislative pressures have contributed significantly to higher education's condemnation of illicit substances.

1. **The Drug-Free Schools and Communities Act Amendments** [103 Stat. 1928] impose upon educational organizations, which receive federal funds, the obligation to create drug and alcohol programs for both students and employees. Implementing regulations [34 C.F.R. Part 86] require promulgation of a policy; biennial review of program effectiveness; enforcement of the standards established in the policy. (Notably, drug testing is not required under the Act.)
2. **The Drug-Free Workplace Act** [41 U.S.C. sec. 701 *et seq.*] applies to all higher educational institutions which enter into federal contracts or receive grants. As the title says, this Act is aimed at drug abuse by employees, so most students are not directly covered, unless employed by their institutions. Indeed, the receipt of a Pell Grant (see Chapter Two) does not in and of itself bring a student individually under the Act. Nevertheless, the Act does provide substantial incentives for the institution to police not only its employees, but also its student body, with regard to possession and use of illegal substances.

3. **The Higher Education Opportunity Act of 2008** adds a requirement to include in the biennial review specific statistics on drug- and alcohol-related violations and fatalities that occur on campus, or as part of the institution's activities, and are reported to campus officials. In addition, the institution must also report on the number and type of sanctions it imposed in response to such violations. (Institutions were already required under this section to annually distribute to students and employees certain information about campus policies, services, and consequences of drug and alcohol abuse, and to review the effectiveness of the institution's program every two years and implement changes as necessary. The review needs to be shared with the secretary of education and the public upon request.)

Indications are that the courts, too, are more ready and willing to support universities in their efforts to interdict illegal substances on their campuses. For example, in ***State v. Nemser,*** *148 N.H. 453, 807 A.2d 1289 (New Hampshire Supreme Court, 2002)*, a Dartmouth College undergraduate was charged with possession of marijuana. [*See* RSA 318-B:2, I (1995).] He moved to suppress the evidence, alleging that the entry and search of his room by Dartmouth Safety and Security (DSS) officers violated the Fourth and Fourteenth Amendments to the federal Constitution, and Part I, Article 19 of the New Hampshire State Constitution. The defendant argued that the DSS officers are agents of the state, to whom the requirements of the Fourth and Fourteenth Amendments and Part I, Article 19 apply.

On these facts, the trial court found:

> [T]he DSS officers (1) do not jointly train with the Hanover Police Department or other law enforcement officers or agencies, (2) do not take specific direction from public law enforcement officials, (3) were not, in the Nemser case, acting at the specific direction or behest of Hanover Police Officers, (4) were not trained or directed by the Hanover Police Department or any other public law enforcement agency in formulating their policy and protocols and, (5) that they were not supplied with any equipment or other accessories or information by the Hanover Police Department to either assist them in or lead them to the discovery of the items seized in the present case." All the same, the court found a sufficient relationship between DSS and the Hanover Police Department to apply constitutional restrictions to the search at issue, and granted the motion to suppress. The State appealed.
>
> When the case worked its way to the Granite State's highest court, the justices reasoned that the Fourth Amendment's prohibition of unreasonable searches and seizures only applied to the campus police in this case if they were acting as agents of the municipal police force. They held, "We conclude that these facts do not support the existence of an agency relationship. We do not discern in them an induce-

> ment by the State to search on its behalf, but rather a grudging acceptance by the Hanover Police Department of the unilateral decisions of a private party over which it believed it had no control. 'Mere knowledge of another's independent action [ ] does not produce vicarious responsibility absent some manifestation of consent and the ability to control.' (citation omitted)

The judicial record with regard to drug testing on college campuses is rather more mixed. In 1994 the California Supreme Court ruled that the NCAA has a compelling interest in the health and safety of student athletes, while the athletes themselves have a diminished privacy-expectation, such that the balance in favor of drug tests prior to championship competitions does not offend either the Fourth Amendment or comparable state constitutional prohibitions of searches and seizures and/or invasion of privacy. The tests at issue were aimed at detecting both steroids and so-called "street drugs." *See **Hill v. NCAA,**, 26 Cal. Rptr. 2d 834 (California Supreme Court, 1994).*

By contrast, in a case decided around the same time, ***University of Colorado v. Derdeyn****, 863 P.2d 929 (Colorado Supreme Court, 1993*), urine tests of university athletes for illicit drugs, incorporated into annual physicals, were deemed to be unconstitutional intrusions. The somewhat-complicated facts of the case are as follows:

The university (CU) began a drug-testing program in the fall of 1984 for its intercollegiate student athletes. CU had since amended its program in various ways, but throughout the existence of the program participation was mandatory in the sense that if an athlete did not sign a form consenting to random urinalysis pursuant to the program, the student was prohibited from participating in intercollegiate athletics at CU. In written descriptions, CU itself always characterized its drug-testing program as "a mandatory program of drug education, testing, and counseling/rehabilitation."

The drug-testing program originally required a urine test for certain proscribed drugs at each intercollegiate athlete's annual physical and also required random urine tests thereafter. Counseling was mandated following a first positive result. The penalty for a second positive result included a seven-day suspension from participation in intercollegiate athletics, and the penalty for a third positive included a minimum one-year suspension. No specific monitoring procedures were prescribed for the collection of the urine samples, and two students testified that during this phase of the program they were not monitored during the act of urination. According to CU's 1984 form describing the program, all test results were sent to the "Team Physician." The intercollegiate student athletes also were required to give their consent to releasing test results to "the Head Athletic Trainer at [CU]; my parent(s) or legal guardian(s) or spouse; the head coach of any intercollegiate sport in which I am a team member; the Athletic Director of [CU]; and the Drug Counseling Program at the Wardenburg Student Health Center."

Sometime later, CU amended its program for the first time. The penalty for a first positive was changed to include suspension for "the current competitive season," and the penalty for a second positive was changed to include permanent suspension from "any activity sponsored by the University of Colorado Athletic Department." Following a first positive, the athlete was also required successfully to complete a substance abuse rehabilitation program as a condition for further participation in intercollegiate athletics. The first amended program also provided that the "collection of the specimen will be observed [sic], and the athlete may be asked to disrobe in order to protect the integrity of the testing procedure."

One male student athlete testified that during this phase of the program the trainer "would hand you a bottle, a screw cap bottle and you and the trainer would adjourn to a restroom where the trainer would physically observe you filling up the bottle with your urine.... I mean that the trainer would actually watch you urinate, you weren't allowed to turn your back; I'm talking about full frontal exposure of your body."

A female student athlete testified, "Some female trainer had to be in the restroom watching you, in the actual stall watching you while you went to the bathroom." Another female student athlete testified, "You came into the track office and the trainer would come in and post all the people's names that were on the team.... That is what we called it, after a while, 'the pee team.' You kind of got flippant about it after a while because it was so embarrassing and everybody had to do it so we made jokes about it so that, you know, it wouldn't be as bad. Then, you would go into the bathroom with one of the trainers because at that time the training room was in the track office so you got one of the trainers and you went to the bathroom and she gave you a coke cup and you peed in the cup with the door open so she could watch and then you take your urine sample and you pour it in the bottle and screw the bottle up and she writes your number or whatever on it and then takes it away."

CU still gave no general or specific assurances of confidentiality of test results. CU's second amended program changed the penalty for a first positive from suspension for "the current competitive season," to suspension for "a twelve month period." In all other relevant respects the program remained unaltered.

CU's third amended program, which became effective August 14, 1988, contained numerous changes. First, it added alcohol, "over-the-counter drugs," and "performance-enhancing substances such as anabolic steroids" to the list of drugs for which students could be tested. Second, the term "athlete" was defined to include "all student participants in recognized intercollegiate sports, including but not limited to student athletes, cheerleaders, student trainers and student managers." Third, random "rapid eye examination (REE)" testing was substituted for random urinalysis, and a urinalysis was performed only after a "finding of reasonable suspicion that an athlete has used drugs," and also at the athlete's annual physical examination. Failure to perform adequately on an REE was considered "*prima facie* reasonable suspicion of drug use [except with regard to steroids]," and the student was required to provide a urine specimen for testing purposes if the student did not perform adequately on the REE. In addition, if a student exhibited "physical or behavioral characteristics indicating drug use including, but not limited to: tardiness, absenteeism, poor heath [sic] habits, emotional swings, unexplained performance changes, and/or excessive aggressiveness," this was also considered reasonable suspicion of drug use, and the student was required to take a urine test. Fourth, urine samples were to be collected "within the Athletic Department facilities," and athletes were "directed to provide a urine specimen in a private and enclosed area" while a monitor remained outside. The monitor would then receive "the sample from the athlete and check[ ] the sample for appropriate color, temperature, specific gravity and other properties to determine that no substitution or tampering has occurred." Fifth, the athletes were required to give their consent to releasing test results to "the Head Athletic Trainer at [CU]; my parent(s) or legal guardian(s), if I am under the age of 21; the head coach of any intercollegiate sport in which I am a team member; the Athletic Director of [CU]; my work supervisor (if applicable) and the Drug Counseling Program at the Wardenburg Student Health Center."

Finally, although CU still gave no general assurances of confidentiality, it did specify in its third amended program that communications between an athlete and physicians at Wardenburg Student Health Center would be confidential. In October of 1986, intercollegiate student athletes at CU filed a class action suit in Boulder County District Court challenging the constitutionality of the drug-testing program as it then existed and seeking declaratory and injunctive relief. Named as defendants were CU, the board of regents of CU, Judith Albino as president of CU, and William Marolt as athletic director, department of intercollegiate athletics. When CU subsequently amended its program, an issue arose as to which version of CU's program, if any, could be challenged at trial.

CU argued that the case was moot because it "would be futile to discuss the merits of a drug-testing policy the University has no intention of reinstating." However, by order, the trial court found that CU and the other defendants had "refused to agree that they will not return to the policy which was initially challenged in this class action. In fact, defendants have indicated that there are circumstances under which they would return to that policy." The trial court concluded "[t]herefore, ... the legality of [CU's] prior drug-testing policy is not moot," and it noted that it had "previously ruled that plaintiffs are to amend the complaint to add allegations concerning the new policy." The plaintiffs filed their amended complaint on March 16, 1989, the same day that the trial court signed the order. In their amended complaint, the plaintiffs sought relief from CU's random drug-testing programs, past, present, and future. Accordingly, at issue in the ensuing trial was the constitutionality of every version of CU's drug-testing program.

On these facts, the high court held, while the university was unable to demonstrate that the consents it obtained from the athletes were not sufficiently coerced to have waived their constitutional rights. Just the same, the justices left the door open for future testing, noting that "we recognize the possibility that in the future CU might be able to devise a program involving truly voluntary consents to drug testing. In such event, CU is free to apply for modification or dissolution of the injunction." Additionally, dissents filed by two justices indicated that these cases are considered very close ones by the nation's judiciaries.

Sources

"Wasting the Best and the Brightest: Substance Abuse at America's Colleges and Universities." [http://www.casacolumbia.org/supportcasa/item.asp?cID=12&PID=155] June 2007.

CHAPTER 7

Student-to-Student Harassment, Discrimination, Hazing, and Violence

For most organizations, customer-to-customer crime is not a serious loss-prevention concern. Two brawlers in a bar will probably find themselves arrested or at least evicted. Two shoppers struggling over the latest version of Play Station will likely suffer a similar fate. While the American common law may entertain a theory or two of liability, such interactions simply are not high on the list of litigation risks of most corporate counsels.

Need we say that institutions of higher learning are different in this regard? Our "customers" are our concerns in ways that only K–12 schools (and perhaps some landlords) can appreciate. When a student poses a threat to his classmates, when a fraternity harasses gays or blacks or Asians on your campus, or when new pledges are induced to binge drink, the university faces serious liability problems.

Students themselves can be held liable for the personal injuries they cause. In days of yore this statement was less solid than it is now, when 18—the age of most freshmen—is deemed to be the age of majority for most purposes. However, this chapter, as all the others, will focus on the institution's liability for student misdeeds.

Student-to-Student Harassment and Discrimination

Federal law prohibits student-on-student sexual harassment

The Supreme Court rules that Title IX reaches hostile acts between students.

By Richard L. Wiener, MLS, PhD, St. Louis University
Audrey T. Feldman Wiener, PhD, St. Louis Family Court

Under Title IX of the Education Amendments of 1972, no education program or activity receiving federal financial assistance may exclude, deny benefits to or discriminate against any person on the basis of sex (20 U.S.C. Sec. 1681.a).

The purpose of the statute is to prevent "discriminatory practices" in education and "to provide...effective protection against those practices."

In *Cannon v. University of Chicago,* 441 U.S. 677, at 704 (1979) and *Franklin v. Gwinnett County Public Schools,* 112 S.Ct. 1028 (1992), the U.S. Supreme Court held that private citizens could collect damage awards when teachers sexually harassed their students. But more recently in *Gebser v. Lago Vista Independent School Dist.,* 118 S.Ct. 1989 (1998), the Court limited the liability of school districts to include only those cases in which "an official who...has authority to address the alleged discrimination and to institute corrective measures on the [school's] behalf has actual knowledge of discrimination in the [school's] programs and fails adequately to respond" (118 S.Ct. 1999). The plaintiff must demonstrate that the official's response shows "deliberate indifference" to "actual knowledge" of discrimination. Instances in which a school administrator had enough information to have inferred that a teacher harassed a student (constructive knowledge) are not sufficient to trigger liability.

Background of the cases

In *Gebser,* teacher Waldrup had sexual relations with student Gebser, who failed to report the incidents to any school administrator. The relationship only became known when a security guard caught Waldrup in the act. The Court held that the district was not liable.

In the 1999 term, the Supreme Court extended the liability of Title IX to include "student-on-student" sexual harassment, *Davis v. Monroe County Bd. of Educ.* (119 S.Ct. 1661). In the case, LaShonda Davis, a fifth-grade student, reported to her mother and teacher that a male classmate made vulgar comments and tried to touch her genital area and her breasts on repeated occasions. The school principal was made aware of the behavior. Despite repeated complaints, the boy was not disciplined and his offensive comments and actions continued, escalating in severity. Finally, he was charged for the misconduct and pled guilty to sexual battery. The 11th Circuit Court of Appeals dismissed a claim for compensatory and punitive damages against the school, holding that Title IX does not provide schools adequate notice that they are liable for sexual harassment of one student by another [*Davis v. Monroe County. Bd. of Educ*., 120 F3.d 1390 (11th Cir, 1997)].

The U.S. Supreme Court agreed with the Eleventh Circuit's conclusion that Title IX does not provide schools notice of liability concerning the actions of others. However, a school's "deliberate indifference" to "known acts of harassment" is itself misconduct prohibited by Title IX which can trigger a private damage action by the plaintiff (Davis, 1999, p. 1671). A school's misconduct causes the plaintiff to be subject to discrimination when the school exercises "substantial control over the harasser" and the context in which the known harassment occurs (e.g., "during school hours and on school grounds," p. 1672). The complained after conduct must be "sexual harassment of students that is so severe, pervasive, and objectively offensive, and that so undermines and detracts from the victim's educational experience, that the student is effectively denied equal access to an institution's resources and opportunities" (p. 1675). Whether a school's response to student-on-student actions rises to the level of misconduct prohibited by Title IX is to be judged by the totality of the circumstances. Actionable conduct will likely go beyond "simple acts of teasing and name calling among school children" (p. 1675), and likely will require more than "one instance of peer-on-peer harassment" (p. 1675).

While, as indicated in the article above, the leading Supreme Court cases spring from the K–12 environment, they are deemed to apply with equal force to high education. Furthermore, individual state laws may serve to extend the reach of Title IX's protections to classes, such as gay and lesbian students, not necessarily protected by federal law at the present time.

A recent example, again drawn from the K–12 environment but pertinent to higher education is ***L.W. ex rel. L.G. v. Toms River Regional Schools Bd.,*** *189 N.J. 381, 915 A.2d 535 (New Jersey Supreme Court, 2007).* In this case, as early as the fourth grade, classmates began taunting plaintiff L.W. with homosexual epithets such as "gay," "homo," and "fag." The harassment increased in regularity and severity as L.W. advanced through school. In seventh grade, the bullying occurred daily and escalated to physical aggression and molestation. Within days of entering high school, the abuse culminated with a pair of physical attacks. Ultimately, L.W.'s unease prompted him to withdraw from his local high school and enroll elsewhere, at the expense of his school district.

The harassment escalated in 1998 when L.W. enrolled at Intermediate West, a school with an enrollment of 1,400 students, for seventh grade. "Almost every single day" classmates directed slurs at L.W. loudly in the halls "so everyone could hear." When asked about his day, L.W. would occasionally reply, "Nobody called me anything today. I had a good day." But, on entering the seventh grade, the maltreatment was no longer limited to verbal disparagement. In the fall, L.W. discovered a piece of construction paper attached to his locker that read, "You're a dancer, you're gay, you're a faggot, you don't belong in our school, get out." L.W. did not immediately report the incident to school officials.

The first reported incident occurred in late January. While in the school cafeteria, a group of ten to fifteen students surrounded L.W. One of those students, R.C., then struck L.W. on the back of the head and taunted him with "the usual" homosexual epithets. L.W. went to the office and called his mother. When she arrived to pick L.W. up, eighth-grade Assistant Principal Raymond McCusker informed her that he would report the incident to seventh-grade Assistant Principal Irene Benn. The next day, L.W. remained home from school, still upset from the previous day's events. His mother called Benn four times that day to determine what action was taken in response. Benn advised L.W.'s mother that McCusker had briefed her on the incident, but because "something had come up," she "did not have time to speak to the children involved." The following day, Benn informed L.W.'s mother that she had spoken with the main participants and determined that R.C., after being called a "whore" by L.W., retaliated against him. Benn counseled both students regarding the inappropriateness of their behavior and warned them of the consequences of future actions. Benn did not punish or reprimand any of the other students involved.

Also in late January, a student approached L.W. in the locker room and, with a crowd of students looking on, said, "If you had a p****, I'd f*** you up and down." L.W. was "[e]mbarrassed, vulnerable, [and] ashamed." L.W. and his mother reported the incident to Benn, but because L.W. did not want any problems performing in the upcoming school play, his mother asked Benn to wait until after the performance to speak with the offending student. However, L.W.'s mother did not follow up with Benn, and no action was taken.

Even the school play was not free of harassment. At every practice, an eighth grade student, R.G., insulted L.W. with derogatory comments. L.W. reported the harassment, and R.G. apologized. Further, as part of a school function, L.W. went to Toms River High School North to watch a dress rehearsal of a school play. There, D.M. mocked L.W. and smacked him on the head with his playbill. L.W. reported the incident. Benn counseled D.M., advising him that further inappropriate conduct would result in more significant consequences. D.M.'s mother was advised of the incident. She apologized to L.W.'s mother and insisted that D.M. write a letter apologizing to L.W.

The insults such as "butt boy, fruit cake, [and] fudge [p]acker" did not abate. The remarks were so frequent in seventh grade that L.W. testified that "[i]f I ma[d]e it through a day without comments, I was lucky." For example, various students pestered L.W. during physical education. When L.W. informed Benn of the badgering, she discouraged the heckling students from using such language and warned them of future consequences if their behavior continued. In addition to reporting the incidents to Benn, L.W. sought the help of his guidance counselor, who urged L.W. to "toughen up and turn the other cheek." L.W.'s mother complained to Benn about the guidance counselor's advice.

The harassment at Intermediate West peaked in mid-March. While standing in the lunch line, M.S., along with two friends, J.A. and C.C., approached L.W., calling him "gay" and "faggot." M.S. then grabbed L.W.'s "private area" and "humped" him, taunting, "Do you like it, do you like it like this?" L.W. escaped, but M.S. followed him and repeated the molestation as classmates watched. L.W. then fled to the school's main office. Benn spoke with all three attackers, told them that their conduct was "inappropriate" and that, if repeated, "It would be dealt with more severely." The assaulting students then returned to class.

L.W.'s mother arrived at school shortly thereafter to pick up her son, who waited in the school's main office while his mother and Benn spoke. Even in the main office, students teased L.W. Following the cafeteria incident, L.W. did not attend school for several days. When he did return, Mark Regan, principal of Intermediate West, Anne Baldi, the school's affirmative action officer, Benn, and McCusker met with L.W.'s mother and aunt. At that meeting, held less than two months after the first reported incident of harassment, Regan informed L.W.'s mother that an "open door policy" would be imposed, permitting her son to leave class and report problems directly to him or Benn any time anyone bothered him. Further, Regan assured L.W.'s mother that her son's teachers would be informed of the situation and L.W.'s special permission to leave class. Finally, Regan stated that harassing students would be dealt with immediately. According to Regan, first-time offenders would be counseled and more drastic action would be taken against repeat offenders.

On his first day back to school, L.W. faced homosexual taunts from his schoolmates, namely, C.C., B.E., and T.L. School officials reacted. Because C.C. was a repeat offender, his family was contacted and he received detention, while Benn and McCusker counseled the first-time offenders on the consequences of their behavior. Later that same day, R.B., P.D., J.P., and T.S. told L.W. that he should "be in a girls['] locker room." As a repeat offender, P.D. was punished with detention, his parents were contacted, and he was warned that he would be suspended if he offended again. The others, all first-time offenders, were counseled. L.W.'s gym locker was also moved closer to the physical education office.

The next month, in April of his seventh grade year, L.W. slapped a female student's buttocks on her dare. Thereafter, the female student's brother, D.R., accompanied by W.K., confronted L.W. in the locker room and said, "I heard [you] smacked my sister on her a**, I don't want you to do that, you're a fag, you don't belong doing that." D.R. then slapped L.W. across his face, ordering him "never to touch his sister again." Laughing and saying, "Faggot...get out of here, we don't want you here," W.K. then "whipped" L.W. over the back of his neck with a silver chain. L.W. reported the incident before going home that day. When his mother arrived, L.W. was crying. He had "welts" on his neck, and his cheek was "all red" from the attack. School officials suspended D.R. and W.K. five days each. L.W. did not return to school for more than a week.

Although unreported, the verbal abuse persisted through the end of the seventh grade, but was of a lesser degree. Eighth grade was a better year for L.W. Although the verbal harassment continued, it was more sporadic. No physical abuse was reported, and, at L.W.'s graduation, L.W. and his mother thanked Regan for "giving L.[W.] a good year." Concerning the lack of physical confrontation during his eighth grade year, L.W. testified that a security guard monitored him between classes approximately 80 percent of the time. However, the guard, a former police officer, testified that he was assigned to the intermediate school generally and that he was not assigned specifically to monitor L.W. Although the security guard was transferred to Toms River High School South when L.W. entered that school as a freshman, the guard stated that the transfer was unrelated to L.W.'s academic progression.

Throughout L.W.'s time at Intermediate West, a school-wide nondiscrimination policy was in effect, one that the district characterized as a "zero tolerance" policy. The district provided students and parents with a handbook of rules, regulations, and policies stating that the district did not discriminate on the basis of numerous characteristics including race, sex, and religion. However, the handbook did not enumerate affectional or sexual orientation. Additionally, the district, which oversaw roughly 18,000 students, maintained a second nondiscrimination policy, an affirmative action overview. That policy was not generally distributed to students and parents; rather, it was maintained by the district's superintendent, principals, and affirmative action office. The affirmative action overview enumerated "affectional or sexual orientation" as a prohibited basis for discrimination.

Benn testified that she explained the school's nondiscrimination policies to students in a class period at the beginning of the academic year. However, E.C., a classmate of L.W.'s, testified that the assembly addressed mostly "fighting" and “yelling in the hall.” To the extent harassment was discussed, according to Benn, no specific reference was made to sexual orientation. The district did not reinforce the discrimination policy through assemblies, letters to parents, or any other widespread communication.

The district employed “progressive discipline” when addressing peer discrimination and harassment. School officials counseled first-time offenders regarding their inappropriate conduct and advised them that more serious consequences would result if the conduct recurred. For a second transgression, the offender earned disciplinary “points.” A third offense could result in suspension. By way of comparison, if a student was more than one minute late for class, the student received three “points” and a detention. Overall, the progressive discipline was student-specific, predicated on the offender’s prior record, not the victim’s identity or history.

On entering High School South, the epithets resurfaced. To avoid the derision he encountered on the school bus, L.W. decided to walk home after school. However, while walking home from school in early September and off school grounds, a car approached L.W. and three students, L.B., J.F., and M.F., exited. M.F. said, “I heard you have a crush on L.B., and that [his] family doesn’t like faggots, [he doesn’t] like faggots.” J.F. pressed L.W., “Well, are you a faggot?” M.F. chimed in, “We don’t like faggots, our whole family doesn’t like faggots.” L.W. yelled, “It’s none of your damn business.” M.F. then punched L.W. in the face, knocking him down. L.W. ran away, crying hysterically, but M.F. chased after him threatening, “If I hear that you said anything about this I’m going to knife you.” L.W. subsequently missed a day or two of school.

In the wake of the attack, L.W.’s mother informed high school officials of the mistreatment her son endured in middle school. According to L.W.’s mother, the educators seemed unaware of L.W.’s past. The district suspended M.F. for ten days, and he later pled guilty to a charge of assault. School officials advised L.W. to take the bus home in the future.

The final incident occurred in mid-September when L.W. went to downtown Toms River for lunch, as many students did. L.T. approached L.W., who was sitting on a curb outside a 7-Eleven convenience store. Unprovoked, L.T. pushed L.W. to the ground and grabbed L.W.’s shirt. L.T. warned L.W. that if he ever heard that L.W. had a crush on him or his friends again that he’d “kick [L.W.’s] a* *.” The aggressor then “completely covered” L.W. with dirt. The district suspended L.T. for ten days.

On her son’s behalf, L.W.’s mother filed a complaint under the New Jersey Law Against Discrimination, N.J.S.A. 10:5-1 et seq., alleging that the Toms

River Regional Schools Board of Education (district) failed to take corrective action in response to the harassment L.W. endured because of his perceived sexual orientation. The director of the Division on Civil Rights held that the district was liable for the student-on-student harassment that L.W. repeatedly endured. The Appellate Division affirmed the Director's decision.

On appeal, the New Jersey Supreme Court considered whether the New Jersey Law Against Discrimination (LAD), which forbids among other things sexual-preference discrimination, could be extended to the plaintiff's situation. The judges held: "Because the Act's broad statutory language is clear, we hold that the LAD recognizes a cause of action against a school district for student-on-student affectional or sexual orientation harassment. We also hold that a school district is liable for such harassment when the school district knew or should have known of the harassment but failed to take actions reasonably calculated to end the mistreatment and offensive conduct. Our conclusion furthers the legislative intent of eradicating the scourge of discrimination not only from society, but also from our schools, thus encouraging school districts to take proactive steps to protect the children in their charge."

In light of such judicial decisions, Rider University in central New Jersey has adopted the following broad anti-harassment policy.

University Harassment Policy

All students, faculty, staff and administrators at the University have the right to expect an environment that allows them to enjoy the full benefits of their work or learning experience. Harassment is any action that may reasonably be expected to threaten, coerce or intimidate an individual or a class of individuals. Where the alleged harassment involves a potential violation of federal or state anti-discrimination laws, the University's affirmative action officer may be called upon to investigate the allegations, using procedures approximating those outlined below under "Sexual Harassment." However, nothing contained in this policy shall be construed either to limit the legitimate exercise of the right of free speech or to infringe upon the academic freedom of any member of the University community.

Sexual Harassment

It is the policy of the institution that no member of the community may sexually harass another. Sexual harassment is defined as unwelcome sexual advances, requests for sexual favors, and/or physical, verbal or written conduct of a sexual nature when:

1. Submission to such conduct is made explicitly or implicitly a term or condition of an individual's employment, education, or participation in University programs or activities, or
2. Submission to or rejection of such conduct by an individual is used as a basis for decisions pertaining to an individual's employment, education, or participation in University programs or activities, or
3. Such speech or conduct is directed against another and is abusive or humiliating and persists after the objection of the person targeted by the speech or conduct, or
4. Such conduct would be regarded by a reasonable person as creating an intimidating, hostile or offensive environment that substantially interferes with an individual's work, education, or participation in University programs or activities.

In the educational setting within the University, as distinct from other work places within the University, wide latitude for professional judgment in determining the appropriate content and presentation of academic material is required. Conduct, including pedagogical techniques, that serves a legitimate educational purpose does not constitute sexual harassment. Those participating in the educational setting bear a responsibility to balance their rights of free expression with a consideration of the reasonable sensitivities of other participants. Nothing contained in this policy shall be construed either to (1) limit the legitimate exercise of free speech, including but not limited to written, graphic, or verbal expression that can reasonably be demonstrated to serve legitimate education, artistic, or political purposes, or (2) infringe upon the academic freedom of any member of the University community. The following procedures apply to instances in which a claim is made of inappropriate behavior that might be interpreted to be sexual harassment.

Informal Procedures

The informal procedures are designed to resolve complaints quickly, efficiently, and to the mutual satisfaction of all parties involved. The Affirmative Action Officer (or designee), with relevant supervisors when appropriate, seeks an outcome that is mutually agreed upon by all parties to the complaint. If it seems appropriate the Affirmative Action Officer will use the services of a counselor to assist in resolving an informal complaint. If the accused is represented by a bargaining agent, the accused may have that agent present at any interview with the Affirmative Action Officer or designee. Records maintained by the Affirmative Action Office arising from informal procedures will not be used for any purpose other than those described above unless an informal complaint results in a formal hearing. Since informal level records represent allegations not supported by formal findings of fact, they will be maintained in a confidential manner separate from any other records for four years. They will be destroyed after that period if no further allegations or formal complaints have been received concerning or by the same individual. Such records shall not be used as evidence of guilt or innocence in any investigation or hearing involving a future complaint involving the same accused. The accused shall be entitled to include a response in the records.

Formal Procedures

If the alleged harassing behavior that triggered the informal complaint has not ceased as a result of informal intervention or is of the kind that contradicts informal efforts, a formal investigation may be initiated. Before a formal investigation, the Affirmative Action Officer (or designee) must explain the process and the relevant avenues of redress to the complainant and the accused. A formal investigation can be terminated with the mutual consent of the parties involved. A formal complaint must be filed in writing within six months of the act of alleged harassment, unless extenuating circumstances require an extension, and must be filed with the Affirmative Action Office. The Affirmative Action Officer (or designee) will notify the president of the union (if the alleged harasser is a bargaining unit member) and the relevant division head as soon as possible after receiving the complaint. The Affirmative Action Officer will provide the accused, the complainant, the union president (when appropriate) or the relevant division head (if the accused does not belong to a bargaining unit), and the Dean of Students (when a student is involved) with a copy of the complaint and this policy. The Affirmative Action Officer (or designee) will investigate the complaint and report the results to the president. The president will initiate disciplinary action, when in his/her judgment it is appropriate, and will inform the accused, the complainant, the union president (when appropriate), the relevant division head, and the Dean of Students (when appropriate) of his/her decision. Implementation and challenge of any disciplinary action will be according to applicable bargaining agreement (up to and including arbitration) or non-bargaining unit disciplinary procedures. Following a determination, records of the formal proceedings will be maintained in the Affirmative Action

Office for four years. The Affirmative Action Office shall maintain a confidential index of dated complaints cross-referenced by name of the accused and the complainant. The Affirmative Action Officer shall have the authority to take all reasonable and prudent steps to protect both parties pending the formal investigation and/or hearing.

Rider University, The Source: Student Handbook of Rider University *(2009) (also published in the Rider University Academic Policy Manual and posted on the university's website) (reprinted with permission.)*

Hazing

Mr. Webster defines "haze" as "to harass by exacting unnecessary, disagreeable, or difficult work… [or] to play abusive or humiliating tricks on, by way of initiation" [Webster's Seventh Collegiate Diction (Springfield: G&C Merriam Co, 1963) at 382]. A more recent edition of the famed dictionary hones in on the subject of this section: "to initiate or discipline by forcing to do ridiculous or painful things" [Webster's New World Dictionary and Thesaurus (N.Y.: Hungry Minds, Inc. 2d ed. 1999) at 292].

This definition is exemplified by the case of ***Brueckner v. Norwich University,*** *169 Vt. 118, 730 A.2d 1086 (Vermont Supreme Court, 1999).* In this case, plaintiff William C. Brueckner, Jr. arrived as an incoming freshman, or "rook," at the Military College of Vermont of Norwich University (Norwich) in August 1990. At the time, he was a twenty-four-year-old, five-year veteran of the United States Navy, having been awarded a four-year naval ROTC scholarship in the amount of $80,000 to attend Norwich. Under the authority and training of Norwich and its leadership, certain upperclassmen were appointed by the university to indoctrinate and orient the incoming rooks, including the plaintiff. These upperclassmen were known as the "cadre." The plaintiff attended Norwich for only sixteen days as a result of his subjection to, and observation of, numerous incidents of hazing. In those sixteen days, the plaintiff withstood a regular barrage of obscene, offensive and harassing language. He was interrogated at meals and thereby prevented from eating. He was ordered to disrobe in front of a female student, although he did not follow the order. He was prevented from studying during some of the assigned study periods, and, on several occasions, cadre members destroyed his academic work with water. Members of the cadre also forced him to squat in the hall as they squirted him with water. He was forced to participate in unauthorized calisthenic sessions, despite an injured shoulder. He was slammed into a wall by a cadre member riding a skateboard in the hall. After cadre members vandalized his room by dumping water in it, plaintiff was ordered to clean up the mess. On two occasions, plaintiff was prevented from attending mandatory ROTC study hall on time, leading him to believe his scholarship status was endangered. One morning, as the plaintiff walked along the corridor in the dormitory, he encountered two cadre members, one of whom asked plaintiff where the plaintiff's nametag was. When the plaintiff responded that he had forgotten it, one cadre member hit the plaintiff hard in the shoulder, which was injured and in a sling. After the other cadre member told the hitter to stop, the hitter struck the plaintiff again in the same shoulder, causing pain and bruises. After reporting the hazing problems to Norwich officials, the plaintiff left the campus, believing that his situation would not improve. He returned briefly once more, then withdrew from Norwich, his scholarship terminated. Norwich investigated the plaintiff's complaints and, as a result, several cadets were disciplined.

The plaintiff brought his action against Norwich for assault and battery, negligent infliction of emotional distress, intentional infliction of emotional distress and negligent supervision. By means of special interrogatories, the jury found Norwich liable on all counts and awarded the plaintiff $100,000 for emotional distress, $8,600 for medical expenses, $80,000 for the lost four-year college scholarship and $300,000 to cover lost earnings (past and future). The jury also awarded $1.75 million in punitive damages. The court denied Norwich's post-trial motions for judgment as a matter of law and for a new trial. Norwich appealed.

The Vermont Supreme Court's Decision

The high court explained that under the settled doctrine of *respondeat superior*, an employer or master is held vicariously liable for the tortious acts of an employee or servant committed during, or incidental to, the scope of employment. Norwich conceded that cadre members acted as its agents in "indoctrinating and orienting" rooks such as the plaintiff. Norwich claimed, however, that the tortious acts complained of were not committed within the cadre members' "scope of employment." Whether a given act is committed within the scope of employment, the court observed (echoing settled American common law), is properly determined by the finder of fact after consideration of the attendant facts and circumstances of the particular case.

To be within the scope of employment, conduct must be of the same general nature as, or incidental to, the authorized conduct. Conduct of the servant falls within the scope of employment if: (a) it is of the kind the servant is employed to perform; (b) it occurs substantially within the authorized time and space limits;

(c) it is actuated, at least in part, by a purpose to serve the master; and (d) in a case in which the force is intentionally used by the servant against another, it is not unexpected by the master. Conduct of a servant is not within the scope of employment if it is different in kind from that authorized, far beyond the authorized time and space limits, or too little actuated by a purpose to serve the master.

In this instance, concluded the court, the cadre were authorized by Norwich to indoctrinate and orient rooks through activities performed at various times of the day and night. A jury could reasonably find members of the cadre were acting in furtherance of their general duties to indoctrinate and orient the rooks and thus within their "scope of employment" at the time of the hazing incidents of which the plaintiff complained.

Norwich argued that, because it had adopted policies against hazing and had instructed the cadre to refrain from mistreating the rooks, the tortious conduct was outside the scope of employment. Norwich contended that ***McHugh v. University of Vermont,*** 966 F.2d 67 (2d Cir. 1992), supported this result. In *McHugh,* the Second Circuit Court of Appeals, applying Vermont law, concluded that an employee who sexually and religiously harassed a fellow employee was not acting within the scope of employment. There, a major in the United States Army and an employee at the University of Vermont's Department of Military Studies told the plaintiff, a female secretary, that his definition of a "secretary" was a "paid whore." The employee repeatedly joked about the plaintiff contracting AIDS, stating that he hoped she would be able to avoid infection. The employee also told the plaintiff that it was "a good day to watch Catholic babies burn." The court rejected the argument that the employee's conduct was within his scope of employment because it was within that scope for him to talk with the plaintiff, either to give instructions or to avoid the awkwardness of silence at work. It held: "It can hardly be contended that [the employee's] alleged conduct furthered the business" of his employer.

Rejecting this analogy, the judges wrote, "The same cannot be said of this case, where the actions involved in hazing rooks may fairly be seen as qualitatively similar to the indoctrination and orientation with which the cadre members were charged. Indeed, Norwich described some of the acts of which plaintiff complained, such as forced calisthenics and questioning at mealtime, as not far removed from the official system of military discipline and training which recruits are expected to endure. The evidence supported the jury's conclusion that the cadre members were acting within the scope of employment."

Although the existence of policies prohibiting hazing did not save Norwich University from liability in this case, no college or university can prevail in the absence of published policies. (Of course, such policies are empty words unless properly promulgated and consistently enforced.) Following is a sample of anti-hazing policies:

Hazing Policy

Introduction and Philosophy

Lycoming College is committed to promoting a campus environment that is just, open, disciplined, and caring. This philosophy supports the educational mission of the institution and our standards for co-curricular programs that facilitate students' development. Lycoming College is opposed to any activity that involves the hazing of any member of the college community.

Definition of Hazing

Hazing is defined as: any action taken or situation created as part of initiation to or continued membership in a student group or organization, which 1) produces or has the potential to produce mental or physical discomfort, harm, or stress; embarrassment; harassment; or ridicule; or 2) which violate College policy, fraternity/sorority policy, or law. This applies to behavior on or off College or organization premises. (Hazing does not include actions or situations that are incidental to officially-sanctioned and supervised College activities.)

Lycoming College, http://www.lycoming.edu/stuaff/handbook/hazingpolicy.htm

---

Hazing Policy

No chapter, colony, student or alumnus shall conduct nor condone hazing activities. Hazing activities are defined as: "Any action taken or situation created, intentionally, whether on or off fraternity premises, to produce mental or physical discomfort, embarrassment, harassment, or ridicule. Such activities may include but are not limited to the following: use of alcohol; paddling in any form; creation of excessive fatigue; physical and psychological shocks; quests, treasure hunts, scavenger hunts, road trips or any other such activities carried on outside or inside of the confines of the chapter house; wearing of public apparel which is conspicuous and not normally in good taste; engaging in public stunts and buffoonery; morally degrading or humiliating games and activities; and any other activities which are not consistent with academic achievement, fraternal law, ritual or policy or the regulations and policies of the educational institution, or applicable state law."

Phi Kappa Theta National Fraternity, http://www.phikaps.org/join/hazing.html

Joint Position Statement against Hazing

Preface

The organizations of the National Pan-Hellenic Council, Inc. (NPHC) are committed to nurturing the ideals of sisterhood and fraternalism in an atmosphere of responsibility and respect. We are also committed to upholding the dignity and self-respect of all persons seeking membership therein. Hazing is antithetical to this commitment and is prohibited by the rules of each NPHC organization. In 1990, the member organizations of the NPHC jointly agreed to disband pledging as a form of admission. At the dawn of a new millennium, we the members of the National Pan-Hellenic Council do hereby reaffirm our unequivocal opposition to hazing and those who seek to perpetuate it.

RESOLUTION

WHEREAS the National Pan-Hellenic Council, Inc. (NPHC) is comprised of local councils drawn from the ranks of 1.5 million college and professional members of the nine historically African-American fraternities and sororities, namely; Alpha Phi Alpha Fraternity, Inc., Alpha Kappa Alpha Sorority, Inc., Kappa Alpha Psi Fraternity, Inc., Omega Psi Phi Fraternity, Inc., Delta Sigma Theta Sorority, Inc., Phi Beta Sigma Fraternity, Inc., Zeta Phi Beta Sorority, Inc., Sigma Gamma Rho Sorority, Inc., and Iota Phi Theta Fraternity, Inc., and the Council of Presidents of these member organizations who come together on issues that promote the common purposes and general good for which these organizations exist; and

WHEREAS these NPHC organizations, operating through chapter located in the United States, the Caribbean, Europe, Africa, and Asia, are proud of their commitment since 1906 to scholarship, community service, leadership and the promotion of sisterhood and brotherhood in an atmosphere of respect and responsibility; and **WHEREAS** these NPHC organizations are likewise committed to promoting the self respect and dignity of all persons seeking membership in the respective organizations; and **WHEREAS** hazing is antithetical to this commitment and is strictly prohibited by the constitution, policies and procedures of each NPHC organization; and **WHEREAS** "pledging" has been officially abolished as a process for membership and pledge "lines" have similarly been abolished; and all members and prospective members are prohibited from engaging in hazing, pledge or pre-pledge "lines"; and **WHEREAS** in 1990, the NPHC organizations issued a joint statement announcing the elimination of pledging and each has instituted within its respective organization, a revised membership development and intake process; and **WHEREAS** each NPHC organization has instituted strong policies against hazing and has taken steps to reinforce and strengthen its stand against prohibited conduct: and **WHEREAS** as we begin this new century and a renewed commitment to the fundamental principles of brotherhood, sisterhood, human dignity and mutual respect, the NPHC organizations desire to make their commitment against hazing abundantly clear and fully intend for every member, prospective member, parent, university and the general public to be aware of the individual and collective position of the organizations against hazing; and **WHEREAS** these NPHC organizations further desire to make known their respective commitment to hold any person who engages in hazing individually and personally liable to the victim and to answer to the law and the organization; and will hold such persons to respond in monetary damages, civil and criminal penalties and severe disciplinary actions by the organization, including expulsion; and **WHEREAS** the definition of hazing has been held to include any action taken or situation created that involves or results in abusive, physical contact or mutual harassment of a prospective Fraternity or Sorority member; and that any such action is considered hazing, whether it occurs on or off the Fraternity or Sorority premises, campus or place where chapters or prospective members meet: and that hazing has also been described to include any action that results in excessive mutual or physical discomfort, embarrassment or harassment; that such activities include, but are not limited to paddling, creation of excessive fatigue, physical or psychological shock, morally degrading or humiliating activities, late work sessions that interfere with scholastic activities and any other activities inconsistent with fraternal law and regulations and policies of the affiliate educational institution and federal, state or local law; and **WHEREAS** such illegal conduct is inimical to the principles for which each organization stands and fails to foster respect for fellow members or preserve human dignity; **BE IT RESOLVED AND RESTATED WITH EMPHASIS ANEW** that hazing, pledging, pledge "lines", pre-pledge "lines" or post-intake hazing are strictly prohibited by these NPHC organizations; and **BE IT FURTHER RESOLVED, RESTATED AND MADE KNOWN** that these NPHC organizations are committed to eradicate the scourge of hazing and to that end that the intake process has been recodified by each organization, which permits the conduct of intake only when specifically authorized by the officer placed in charge of the process and at only such times, places and in the presence of persons specifically authorized and certified to conduct the intake process; that prospective members and the parents of collegiate applicants are advised that hazing is not a requirement for membership, nor is it tolerated; that members and prospective members must attest that they are fully aware of the organization's policy against hazing and will not engage in prohibited conduct and that the organization will fully cooperate with law enforcement authorities and with university officials in the investigation and prosecution of hazing or other illegal activity; that members and applicants for membership are also put on written notice that they will be held responsible to the organization for violation of policies against hazing and the organization will pursue full remedies allowed by the law to obtain indemnification for damages caused by the actions of the members or applicants who participated in illegal, unauthorized or prohibited conduct despite notice to refrain from such conduct; that each organization shall enforce severe penalties, including expulsion, for proven violations of its policies against and impose sanctions against a chapter involved and cooperate with the university in implementing sanctions by the university; that members and applicants for membership shall be required to immediately notify the national office of the Fraternity or Sorority, the local chapter advisor, university officials and law enforcement officials of any observed hazing incident or improper activity believed to be in violation of the policy against hazing, without fear of reprisal and their application for membership will not be affected by so doing; and, indeed, failure to report known violations may disqualify a candidate for membership; and, finally, that these NPHC organizations shall continue to encourage their members to participate in activities which promote high scholastic achievement, sisterhood, brotherhood, loyalty and leadership; and shall continue to affirm sound values and the worth of every member working together to accomplish organizational goals and serve the community.

National Pan-Hellenic Council, http://www.zphib1920.org/policy/NPHC%20Joint%20Position%20Statement%20Against%20Hazing%20(2003).pdf

Violence

Sexual Assault

The Catholic Church is not the only organization to learn in the last decade that a failure to act effectively upon a sexual assault complaint can come back decades later to embarrass you. On March 14, 2007, a recovering alcoholic named William Beebe was sentenced in the Charlottesville Circuit Court for a rape he committed at the University of Virginia in 1984. At the time, says victim Liz Seccuro, she woke up in a frat house, after passing out from a doctored drink, and reported the assault to a dean and the campus police. She added in a press conference following the sentencing hearing that the university officials treated her claim "dismissively." UVA spokeswoman Carol Wood issued a statement saying Seccuro is "a courageous woman who was determined to see this through, and today justice was served on her behalf."

The bizarre post-script to the two-decade-old crime began when Beebe, mounting the ninth step of the Alcoholics Anonymous recovery program, wrote a letter to Seccuro in which he confessed the crime. The AA program calls for participants to make amends to those they have harmed. An exchange of emails ensued in which Beebe wrote, "I want to make clear that I'm not intentionally minimizing the fact of having raped you. I did." Although Seccuro said she forgives Beebe, she added that an apology wasn't enough to compensate for the severe disruption she suffered in her own life.

After she reported Beebe's admission to the Charlottesville PD, Beebe was arrested in Las Vegas and extradited to Virginia, where there is no felony statute of limitations. At first prosecutors reportedly wanted to charge him with rape and seek a life sentence. However, when it came out that others also had raped the victim, Beebe was permitted to plead to the lesser offense. Although even that brought a ten-year prison term, the judge suspended all but 18 months of incarceration. In return Beebe, when released, will devote 500 hours to alcohol-abuse and date-rape training on college campuses.

UVA hasn't said whether it will be on Beebe's community-service circuit.

Campus Killers

When Will These Classroom Killings Stop?

By Jim Castagnera

On Monday a crazy gunman opened fire in a Virginia Tech residence hall and a little later in a classroom across campus, killing some 30 people in what is being labeled "the deadliest shooting rampage in U.S. history." The gunman subsequently was killed, bringing the death toll to 31. As I wrote this column, no one knew the murder's motive.

Virginia Tech's president was quoted by the Associated Press as saying, "Today the university was struck with a tragedy that we consider of monumental proportions. The university is shocked and indeed horrified."

In 21st century America we have almost come to accept these horrible mass murders as natural disasters. This community has been hit by a hurricane. That one has been torn up by a tornado. Oh, and that one over there has been blasted by a madman with a gun. The Tech student body no doubt will be afforded free access to "grief counselors."

We used to say, "Everybody talks about the weather, but no one does anything about it." Should we now say, "Everybody talks about gun violence, but no one does anything about it?" Living here in suburban Philadelphia, I watched as the City of Brotherly Love averaged one homicide per day in 2006. Philly passed the 100-homicide mark during the first quarter of '07, suggesting it well may be on its way to breaking last year's record. Here, too, students are, often as not, counted among the innocent victims of gun violence gone out of control.

Yeh, I know... guns don't kill people, people kill people. But these killers are better armed than ever before. When I was a Franklin and Marshall College student a lifetime ago, I witnessed plenty of fights, often of the town v. gown variety. A group of fraternity punks, such as myself, might get a bit rowdy in a local tavern. The blue-collar crowd at the opposite end of the bar might take umbrage. The upshot might then be a quick exchange of fisticuffs. On a rare occasion a knife or a broken bottle could come into play.

My point is: almost nobody carried a gun.

By contrast today, if you are confronted by a belligerent bar fly, run for your car.

Odds are better than even the guy is packing.

No need to look for trouble in a local bar, however. Virginia Tech is not the only school where guns have gotten into classrooms. Just last year a local high school student entered one of our county's Catholic high schools, discharged his father's AK-47, then shot himself. We could only be grateful that the troubled youth didn't first kill his classmates, making Delaware County the scene of a new Columbine massacre.

The Canadian college professor Marshall McLuhan—best known during my college days for saying, "The medium is the message"—asserted that Americans live in "Bonanzaland," i.e., the Wild West of the 1880s. Well, folks, that time is long past. Our K–12 schools have rightly adopted zero-tolerance policies toward weapons in their halls and classrooms. Colleges, too, have clamped down on violence—even the fisticuffs of my era.

Obviously, this isn't enough.

Neither are grief counselors enough.

The Second Amendment to the U.S. Constitution may give us all the right to bear arms, though some judges and scholars have questioned the Supreme Court's reading of that bit of the Bill of Rights. Regardless of what rights we want to read into the Second Amendment, I say our daughters and sons have a higher right: to enjoy and benefit from their educations without looking over their shoulders and wondering whether today is the day their classroom is riddled with bullets.

I don't have the answer, folks. I just know in my guts that, until we dispense with the grief counselors and the platitudes, and get mad as hell about travesties like this latest massacre at Virginia Tech, the killing is just going to continue.

Source: News of Delaware County *(PA) (Copyright, James Ottavio Castagnera, 2007).*

Case Study No. 1: University of Texas (1966)

In August 1981, just out of law school and fresh from a bar exam, I, one of your two authors, reported for duty as an assistant professor of business law at UT-Austin. Not long into the fall semester, I learned that when the Texas Longhorns won, the 307-foot tower dominating the campus glowed burnt-orange. As attractive as the tower was, I also soon learned that it was closed to visitors. By contrast, back in 1966 the 28th floor observation deck hosted some 20,000 tourists annually.

Then, on August 1, 1966, a 25-year-old ex-marine named Charles Joseph Whitman, having murdered wife and mother the night before, climbed the tower and shot some 45 passers-by. He managed to kill 14, before being shot to death himself. The university closed the tower for two years, then closed it again in 1975 following a series of sporadic suicide jumps from its heights.

Addressing what went wrong before and during the tower massacre changed the way not only the University of Texas but all of higher education thinks about and tries to deal with dangerous people on our campuses.

On March 29, 1966, Whitman—by then a student at UT—was referred to Dr. M.D. Heatly on the university's health center staff. Dr. Heatly opened his report, "This massive, muscular youth seemed to be oozing with hostility." Whitman admitted "that he had on two occasions assaulted his wife physically."

He told Heatly that in the marines he'd been court-martialed for fighting. Most remarkably, Heatly recorded, "Repeated inquiries attempting to analyze his exact experiences were not too successful with the exception of his vivid reference to 'thinking about going up on the tower with a deer rifle and start shooting people.'" The good doctor's solution? "No medication was given to this youth at this time and he was told to make an appointment for the same day next week, and should he feel that he needs to talk to this therapist he could call me at any time during the interval."

Within days of the August 1st shootings, the Hogg Foundation for Mental Health, founded decades earlier on the UT campus, ramped up efforts to improve availability of services for psychologically troubled members of the campus community. Student-counseling services were expanded, including services aimed specifically at patients in "crisis situations."

Today, every campus has its counseling center and its policies on threats of violence and suicide. Yet costly, high profile lawsuits involving students' violence toward themselves and others abound. Universities still struggle with whether to treat or expel such students. And, as the VTU tragedy demonstrates, identification and prevention remain elusive goals.

According to author Gary Laverge, who wrote a book about the tower shootings, "The university [in 1966] had no real police department—only a few unarmed men who spent most of their time issuing parking permits."

Today, the UT System Police website states, "Our official creation as a police agency occurred in 1967 and was largely the result of a sniping incident on August 1, 1966 on the UT-Austin campus.... During the 1967 session of the Texas Legislature, members of the House and Senate in a near unanimous action answered a growing need on Texas college campuses for adequate police protection." Article 2919j of the Texas Civil Code authorizes the Lone Star State's public colleges and universities to commission their security personnel as "peace officers." Countless campuses across the country followed suit, so that—for example—Philadelphia's Temple University on the city's dangerous north side boasts one of Pennsylvania's largest police forces. Meanwhile, most U.S. cities—similarly taking their lead from Austin, Texas—have created SWAT teams.

Nonetheless, campus police and city SWAT teams are no silver bullet or magic shield, when pitted against a determined mass killer.

Meanwhile, the U.T. Tower was once again reopened in late 1998, following $500,000 worth of renovations to prevent jumping. Tours today are by appointment only.

Case Study No. 2: Dawson College (2006)

When the police use profiling, it's condemned as racist. When the customs service does it, it's similarly assailed as discriminatory and unconstitutional. Still, it's being done. *Travel & Leisure* magazine reported in January, "The Transportation Security Administration (TSA) recently began rolling out a new security program, Screening Passengers by Observation Techniques (SPOT), at dozens of airports around the country." *Time* magazine explained, "TSA employees will be trained to identify suspicious individuals who raise red flags by exhibiting unusual or anxious behavior, which can be as simple as changes in mannerisms, excessive sweating on a cool day, or changes in the pitch of a person's voice." Although such techniques invariably arouse the ACLU, should colleges and universities consider adopting them?

Before you answer, consider the case of Dawson College. On September 13, 2006, Kimveer Gill parked his car in downtown Montreal, removed a cache of weapons from the trunk, forced a passerby to carry his extra ammunition, and walked the short distance to the college's campus. At the main building's back entrance he opened fire on students standing on the steps. His hostage ran off with the extra ammunition as Gill entered the building and walked to the cafeteria, where he immediately shot two students. Ordering the others in the room to lie on the floor, he continued firing randomly until police arrived. Taking two more hostages, he attempted to escape until, shot in the arm, he took his own life. The toll: one student dead, 19 more wounded.

Police later found Kimveer Gill's profile posted on a website called VampireFreaks.com [www.vampirefreaks.com]. In the accompanying photo he wears a black leather trench coat and sports a Beretta Cx4 Storm semi-automatic carbine, one of four guns he took to Dawson College. Visit VampireFreaks.com today and you can purchase "cyber-gothic clothing" on a related link called clothing@F—TheMainstream, and read featured interviews with "Velvet Acid Christ," "Zombie Girl," and "Grendel." Gill's own VampireFreaks screen name was "fatality 666." His last login was at 10:35 AM on the day of the shootings.

In the aftermath of the Dawson College shootings, the so-called "Goth" subculture came under sharp attack in the media. Hardly a high school or a college on the North American continent is without its clique of Goth enthusiasts in their leather, chains, piercings, tattoos, and bizarre hairstyles. Operators of Goth shops and websites found themselves defending the lifestyle and adamantly disavowing violence. Some expressed shock at the 55 graphically violent pictures posted on Gill's VampireFreaks web page.

Gill also turned out to be a big fan of the video game "Super Columbine Massacre RPG." Go to the game's web site [www.columbinegame.com] today and you'll find this statement about the Virginia Tech massacre (Case Study No. 3, below): "This week, the press is awash with stories about the shooting at Virginia Tech—the deadliest in recent history. Will we remember this tragedy in a week? In a month? In the years to follow? I certainly hope so. I hope we can learn from such sobering events as Virginia Tech, as Dawson College, Ehrfurt, Columbine and all the other horrific shootings modern society has endured. So often the potential for another shooting is just around the corner should we forget the lessons history has to offer us. This process of reevaluation, introspection, and a search for understanding is the value I believe my video game offers to those who play it." The author, site owner Danny Ledonne, is said to have vomited when he learned that Gill was a fan. Presumably Gill wasn't participating for "reevaluation, introspection, and a search for understanding."

VampireFreaks and Super Columbine Massacre persist on the web, despite their appeal to the Kimveer Gills out there. No one has definitively proven a clear cause-effect relationship (albeit the Alabama Supreme Court last year reinstated a $600 million lawsuit against the makers of a video game called "Grand Theft Auto," which the plaintiffs blame for the shooting deaths of two police officers and a dispatcher in 2003).

As Goth enthusiasts and video gamers alike point out, tens of thousands of adherents never commit a violent crime. In the absence of a clear causal connection between violence-glorifying cults and games on one hand and campus shooters on the other, academic freedom argues against profiling Goths and gamers as potential threats. And yet, as horrific incidents multiply down the decades, administrators might be forgiven for considering closer scrutiny of students who fall into these categories.

Case Study No. 3: Virginia Technical University (2007)

The panel investigating the VTU massacre met for the first time on Thursday, May 10, 2007. Present was no less a political light than Virginia Governor Tim Kaine, who commented that "we owe it to the victims" to learn all there is to know about the tragedy. He charged the eight-member commission, chaired by retired State Police Superintendent W. Gerald Massengill, to learn all it can about, among other things, the killer's mental state and mental-health treatment.

In 1966 (as pointed out in Case Study No. 1, above), UT-Austin's resident psychiatrist conducted a session with the tower sniper some three months before the troubled ex-marine climbed to the 28th floor observation deck and shot 45 passers-by. The doctor's notes eerily reported the 25-year-old Whitman's fantasy of shooting at people from the tower.

A decade later, in ***Tarasoff v. Regents of the University of California,*** *551 P.2d 334 (1976),* the California Supreme Court enunciated a duty-to-warn rule, which has been adopted over the past 30 years by much of the American common law. The decision established an obligation among mental-health professionals to warn the known, intended victim of a patient, doctor-patient privilege notwithstanding.

In 1995 the Virginia Supreme Court had occasion to consider the *Tarasoff* rule. In ***Nasser v. Parker,*** *455 S.E.2d 502 (1995),* the Commonwealth's high court stated that "we disagree with the holding of *Tarasoff* that a doctor-patient relationship or a hospital-patient relationship alone is sufficient, as a matter of law, to establish a 'special relation'" with the patient sufficient to fix liability upon the doctor who declines to warn. Under this Virginia precedent, the mental-health caregiver must "take charge" of the mentally ill individual in order to implicate duty-to-warn liability.

In the VTU killer's case, reports indicate that police first investigated the future mass murderer in November 2005, following up on another student's harassment complaint. Cho was directed to the university's Office of Judicial Affairs. The complainant declined to press charges, saying that Cho's unwelcome attentions were merely annoying, not truly harassing.

A month later another female student filed a complaint against Cho with the VTU PD. This time, after the campus police interviewed Cho, another student called to claim that Cho appeared to be suicidal. This call resulted in issuance of a detention order. The troubled young man was subsequently evaluated at Carilion St. Albans Behavioral Health, an independent mental-health facility. Following this counseling intervention, say police, they received no more student complaints about Cho.

Also in the fall of 2005, a VTU poetry professor had Cho removed from her class. Nikki Giovanni told media she found the young man's poetry so intimidating and his presence so menacing that, when two students who shared her anxiety stopped attending class, she moved to remove Cho. Describing Cho as "mean," she told CNN, "I knew when it happened that that's probably who it was."

These facts prompt the questions: In the fall of 2005 should Cho have been removed from more than just Giovanni's poetry class? Should he have been kept in custody—institutionalized—when he was taken to the mental-health facility?

A May 8th editorial in the *Roanoke Times* complains of "No Teeth in Mental Health Laws in Virginia." The piece goes on to contend that Cho's fall 2005 release from custody was inappropriate because he was diagnosed as "depressed and imminently dangerous." In eerie emulation of the UT psychiatrist's suggestion that tower-sniper Whitman make an appointment for the following week, Cho was ordered to pursue outpatient treatment and then released. As with Whitman, Cho's next appearance on the radar screen was gun in hand.

The ultimate question is whether on these facts VTU assumed any legal liability vis-à-vis Cho's victims and their families in terms of a future wrongful-death action. Though the young man's meanness and intimidating behavior in Professor Giovanni's poetry class fit a profile of a potential menace to the campus community, profiling alone cannot form the basis of legal liability for the university. Indeed, whether profiling has any future in campus security is a problematic issue at best.

Under the Virginia Supreme Court's variant of the *Tarasoff* rule, VTU may well be found to have "taken charge" of Cho in 2005. Although he named no specific victims, whom Judicial Affairs and campus police could have warned, the Commonwealth's courts may prove to be sympathetic to injured survivors or the parents of the deceased victims, who choose to sue. The Commonwealth's highest court ultimately may be called upon to determine whether such anticipated wrongful-death actions are capable of prevailing under Virginia common law.

In the wake of the VTU tragedy, numerous institutions have developed "Active Shooter Response" plans.

Active Shooter Response

Since the recent tragic events at Virginia Tech, many people have asked what they should do if caught in an "active shooter" type incident on campus. These kinds of situations are always unpredictable but there are things that should be immediately done to protect oneself.

If it is possible to do so safely, exit the building immediately when you become aware of an incident, moving away from the immediate path of danger, and take the following steps:

Notify anyone you may encounter to exit the building immediately.

1. Evacuate to a safe area away from the danger, and take protective cover. Stay there until emergency responders arrive.

2. Call **911** and the **Rider University Public Safety Department at (609) 896-7777**, providing each dispatcher with the following information:
    a. Your name
    b. Location of the incident (be as specific as possible)
    c. Number of shooters (if known)
    d. Identification or description of shooter(s)
    e. Number of persons who may be involved
    f. Your exact location
    g. Injuries to anyone, if known
3. Individuals not immediately impacted by the situation are to take protective cover, staying away from windows and doors until notified otherwise.

If you are directly involved in an incident and exiting the building is not possible, the following actions are recommended:

If you are not in your room, then go to the nearest room or office.

1. Close and lock the door.
2. Turn off the lights.
3. Seek protective cover. Stay away from doors and windows.
4. Keep quiet and act as if no one is in the room.
5. Do not answer the door.
6. Call **911** and the **Rider University Public Safety Department at 609-896-7777** if it is safe to do so, providing each dispatcher with the following information:
    a. Your name
    b. Your location (be as specific as possible)
    c. Number of shooters (if known)
    d. Identification or description of shooter
    e. Number of persons who may be involved
    f. Injuries if known
7. Wait for police to assist you out of the building.

The Lawrence Township, Princeton Borough, and Princeton Township Police Departments are trained and equipped to respond to an emergency incident of this nature. During the initial phase of the incident, the police will evaluate the situation to determine the best course of action for the safety of the Rider community. Once the police respond, they will be responsible for all tactical operations. Rider University will provide available service assistance.

Follow up assistance is encouraged from available on campus resources (i.e., Student Health, Counseling, Residence Life, Public Safety, Dean of Students, Human Resources).

Courtesy of Rider University Department of Public Safety
(Reprinted with permission of Rider University.)

Impact of the Higher Education Opportunity Act (HEOA)

After student loans, student safety may reasonably be ranked the second most-serious concern of Congress, as reflected in the HEOA. The statute contains numerous, detailed provisions:

Disclosure of On-Campus Crimes

The federal Clery Act already required college and university officials to report incidents of campus crime. The HEOA amends the older federal law by:

- Requiring information to be provided to students and employees in the institution's annual security (Clery) report regarding any agreements with state and local law enforcement agencies for the latter's investigation if alleged criminal offenses on campus
- Adding four additional crimes (larceny, simple assault, intimidation, and destruction or damage of property by vandalism) to the list of annually reportable on-campus crimes, if the offenses were motivated by bias or hate, i.e., if the victim was intentionally selected on the basis of race, gender, religion, sexual orientation, ethnicity or disability.
- Requiring a statement of current campus policies on emergency response and evacuation procedures, which procedures must be tested at least annually, in order to deal with immediate threats to student and staff health and safety.

Missing Persons

Every college and university which offers campus housing must:

- Create a Missing-student notification policy which permits resident students to register contact persons, who will be notified within 24 hours of when the student is determined to have gone missing
- Advise every non-emancipated (under 18) student that a custodial parent or guardian must be so notified
- Advise all students that the appropriate law enforcement agency will be notified within 24 hours of the student going missing
- Initiate emergency contact procedures to alert the campus community that a student has gone missing

Fire Safety

Colleges and universities must publish an annual fire-safety report which includes:

- Number and cause of every fire
- Number of fire-related injuries that resulted in medical-facility treatment
- Number of fire-related deaths
- Value of property damaged by fire
- Description of each residence hall's fire-safety system
- Number of mandatory fire drills
- Policies on electrical appliances, smoking, open flames, evacuation procedures, and fire-safety education
- Plans for future fire-safety improvements

CHAPTER 8

Physical, Mental, and Learning Disabilities

Overview

"Today, there are more students with documented disabilities in higher education than ever before—140,142 freshmen reported having a disability in 1996 (HEATH Resource Center, 1998). That figure represents over 9% of all freshmen (HEATH Resource Center, 1998), as compared with only 2.6% in 1978 (HEATH Resource Center, 1995). Although the process has been slow, colleges and universities (hereafter referred to as '11 colleges') have made their programs more and more accessible, sometimes in good faith, sometimes due to coercion by federal agencies and courts. Only modest progress was made between 1973 (the passage of Section 504 of the Rehabilitation Act) and 1990 (the passage of the Americans with Disabilities Act; ADA); however, once the ADA was passed and amended and regulations were promulgated, institutions that had made little or no progress in making their buildings and programs accessible increased their efforts. Presumably, this increase in part is because of the slightly broader coverage of the ADA, publicity surrounding the passage of the ADA, an increase in the number of administrative appeals and lawsuits, and growth in the number of students requesting accommodation. The greater demand for accommodation can be attributed primarily to the fact that many current college students received either an Individualized Education Program (IEP; as is required by the Individuals with Disabilities Education Act of 1990; IDEA) or a service plan (as is required by Section 504) while in elementary and secondary schools, and have become increasingly aware of their rights to accommodation while in higher education.

"Of particular significance in recent years has been the growth in the number of students with learning disabilities. Over 35% of the freshmen in 1996 who reported having a disability were purported to have a learning disability—an increase from 24.9% in 1991 (HEATH Resource Center, 1998). The growth in the number of students with learning disabilities has created a new challenge to professors and colleges. Over the years, there has been considerable resistance by professors to alter the way they instruct, particularly if such alteration were to accommodate a student with a mental, as compared to a physical, disability. Many professors prefer that all students meet the same set of requirements, within the same time period (see, e.g., *Morse v. University of Vermont,* 1992), and in the same way, and are ill-prepared either to adapt their instruction to address the individual needs of students or to identify appropriate, fair, and reasonable accommodations. This situation is ameliorated somewhat by the assistance provided by administrative units such as Student Disability Services (SDS). This and similar units are responsible for reviewing documentation provided by students and for making a determination as to eligibility status and appropriate accommodations and adjustments, if any. However, such units often are inadequately funded, given the growth in the number of students requesting accommodation, and seldom have experts on staff who are knowledgeable about the wide range of disabilities that colleges are now attempting to accommodate."

College Students and Disability Law

By Stephen B. Thomas (2000)

The ADA is a comprehensive piece of civil rights legislation for individuals with disabilities; Title I of the act, which applies to employment, prohibits discrimination against individuals who are otherwise qualified for employment. The act became law on July 26, 1990, effective two years after that date for employers with twenty-five or more employees and three years from that date for employers with fifteen or more employees. http://www.dol.gov/esa/regs/statutes/ofccp/ada.htm provides the full text of the Americans with Disabilities Act.

Coverage

The ADA applies to both private and public sector employers with fifteen or more employees but does not apply to most federal government employers, American Indian tribes, or bona fide private membership clubs. The Congressional Accountability Act of 1995 [Pub. L. 104-1, 109 Stat. 3] extended the coverage of the ADA and the Rehabilitation Act to the employees of the House of Representatives, the Senate, the Capitol Guide Service, the Capitol Police, the Congressional Budget Office, the Office of the Architect of the Capitol, the Office of the Attending Physician, and the Office of Technology Assessment. The Presidential and Executive Office Accountability Act [Pub. L. 104-331, 110 Stat. 4053] extended coverage of the ADA and the Rehabilitation Act to the Executive Office of the President, the Executive Residence at the White House, and the official residence of the Vice President. United States employers operating abroad or controlling foreign corporations are covered with regard to the employment of U.S. citizens, unless compliance with the ADA would cause the employer to violate the law of the foreign country in which the workplace is located.

The U.S. Supreme Court, in a 5-4 decision, ruled that the Eleventh Amendment of the U.S. Constitution gave the states immunity from individual suits for damages under the ADA, *Board of Trustees of the University of Alabama v. Garrett* [531 U.S. 356 (2001)]. The Court's reasoning in Garrett was consistent with its earlier decision in *Kimel v. Florida Board of Regents* [528 U.S. 62 (2000)].

Provisions

The ADA prohibits covered employers from discriminating in any aspect of employment because of disability against an otherwise qualified individual with a disability. Illegal discrimination under the ADA includes:

...limiting, segregating, or classifying employees or applicants in a way that adversely affects employment opportunities because of disability, using standards or criteria that have the effect of discriminating on the basis of disability or perpetuating discrimination against others, excluding or denying jobs or benefits to qualified individuals because of the disability of an individual with whom a qualified individual is known to associate, failing to make reasonable accommodation to the known limitations of an otherwise qualified individual unless such accommodation would impose an undue hardship, failing to hire an individual who would require reasonable accommodation, and failing to select or administer employment tests in the most effective manner to ensure that the results reflect the skills of applicants or employees with disabilities.

The ADA also prohibits retaliation against any individual because the individual has opposed any act or practice unlawful under the ADA or because the individual has filed a charge or participated in any manner in a proceeding under the ADA. The act also prohibits coercion or intimidation of, threats against, or interference with an individual's exercise of or enjoyment of any rights granted under the act.

Qualified Individual with a Disability

The ADA and the Rehabilitation Act impose obligations not to discriminate against otherwise qualified individuals with disabilities. According to the Supreme Court decision in *Southeastern Community College v. Davis* [442

U.S. 397 (1979)], a person is a qualified individual with a disability if the person "is able to meet all ... requirements in spite of his disability." The individual claiming to be qualified has the burden of demonstrating his or her ability to meet all physical requirements legitimately necessary for the performance of duties. An employer is not required to hire a person with a disability who is not capable of performing the duties of the job; however, the regulations under the act require the employer to make "reasonable accommodation" to the disabilities of individuals.

The ADA defines "qualified individual with a disability" as "an individual with a disability who, with or without reasonable accommodation, can perform the essential functions of the employment position that such individual holds or desires." When determining the essential functions of a job, the court or the EEOC, which administers and enforces the ADA, is to consider the employer's judgment as to what is essential; if a written job description is used for advertising the position or interviewing job applicants, that description is to be considered evidence of the essential functions of the job.

In *Cleveland v. Policy Management Systems* [526 U.S. 795 (1999)], the Supreme Court held that an individual who applies for Social Security disability benefits may still be a "qualified individual with a disability" within the meaning of the ADA. In *Albertsons, Inc. v. Kirkingburg* [527 U.S. 555 (1999)], the Supreme Court held that a truck driver who was not able to meet federal safety standards for commercial motor vehicle operators was not "a qualified individual with a disability" under the ADA; the employer was not required to participate in an experimental program that would have waived the safety standards.

Definition of Disability

The ADA defines "individual with a disability" very broadly: Disability means, with respect to an individual,

(a) a physical or mental impairment that substantially limits one or more of the major life activities of such individual;
(b) a record of such an impairment; or
(c) being regarded as having such an impairment.

Employees who use illegal drugs are not protected by the ADA, nor are alcoholics who use alcohol at the workplace or who are under the influence of alcohol at the workplace. Individuals who are former drug users or recovering drug users, including persons participating in a supervised rehabilitation program and individuals "erroneously regarded" as using drugs but who do not use drugs, are under the ADA's protection.

The definition of disability under the ADA includes infectious or contagious diseases, unless the disease presents a direct threat to the health or safety of others and that threat cannot be eliminated by reasonable accommodation. Temporary or short-term nonchronic conditions, with little or no long-term or permanent impact, are usually not considered disabilities. The act's protection does not apply to an individual who is a transvestite, nor are homosexuality, bisexuality, or sexual behavior disorders such as exhibitionism or transsexualism considered disabilities. Compulsive gambling, kleptomania, pyromania, and psychoactive substance use disorders resulting from current illegal use of drugs are also not within the definition of disability.

In *Sutton v. United Air Lines, Inc.* [527 U.S. 471 (1999)], the Supreme Court held that when determining whether an individual has a disability that substantially limits one or more major life activities, a court must also consider the existence of corrective, mitigating, or remedial measures that may reduce the effect of the disability. Sutton sought a job as a commercial airline pilot but suffered from severe myopia, which rendered her vision at 20/200 or worse in each eye. With corrective lenses (either glasses or contact lenses), however, her vision was functionally equivalent to normal vision. Although her vision problems disqualified her from serving as an airline pilot, the Court held that she was not disabled within the meaning of the ADA definition. Her corrected vision did not substantially limit her in any major life activity, and her myopia was therefore not a disability within the meaning of the ADA. Sutton also claimed that her condition prevented her from being a commercial pilot and thus substantially limited her ability to work, which is a major life activity. The Court rejected that argument, holding that a disability must preclude an individual from a class or range of jobs, rather than simply disqualifying her from a particular or specialized job, to substantially limit her ability to work.

A person claiming protection of the ADA must have a disability, but the mere existence of such a disability is not, in itself, sufficient to establish ADA coverage. The individual's disability must "substantially limit one or more major life activities" for the individual to be disabled within the meaning of the ADA. In the following case, the U.S. Supreme Court considered what an individual must demonstrate in order to establish that the disabling condition substantially limits one or more major life activities.

Universities have a lot to think about when it comes to the sensitive issue of disability. The Americans with Disabilities Act (ADA) prohibits discrimination and in many cases calls for an institution to provide necessary accommodations. These broad definitions are often difficult to apply to individual cases.

Under ADA, not every condition, physical or mental, qualifies a person as legally disabled. The degree of a disability is taken into consideration, namely how limiting the disability is in at least one major life activity. If the student in question's ability to, for instance, walk or work is "substantially" limited, he/she is eligible by law to receive accommodations. If the negative effects of the disability are only "minor," universities are not obligated to provide special services.

Once a student is deemed eligible, "a college is required only to provide reasonable accommodations, not to lower its academic standards." Stephen M. Shore, a UMass graduate with Asperger's syndrome, ran into trouble while pursuing a doctorate in music at Boston University. Mr. Shore was a high achiever in the field of music—he had been able to teach himself to play a number of instruments before high school. However, he often didn't even know where to begin with basic research papers during his time at UMass. This apparent paradox is actually typical of Asperger's, as is an "extremely literal way of thinking."

At Boston University, Mr. Shore was forced to leave the music program when he failed to pass certain tests on music genres. He had no trouble with more structured genres, but others, like the Romantic era, proved impossible for him to comprehend. Mr. Shore requested that certain test questions be rephrased. The request was denied because, according to the university's office of disability services, Boston "provides Asperger's students with assistance on social interaction and time management, but nonetheless requires them to meet the same academic standards as other students." The decision was never challenged, but the university maintains that it was "academically correct."

Under the ADA, universities are only required to provide reasonable accommodations. Accommodations that lower the institutions academic standards or diminish the integrity of its curriculum are not considered reasonable. Common examples include extra time for tests, leaves of absence, preferential seating, and extended deadlines for the completion of a degree program. Accommodations also need only be granted when deemed fitting of the student's disability.

Reprinted with permission of "LD Online," WETA Public Television, Arlington, VA
http://www.ldonline.org/article/6082

Americans with Disabilities Act Amendments Act (2009)

Already identified by the acronym "ADAAA," the new statute is intended to "restore protections for the broad range of individuals with disabilities as originally envisioned by Congress." What this statutory pronouncement of purpose means in practical terms: the express overruling of two U.S. Supreme Court decisions, which collectively cut back the ADA's reach in the American workplace.

1. *Sutton v. United Airlines,* 527 U.S. 471 (1999) held that mitigating and corrective measures, allowing individuals to cope with or control their impairments, might be deemed sufficiently effective as to eliminate the disability for purposes of ADA coverage.
2. *Toyota Motors v. Williams,* 534 U.S. 184 (2002) determined that "Merely having an impairment does not make one disabled for the purposes of the ADA."

These two decisions have proven themselves to be a deadly duo, enabling employers to prevail in a majority of motions to dismiss ADA claims in federal district courts, since the increasingly conservative high court handed them down.

While the conservative "Supremes"—Chief Justice Roberts and Associate Justices Thomas, Scalia, Alito and Kennedy (the same majority which decided *Pyett* on April 1st) control the judiciary—Congress has been regained by the Democrats. Long chafing under the yoke of *Sutton/Toyota*, the Dems' constituents prevailed in the passage of he ADAAA. The new law's main features:

1. "Disability" should be defined broadly, creating a sort of legal presumption in favor of the plaintiff/employee.
2. Mitigating measures, such as medications and prosthetic devices, must be ignored when deciding whether or not a disability exists.
3. Episodic conditions, as well as those in remission, now may qualify as "disabilities."
4. Unless the condition is transitory, i.e., of six months or less in duration, or very minor, a plaintiff/employee may rely on it to successfully sue under the "regarded as" prong of the ADA's disability categories.
5. "Major life activities" are now expressly defined to include standing, bending and lifting; thinking, concentrating, reading and communicating; and all "major bodily functions."

According to Pepper Hamilton LLP, an international law firm headquartered in Philadelphia, "As more individuals fall within the protections of the ADA and as the courts wrestle with the new definitions under the Act, we expect to see more claims filed with the Equal Employment Opportunity Commission and increased litigation." Adds another international law firm, Morgan Lewis, "Thus, the ADAAA is expected to alter in a major way how employers handle disability issues both in the workplace and in litigation."

Attorney Salome Heyward, a nationally recognized expert on student-disability law, commented in an April 3, 2009, lecture at the University of Pennsylvania (attended by your author), "Every civil rights statute has the same lifespan. We enact them, then we set about finding the loopholes." Applying this theorem to the ADA, she claimed, "The lawyers hijacked the law and turned it against the people it was supposed to protect."

How did we get there?" she asked rhetorically. Her answer: "Under section 504 of the Rehabilitation Act, we didn't spend a whole lot of time fighting about" what was a disability. The ADA, however, reached out and touched private business, "which applies a cost-benefit analysis" to everything. "They figured out, if we can prove someone is not disabled, then we win."

Standing alone, explained Heyward, the definition of disability is "just a bunch of words, that don't mean anything in a vacuum." Along came the EEOC, which stated that an impairment is a significant restriction on a major life activity, when the claimant is compared to average people. In *Sutton,* the plaintiff wanted to be a pilot, but was denied the opportunity because she wore glasses. Writing for the majority of the high Court, Justice O'Connor concluded that, under the EEOC definition of disability, Sutton was not disabled. Her glasses corrected the physical shortfall, albeit she still was disqualified by the potential employer from pursuing her chosen career. O'Connor even wondered aloud if working was a major life activity. Recalled Heyward, "I had visions of lawyers dancing in the street."

"It was open season" after *Sutton,* she asserted. She cited a case concerning a grand mal seizure, where according to Heyward, the Court asked the question, "Is consciousness a major life activity?" Another case, she said, required five reported decisions to determine whether a learning disability, which prevented a law school graduate from successfully attempting the bar exam, an impairment of a major life activity. Concluded Heyward, "If it takes five reported decisions to answer this, the standard is a failure."

"Congress thought that, because the Rehab Act had been around for 15 years," said Heyward, "the ADA would mirror section 504." In the ADAAA, Congress "specifically called out the EEOC and its definition, saying it's not an appropriate definition. *Sutton* and *Toyota* were expressly overruled." The Act's preamble essentially directs us to back "to how we did things under the Rehab Act." To understand what that means, suggested Heyward, we might do well to recall the seminal case of *School Bd. of Nassau County, Fla. v. Arline*, 480 U.S. 273 (1987):

Facts. Section 504 of the Rehabilitation Act of 1973 provides that no "otherwise qualified handicapped individual," as defined in 29 U.S.C. § 706(7), shall, solely by reason of his handicap, be excluded from participation in any program receiving federal financial assistance. Section 706(7)(B) defines "handicapped individual" to mean any person who "(i) has a physical ... impairment which substantially limits one or more of [his] major life activities, (ii) has a record of such an impairment, or (iii) is regarded as having such an impairment." Department of Health and Human Services (HHS) regulations defined "physical impairment" to mean, *inter alia,* any physiological disorder affecting the respiratory system, and define "major life activities" to include working. Gene Arline was hospitalized for tuberculosis in 1957. The disease went into remission for the next 20 years, during which time she began teaching elementary school in Florida. In 1977, and again in March and November 1978, she had relapses. After the latter two, she was suspended with pay for the rest of the school year. At the end of the 1978–1979 school year, the school district discharged her after a hearing, because of the continued recurrence of tuberculosis. After she was denied relief in state administrative proceedings, she brought suit in federal district court, alleging a violation of § 504. The district court held that she was not a "handicapped person" under the Act, but that, even assuming she were, she was not "qualified" to teach elementary school. The court of appeals reversed, holding that persons with contagious diseases are within § 504's coverage, and remanded for further findings as to whether respondent was "otherwise qualified" for her job. The Supreme Court granted *certiorari.*

Holdings. Writing for the majority, Justice Brennan held:

1. A person afflicted with the contagious disease of tuberculosis may be a "handicapped individual" within the meaning of § 504.
    a. Arline was a "handicapped individual" as defined in § 706(7)(B) and the HHS regulations. Her hospitalization in 1957, for a disease that affected her respiratory system, and that substantially limited "one or more of [her] major life activities," established that she has a "record of ... impairment."
    b. The fact that a person with a record of impairment is also contagious does not remove that person from § 504's coverage. To allow an em-

ployer to justify discrimination by distinguishing between a disease's contagious effects on others and its physical effects on a patient would be unfair, would be contrary to § 706(7)(B)(iii) and the legislative history, which demonstrate Congress's concern about an impairment's effect on others, and would be inconsistent with § 504's basic purpose to ensure that handicapped individuals are not denied jobs because of the prejudice or ignorance of others. The Act replaced such fearful, reflexive reactions with actions based on reasoned and medically sound judgments as to whether contagious handicapped persons are "otherwise qualified" to do the job.

2. In most cases, in order to determine whether a person handicapped by contagious disease is "otherwise qualified" under § 504, the district court must conduct an individualized inquiry and make appropriate findings of fact, based on reasonable medical judgments given the state of medical knowledge, about (a) the nature of the risk (e.g., how the disease is transmitted), (b) the duration of the risk (how long is the carrier infectious), (c) the severity of the risk (what is the potential harm to third parties), and (d) the probabilities the disease will be transmitted and will cause varying degrees of harm. In making these findings, courts normally should defer to the reasonable medical judgments of public health officials. Courts must then determine, in light of these findings, whether any "reasonable accommodation" can be made by the employer under the established standards for that inquiry.
3. Because the district court did not make appropriate findings, it is impossible for this Court to determine whether respondent is "otherwise qualified" for the job of elementary school teacher, and the case is remanded for additional findings of fact.

Arline and the ADAAA

Concluded Heyward in her April 3rd remarks at Penn, "*Arline* calls for a case-by-case, individualized inquiry." Furthermore, under the amendments, "We can no longer cherry pick those factors that support our position. For instance, one standardized test score cannot be the 'Holy Grail.' We must do a balancing" of all the available evidence in a particular case. Considerations specifically highlighted by Heyward included:

1. Objective medical evidence of the nature and severity of the alleged impairment, provided by qualified experts, will rule. Exemplifying bogus

claims, she added, is so-called "test anxiety." "When I took the bar exam with 1,400 others in the same room, we all had test anxiety," she recalled with a smile. This in itself is not a disability, unless the claimant can document an "underlying psychotic condition."

2. What is the claimant's present level of performance? Heyward cited a case concerning Philadelphia's Temple University in which a student tried to connect her alleged anorexia to her failure to pass one class. However, she had done well in all her other courses. Overall, her present level of performance, concluded Heyward, belied her disability claim.
3. What impact does the disability have on a major life activity? Congress, said Heyward, has now made it clear that working and learning are major activities, something that the common law had called into question. However, the courts are directed to look to "broad ability" to perform the life activity.
4. Who is the average person to whom the claimant should be compared? Heyward argued that the comparison should be made to similarly situated people. Thus, a college student should be compared to other college students, not to the public at large. The same would seem to be true of an allegedly disabled professional person.
5. When evaluating a disability, consider past performance, as well as the compatibility of a claimant's statements and behavior. Remember, Heyward cautioned, that persons from minority groups may never have been diagnosed as disabled, when in the K–12 system, due to limited school-district resources.
6. Asperger's syndrome and autism are on the rise in American society. Returning war veterans are manifesting post-traumatic stress disorders. "'Traditional counseling' of troubled students and employees is no longer an effective model" in the post-Virginia Tech world, she said. I agree.

Checklist: Disability-Litigation Prevention Guidelines

1. Establish and publish reasonable and sufficient guidelines for students to follow in their efforts to document a disability (e.g., a former IEP; documentation from an appropriately licensed professional).
2. Review financial aid practices and remove where possible any provisions that result in discrimination against, or otherwise adversely affect, students with disabilities.
3. Review admission procedures to ensure that they do not arbitrarily deny or unnecessarily delay the admission of students with disabilities.

4. Make reasonable efforts to keep abreast of new technologies and instructional methodologies that may assist a student with a disability to be otherwise qualified.
5. Within the Student Disability Services (SDS) staff, employ one or more individuals who has knowledge of disability law and assessment of disabilities in adults.
6. Ensure that SDS is sufficiently staffed and adequately funded to address the increasing number of inquiries and demands for accommodation.
7. Engage in the in-service training of administrators, staff, and professors regarding the need for accommodation and access.
8. Periodically assess buildings and grounds to determine accessibility.
9. Examine academic and disciplinary procedures to eliminate those that would impermissibly discriminate against students with disabilities.
10. Handle inquiries and requests for accommodation in a timely fashion.
11. Investigate allegations of noncompliance and discrimination promptly and efficiently.

Reprinted with permission of "LD Online," WETA Public Television, Arlington, VA
http://www.ldonline.org/article/6082

Physical Disabilities

Service Animals

It is well known that the ADA says colleges must accommodate students requiring the assistance of a guide dog. The dog may remain on campus with the student regardless of any campus policy otherwise forbidding pets. Guide dogs, while the most common example, are not the only animals allowed under ADA. All "service animals," which ADA defines as "any guide dog, signal dog, or other animal individually trained to do work or perform tasks for an individual with a disability," are fair game.

Recent requests for permission to have snakes, ferrets, and cats on campus have caught colleges off guard. The grounds for this odd trend are "emotional support." Students suffering from mental illnesses such as depression, bipolar disorder, and schizophrenia claim that their pets provide them with "psychiatric service," qualifying them as service animals under ADA. Many colleges are skeptical, and the courts have yet to make a clear decision. In the meantime, uncertainty has led to a wide range of reactions; some colleges are refusing all requests while others are "too quick to accommodate even unreasonable requests, fearing lawsuits."

In general, the ADA and the Fair Housing Act have been interpreted as applying only to those animals that perform concrete tasks. With one exception, emotional support has never been included. That exception, however, directly supports the positions of many students demanding to bring their pets on campus. A 1994 case saw a judge order an apartment complex to allow a woman with depression keep her dog, disregarding their no-pet policy.

At universities, the decision is usually more complex. Many students not only wish to keep their "service" animals in their dorm rooms, they want to bring them to class. This of course has administrators worried about the animals causing distractions and in the long run turning the campus into a zoo. Some schools also argue that some animals, such as snakes or certain dogs, might violate campus health and safety policies. A disability consultant cites an example in which a student once asked to leave her pit bull–rottweiler mix at the campus day-care center.

Rutgers University in New Brunswick (NJ) reached the decision of partially accommodating five psychiatric-service animal requests. The dog, snake, and three cats in question were given permission to live on campus with their owners in the university's garden-style apartments. Such animals are still not allowed to stay in standard dormitory buildings in sight of other students with allergies and phobias.

Whatever the decision, all colleges should clearly spell out their policy and differentiate between service animals and emotional-support animals. A good policy clearly defines the two and explains the duties of the disabled party, as well as those of other students and faculty members. Any areas off-limits to the animals must be included. For example, the University of Wisconsin at Madison does not allow animals in laboratories (with exceptions), mechanical rooms, or any other potentially dangerous places. Lastly, the policy should spell out grounds for removal of service animals from the campus. (See University of Wisconsin at Madison website for example policy.)

At the moment, the ADA does not explicitly say that colleges must accommodate animals not falling into the traditional service category. Administrators should prepare for the possibility, though. The amount of research and case studies is still insufficient to be conclusive, but more and more mental health professionals are accepting the idea that animals can have positive effects on the mentally ill. It is already common knowledge that elderly people benefit from an animal's presence, and studies have proven animals' ability to lower one's blood pressure. It is not unthinkable that a dog could comfort and reassure its owner during a panic attack or a wave of depression. A revision to the ADA could in the near future deem a therapist's note justification for a student to keep his/her "pet" on campus.

Gallaudet University: A Case Study in Reverse Discrimination?

In September and October of 2006, student demonstrations at Gallaudet University, the only liberal-arts college specifically designed for the higher education of students who are deaf or hard of hearing, in Washington, D.C., created such a frenzy that many were comparing it to the student revolution of the 1960s. Characterized by passionate student protestors, boycotting and canceling of classes, the occupation of campus buildings, and finally, mass arrests, the campus was completely shut down for three days, but classes were ultimately canceled for at least two weeks due to protestors' lockouts and threats. The origin of all this chaos and anger? The appointment of Jane K. Fernandes as president of the university—a woman deemed by many of Gallaudet's students and some of its administrators as "not deaf enough" to serve the school.

On October 29, Fernandes, who had been unanimously selected from the board of trustees after beating out 24 other applicants, had her contract revoked by the trustees after weeks of upheaval. Despite having been born deaf, having a deaf mother and brother, and devoting her career to deaf education, Fernandes was considered "not deaf enough" because she grew up learning to use her voice and was not a native user of American Sign Language (ASL), which she didn't learn until the age of 23. Fernandes could be described as a user of Pidgin Signed English (PSE), which is a mix of English and ASL—thus, she cannot speak the way users of pure ASL can, in a manner that is completely separate from English or any spoken language. Furthermore, Fernandes used both her hands and her voice to communicate, something that was seen as politically incorrect to those who support "pure" deafness—a belief that the deaf are a linguistic and even ethnic minority, that deaf people should never wish they can hear or speak, and that the deaf should speak fluent ASL and nothing else.

Deaf activists model their ideas after the civil rights movement, proclaiming themselves a separate culture defined by their language and shared experiences. They aim to have deafness seen as a social group instead of as a biological deficiency or a handicap. However, by defining themselves as a linguistic minority or culture, deaf activists are forced to form rigid perceptions of who is deaf and who isn't, consequently shutting out those who were taught orally, were not born deaf, use cochlear implants, are only partially deaf or hard of hearing, did not have the means to learn ASL, or do not use ASL for any other reason. In short, strict interpretation of deafness creates the image a "pure" or perfect deaf person, and ultimately imitates, in the words of one pundit, "the worst aspects of racial profiling." These terms end up reducing the rights of many people.

At Gallaudet, the main disagreement between protestors and Fernandes existed in the idea of "Total Communication," which says that students and professors should be able to use any form of communication that works best for the situation. Fernandes wrote in an email interview, "As [Gallaudet is] a federally funded university… I strongly believe that every deaf, hard of hearing or deaf-blind child in the United States, regardless of schooling, family background, language or communication choices… or other differences, has a rightful place at Gallaudet." Protestors believed that ASL should be used as the sole language for the deaf in order to preserve the purity of the language and uphold respect for it and its associated culture, but this position created concern for many students who, although deaf, might only have been novices at ASL. Many professors who supported the idea of an ASL-only school had already put the policy into effect in their classrooms, despite Gallaudet's opposing rules, making it difficult for many students to learn.

The ASL-only policy was not the first time students forced a decision upon Gallaudet. In 1988, a hearing woman was given the position of president, but resigned after only three days because of a student protest that insisted upon the selection of a deaf president. Thus, some people wondered if the school had made a mistake in ultimately allowing its students to select the university's administrator. However, the 1988 protest had been far less personal and offensive than the ordeal Fernandes was put through.

In the fight to have Fernandes fired, students attacked Fernandes' signing skills and her apparent lack of "deaf purity" and "deaf pride." However, protestors also attacked her personal life, citing her appearance, marriage, family, and social skills as detrimental, saying that she was not a people person and that she probably married her husband in order to get a job at the university. These accusations stemmed almost solely from discrimination based on her limited use of ASL.

Is it possible for a university such as Gallaudet to be guilty of reverse disability discrimination? At first glance, the applicable statutes, notably the ADA, would seem to say "no." To be covered by the protections of the ADA, let us remind ourselves, an individual must be

1. Physically or mentally impaired in a way that substantially limits some major life activity;
2. Have a record of suffering from such an impairment; or

3. Be regarded as having such an impairment.

A job applicant or employee whose hearing falls within the normal human range would seem to fall outside this definition.

However, if one looks more closely at the third of these mutually exclusive criteria, one might well wonder if the deaf majority at Gallaudet do not indeed deal with unimpaired applicants and employees as if it is they who are disabled.

The legal theory of reverse disability discrimination has not gained much, if any, traction in the American common law. For example, in ***Johnson v. University of Iowa,*** *431 F.3d 325 (U.S. Court of Appeals, 8th Circuit, 2005),* a father challenged the university's policy of providing disability leave to biological mothers while denying the same benefit to new fathers. Johnson's case was more in the nature of a reverse sex-discrimination claim. But in essence it turned upon the court's conclusion that most newly delivered biological mothers are indeed disabled during the first six weeks or so after giving birth, while the same cannot be said of biological fathers. Thus, the case can be read—at least inferentially—as rejecting a claim of reverse disability discrimination, i.e., denying new fathers the same leave as afforded to new mothers on the ground that they are not physically impaired from returning to work. The court held that, because Johnson had no inherent legal right to paternity leave, not only his sex-discrimination, but also his "equal protection of the law" claims must fail.

In ***Dewyer v. Temple University,*** *89 Fed. Appx. 811 (U.S. Court of Appeals, 3d Circuit, 2004),* although the court affirmed dismissal of the plaintiff's ADA claim, the judicial panel's characterization of a "regarded as impaired" claim is illuminating:

"A person is regarded as disabled if the person:

1. Has a physical or mental impairment that does not substantially limit major life activities but is treated by the covered entity as constituting such limitation;
2. Has a physical or mental impairment that substantially limits major life activities only as a result of the attitudes of others toward such impairment; or
3. Has [no such impairment] but is treated by a covered entity as having a substantially limiting impairment."

The third prong of this Third Circuit test is particularly intriguing. Is it not the case that hearing applicants and employees, denied equal treatment by Gallaudet, are being "treated by a covered entity as having a substantially limiting impairment"? Admittedly, the court goes on to say that "In order for a case to fall under the 'regarded as prong,' an employer must 'regard the employee to be suffering from an impairment' within the meaning of the statutes," citing another of its precedents, Rinehimer v. Cemcolift, Inc., 292 F.3d 375, 381 (3d Cir.2002). However, as we have noted above, many deaf persons—students, professors and administrators alike—regard their own impairment as a cultural, rather than a physical, phenomenon, and by logical extension of this view, consider hearing persons to be at a distinct disadvantage within the campus culture of Gallaudet.

Mental Disabilities

Psychological Disabilities

The grey area of psychological disabilities, such as depression and bipolar disorder, makes it especially difficult for universities to know what is required of them. Officials cannot always recognize the disability through physical symptoms, and requested accommodations often have a more direct effect on the academic standards of a university. This can require a more detailed analysis of a case, but the basic standards of ADA can still be relied on through correct interpretation.

Amir v. St. Louis University, *184 F.3d 1017 (U.S. Court of Appeals, 8th Circuit, 1999).* Guy Amir, diagnosed with obsessive-compulsive disorder, had had academic difficulties from the beginning of his studies at SLU's Medical School. He was allowed a leave of absence during his first year in the program and returned without further problems until the clinical phase of his studies. The worsening of his disorder at that time resulted in a physician at SLU's clinic, Robin Park, M.D., to urge Amir to seek help through hospitalization. When he tried to return, he was at first denied by Dr. Park due to "prolonged absence."

After filing a grievance in which "Amir alleged that Dr. Park coerced him into hospitalization and discriminated against him based upon his disorder," Amir was allowed to return and finish his studies. His grievance, however, was rejected, and he was to complete his clinical phase under Dr. Park. Although Amir passed each portion of the clinic, Dr. Park failed him based on a new grading policy instated shortly before Amir's return. The new policy "allowed a supervisor greater discretion in issuing a student a failing grade," and was instated by the department Dr. Park resided over as chairman.

This was not sufficient evidence for the Eighth Circuit Court of Appeals to deem Dr. Park's behavior discriminatory or related to Amir's disability. Amir's other requests to complete his studies at another institution and to receive a passing grade were also found to be unreasonable. SLU did not allow Amir to study elsewhere based on general academic policy not specific to his case, and the denial of a passing grade was an "academic decision." The court ruled that all of Amir's requests were "not logically related to the functional aspects of the disability" and asked SLU to significantly alter or lower its academic standards and policies. All requests were denied.

Learning Disabilities

Learning disabilities, such as dyslexia and attention-deficit disorder, are dealt with in a manner similar to psychological disorders. Accommodations may be made to the extent that academic standards are not lowered and the key goals or activities of a course are not fundamentally altered.

Wynne v. Tufts University School of Medicine, *507 U.S. 1030 (U.S. Supreme Court, 1993).* After failing the majority of his classes in his first year at Tufts, Steven Wynne was diagnosed with dyslexia and granted accommodations by the university. Tufts allowed Wynne to repeat the classes he had failed "with the assistance of counseling, tutors, note-takers, and taped lectures." He was also required to audit the classes he had only narrowly passed. Tufts refused to offer Wynne an alternative to multiple-choice exams, with which Wynne had significant difficulty on account of his disability.

Wynne this time managed to pass all but two courses; he was allowed the opportunity to retake the final exam for each. He passed one but failed the other. Based on these results, Wynne was officially dismissed from Tufts.

Wynne filed a complaint with the Office of Civil Rights based mostly on Tufts's refusal to accommodate his request for non-multiple-choice testing. The 1st Circuit Court of Appeals went back and forth with the case, but ultimately ruled in favor of Tufts. Tufts's explanation that "critical thinking skills were taught by use of multiple choice exams" justified the conclusion that such a change in curriculum was too significant and would lower Tufts's academic standards. Removing multiple-choice exams would have made it impossible for certain basic requirements to be met.

Important to note in the above case is how Tufts went about establishing the basis for their decision to deny Wynne's request. When presenting their case before the 1st Circuit, Tufts was able to show:

1. The appropriate university officials with pertinent responsibilities and experience had considered the requested accommodation.

2. These officials had considered (a) the potential effects of the requested accommodation on the academic program and institution and (b) the availability of alternatives.
3. The conclusion that the requested accommodation was unreasonable had been reached in a rational and thoughtful manner.

In contrast, the University of Colorado's decision to deny medical residency to an applicant with multiple sclerosis was ruled unjustified by the 10th Circuit in ***Pushkin v. Regents of the University of Colorado,*** *658 F.2d 1372 (U.S. Court of Appeals, 10th Circuit, 1981)*. The interview committee at Colorado had reached the conclusions that Dr. Pushkin, the applicant, would not be able to handle the stress or tasks of the position at Colorado's Psychiatry unit. However, because these conclusions were based on nothing more than the committee's initial impressions after their 45-minute interview with Dr. Pushkin, the court ruled in Pushkin's favor. The lack of thought and consideration that Colorado invested in their decision justified Pushkin's case and allowed the court to conclude that the interview committee had based its decision largely on stereotypes associated with multiple sclerosis.

Determining the severity of a student's learning disability can be even more difficult than that of a psychological disability. It is still debated "whether a student should be compared with the general population or against other undergraduate or graduate students when determining if he or she has a disability." Many argue that, based on the statistic that only about one third of the age 18–24 population is enrolled at a university, the learning disabled are high achievers when compared with the rest of their age group. Comparing them with the average non-disabled college student would be a completely different story.

Wong v. Regents of the University of California, *410 F.3d 1052 (U.S. Court of Appeals, 9th Circuit, 2005)*. Andrew H.K. Wong was dismissed from the University of California at Davis's medical school after failing to meet academic requirements during his third year clinical clerkship. He filed suit on the grounds that he had been denied appropriate accommodation for his learning disability. The 9th Circuit Court of Appeals ultimately reached their decision after comparing Wong to the general population.

The court cited Wong's academic history, which was "filled with contradictions." His disability was first identified in kindergarten, but he was then found to be gifted in elementary school. He was later put into an assisted learning class and often requested extra time for assignments and exams in high school and at college. Nonetheless, Wong graduated from San Francisco State University with

Magna Cum Laude and a GPA of 3.54. He then earned his master's at the same institution in cellular/molecular biology.

After failing the Medical College admission test three times, Wong passed and completed his first two years at Davis with a solid grade average—all without special accommodation. His grades then plummeted at the start of his third year. It was then that Davis's Disability Resource Center first diagnosed Wong "as having a learning impairment that limited his ability to process and communicate information." In response, Wong was granted substantial accommodations until UC called one of his requests "unreasonable, unfair, and contrary to the purposes of the curriculum." Wong failed his following clerkship and was deemed unqualified to continue at the medical school.

"Wong's prior academic success…was viewed as fatally inconsistent with his claim to be disabled" by the 9th Circuit. Wong had demonstrated in the past that he was capable of learning as well as or better than the average member of the general population. The decision supports the position that students with learning disabilities can be best weighted against the general population. This is the direction in which the courts have recently been going.

Depression and Suicidal Tendencies

In April 2006, a settlement was reached between the Massachusetts Institute of Technology and the parents of student Elizabeth H. Shin. In 2000, Ms. Shin took her own life after making suicidal threats. Based on grounds that MIT had known of Ms. Shin's imminent danger to herself and failed to take appropriate action, her parents sued the university for $27 million. A similar decision was reached in the he 2002 student suicide case ***Schieszler v. Ferrum College**, 236 F. Supp. 602 (U.S. District Court, W.D. Virginia, 2002)***. Also settled outside the courtroom, a Virginia federal court had "found that Ferrum officials had a legal duty to ensure the safety of the deceased student, Michael Frentzel, because they knew of the 'imminent probability' that he would try to harm himself." These cases have resulted in controversial policy changes by many other universities now worried about liability.

Mandatory-leave policies are many schools' answer to potentially suicidal students. Gary Pavela, director of judicial programs at the University of Maryland at College Park and author of *Questions and Answers on College Suicide: A Law and Policy Perspective*, sees this reaction as based purely on a risk-management perspective. It ignores the educational responsibilities of institutions, which include working with and helping their students through difficult times. In October 2004, Jordan Nott was one such student suspended from his university (George Washington University) after reporting his depression to the campus hospital. "I thought it took a lot of courage to say I need help, I need to talk to someone, I want to be healthy, I want to be happy. But this was something that made me feel even worse," said Nott after receiving the news from an administrator.

Such a policy is not only ethically questionable, but it can now result in exactly what institutions are trying to avoid: lawsuits. A university like George Washington may dodge a liability case similar to that of MIT. However, George Washington is now being sued on the grounds that such a mandatory leave policy is in violation of federal disability law, which also protects individuals with mental health issues. "If you live by risk management, you can die by risk management."

In 2004, Bluffton University handled a student who had attempted suicide in a similar manner. The university refused to take the student's bipolar disorder into account and did not allow her to appeal. In 2005, the civil-rights office wrote to the university in response. In the letter the office acknowledges that universities may address "the dangers posed by an individual who represents a 'direct threat' to the health and safety of self and others, even if such an individual is a person with a disability." However, the office also writes, "to rise to the level of a direct threat, there must be a high probability of substantial harm and not just a slightly increased, speculative, or remote risk." The university's decision may not be based on "unfounded fear, prejudice, or stereotypes."

In the George Washington case, Nott has argued that he never made a suicide threat or did anything else to indicate he could be suicidal at any time, including the night he was admitted into the campus hospital. This greatly contrasts the case of Ms. Shin, who had already attempted suicide before and told her dorm supervisor of her intent to do so again. There is no evidence to indicate that Mr. Nott was behaving in a manner at all like that of Ms. Shin, which will make it difficult for George Washington to claim that the grounds for Nott's dismissal were anything other than the "unfounded fear" described above. Nott was depressed and in need of help, but a "direct threat"?

Mr. Pavela recommends using discipline "as a lever to get them [students] the help they need—but not using discipline as a hammer." In this way, students are threatened with suspension if they don't seek help. Such punishment should only be used as "a last resort" to use the words of Bill Haggard, associate vice chancellor for student affairs at Western Carolina University. The university's policy stems from its early attempts to get students with eating disorders to seek treatment. Students often refused in the past, but the policy has since created the necessary "leverage to encourage students to get help." The policy seems to be effective as even a single student has yet to be dismissed.

Sources

Allen, Charlotte. "Identity Politics Gone Wild: The Deaf Culture Wars at Gallaudet University." *The Weekly Standard*, 2007, 012(28).

Davis, J. Lennard. "Deafness and the Riddle of Identity." *Chronicle of Higher Education*, Jan. 12, 2007, p. B6.

HEATH Resource Clearinghouse, http://www.heath.gwu.edu/

CHAPTER 9

Privacy Rights and Intellectual Property Issues

In a world that is changing so much and so quickly, the rules that govern it are forced to do the same. Privacy rights and intellectual property laws are no exception, and they are two issues that cannot be ignored by universities.

The first issue of privacy rights in regard to students' records has a very direct impact on higher education. The Federal Educational Rights and Privacy Act of 1974 (FERPA) provides the guidelines concerning educational records, student and parent access to them, and the obligation of universities to protect that information. The U.S. education system has had more than 20 years to test these boundaries with recent circumstances demonstrating new interpretations.

With intellectual property, two areas apply on a large scale to universities. The first is written media. Plagiarism has been a matter of concern for a long time, and it isn't difficult to imagine that it is an exceptionally large problem on campus. With the Internet have come new rules and possibilities when it comes to information and, therefore, also plagiarism. This topic is covered thoroughly in Chapter Five.

The second area is perhaps not as obviously an issue for universities. Piracy of copyrighted audiovisual media has increased immensely since the Internet's debut. Of course on-line downloading and copying of songs and movies occurs off campus, but a particularly large amount of attention is being paid to higher education institutions by organizations fighting these crimes. With the advanced on-line networks most competitive universities offer, it is no wonder that many students choose to take advantage of the opportunity to create enormous digital libraries at virtually no cost. But to what degree are universities responsible for enforcing copyright law?

Students' Privacy Rights and the Federal Educational Rights and Privacy Act (FERPA)

FERPA was passed in 1974 and amended in 2009 to help colleges, students and other third parties understand their rights of access to student records. The law pertains to all schools receiving funds from the U.S. Department of Education.

At first glance, it may seem cut and dry. Students and parents have access to their records at any time, and the university is obligated to protect the data from anyone else. However, the law, like most laws, is not that simple and leaves room for much more interpretation (U.S. Department of Education, 2005).

University students are guaranteed access to their records within a 45-day period of request, but the school is not required to offer a hard copy. If the student is located far enough away from the campus to hinder visiting, the university may choose to send the records to another institution in the student's area where the documents can then be viewed. Many universities do offer hard copies of student records with, of course, the applicable copy fees (Lipka, 2006).

Parents and guardians have no guaranteed access to a student's records. Should they request this access, the student must first be claimed as a dependent on their tax return. Even then, the university does not have to comply. FERPA more or less says that universities may choose when they do or don't want to offer records to parents and guardians. LeRoy S. Rooker, director of the Family Policy Compliance Office at the U.S. Department of Education, notes that, while it is a school's right to conceal a student's records from these third parties, for public-relations reasons, it is generally in the school's interest to maintain "institutional consistency on what kinds of records are or are not disclosed." The same can apply to the issue of hard copies (Lipka, 2006).

Exceptions to FERPA include allowing appropriate officials to view records for legitimate legal, health or safety reasons. One recent example is an antiterrorism investigation following September 11, 2001. The FBI received information about students who had applied for financial aid in order to determine whether suspected terrorists were using student identities to obtain federal money. The investigation was within the legal limits of FERPA; in fact, the government is more or less guaranteed access to all information on Fafsa forms. Only if the university adds information to the form can a violation of FERPA be considered (Selingo, 2006).

This investigation, which was discovered around the middle of 2006, is of particular interest now due to a controversial new system proposal for tracking student records. The most controversial issue at the moment is government access to student records for the purpose of tracking individual student progress and evaluating institutions. The federal government has been considering a plan to follow student progress and more accurately determine university statistics since 2004 (Gidjunis, 2004).

The unit-record system, which was put into motion by the Bush administration and Republican Congress leaders, would give the government the right to track any individual's educational progress upon enrolling at a higher education institution. The new system would replace Ipeds, surveys of colleges that report on figures such as enrollment, tuition and faculty salaries. Many now consider Ipeds inadequate. They focus only on colleges' full tuition prices and not what students actually pay after financial aid. They also do not follow transfer students; "those who earn a bachelor's degree from a four-year college other than the one in which they first enrolled are counted as dropouts" (Gidjunis, 2004).

The proposed system should, of course, take these things into account because it literally would follow a student's every move with access to personal, academic, financial aid and enrollment data. Private colleges are especially against the new system due to concern that student data is at enough risk as it is. The system was first proposed at a time when identity theft was already an increasing problem, and the removal of social security numbers and other personal data from student records was being considered. The new policy is a step in the opposite direction (Gidjunis, 2004).

A poll in 2006 showed that the majority of Americans are against the unit-record system (Walters, 2006). On the other hand, schools like the University of Georgia have replaced student IDs with biometric scanners. Students must place their hands on sensors to gain access to the university library, gym or cafeteria. The biometric data is, consequently, also a part of the University of Georgia's files (Kiernan, 2005).

The 2009 FERPA Amendments:

- Redefine "personally identifiable information"
- Rule out disclosure of educational records to a student's former school for evaluation or accountability purposes
- Allow limited authorization for studies to improve instruction.

Case Study: Ohio University Security Breach

In April 2006, the FBI brought a security breach to the Ohio University's attention. The administration at first thought that the breached server did not contain any sensitive data, but upon further investigation they discovered that 35 Social Security numbers had been exposed. Things turned far grimmer when IT found an alumni-relations office server had been unintentionally left online. Hackers had broken into the server in March 2005 and had been using it for music file sharing. What this meant for Ohio University was that "300,000 files containing personal information about alumni and university staff members, including 137,000 Social Security numbers, had been exposed for more than a year."

And that was not all. Three other servers/computers had also been breached over the 13-month period. Thousands of tax forms, medical records, a dozen credit card numbers and even more Social Security numbers had been made available to hackers.

Some $77,000 was spent notifying hundreds of thousands of alumni of the security breach through e-mails and letters. In the three weeks following the discovery of the breach, Ohio University spent $750,000 re-securing its main servers. A consultant was also hired to determine how and why the breach occurred.

In short, the disaster was attributed to negligence. Ohio University had not been providing sufficient funds to maintain security of its electronic files, and its IT departments were disorganized and inefficient. There is also evidence that Ohio University had seen warning signals before the incident, including a student who accidentally stumbled upon sensitive student data, but failed to act.

In addition to the over $800,000 spent directly after the shock, Ohio University quickly invested $4 million in its IT program. Two system administrators were fired, and the IT chief information officer resigned. Eight hundred angry e-mails and letters were received from alumni, and, as stated in many of the complaints, the university lost many regular donors. Ohio University so far faces one potential class-action lawsuit and knows of more than thirty other cases of identity theft among alumni.

The breach was a big wake-up call not only for the Ohio University but the higher education world in general. The costs and ramifications have so far been great, and it is yet to be a closed case. Although it is doubtful that a link between much of the identity theft and the incident can be proven, the university has certainly suffered a terrible blow to its reputation, a public relations nightmare.

Advice. Computers and Internet have proven to be practical for a variety of jobs, but they are luxuries that require caution. Organizations responsible for sensitive data must exercise extreme caution. The Ohio University breach may be the biggest to date, but it is not an isolated incident. Eighty other universities' systems have been hacked into in the last two years. Many, such as the University of San Diego, are well-financed institutions.

Universities are by nature difficult to secure. They are decentralized and store information in different computers and systems across the campus. One student's information can be available on several databases concerning library fines, enrollment, meal plans and campus activities. Ohio University has introduced a plan for tightening IT security. Social Security numbers will be used within fewer databases, a strong and clear structure will be created in the IT departments and the necessary security levels will be maintained for sensitive data.

Educause, a higher education technology organization, recommends that such policies be standards at universities. Rodney J. Peterson, a policy analyst at Educause, points out that "the challenge for college system administrators is to develop security policies that protect the institution's data but are flexible enough to accommodate its varied missions" (Wasley, 2006). It is unlikely that colleges can offer 100% security of data without turning into police states. Some college officials believe that there is no way to be sure all systems are safe. "No matter how much we invest in technology, no matter how good our IT staff is, there's nothing we can institutionally do to protect ourselves completely," says Dennis A. Trinkle, chief information officer of Valparaiso University (Foster, 2006).

Many states have adopted laws requiring public and private colleges to notify individuals affected by data breaches. Although not yet mandatory, many colleges invest in offering credit-monitoring services to clients whose data was exposed. As shown by Ohio University, these are costly measures, but they may only be the beginning. Should the case against Ohio University be certified as a class-action lawsuit (the first of its kind), hundreds of thousands of people would be eligible to receive damages for the university's failure to secure their data (Foster, 2006).

Based on these circumstances, some institutions have invested in cyber-insurance policies similar to those used by banks, hospitals and retailers. The number of colleges to buy policies has gone up this year, but it is still relatively rare. Many still feel there is not enough evidence of financially significant breaches to justify cyber-insurance. The general opinion seems to be that there isn't enough information to be sure one way or the other. The decision for a class action in the Ohio University case would most likely provide the turning point and put cyber-insurance on its way to becoming a higher education standard (Foster, 2006).

The near future should offer more concrete facts regarding the issue, but until then, a cyber-insurance policy is certainly a safe move. It should not, however, replace solid Internet security. Insurance may cover the financial costs of data theft, but not the damage done to a school's reputation and public relations.

Intellectual Property

"The concept of intellectual property is almost dead thanks to the Internet" (Khanna, 2004). That is a grim statement that cannot be ignored. The Internet has changed our world enormously, opening new doors of communication and access to knowledge. Such privilege does not come without responsibility, as the degree to which it can be taken advantage of is enormous. The idea of intellectual property is to treat knowledge like private property, using copyrights, trademarks and patents to enforce the notion.

Some see turning intellectual property into private property as an "enclosure of the commons" that hinder the advancement of science and democracy (Monaghan, 2005). On the other hand, one of the first statements of fair use dates back to the Talmud. It is written that a person "who reports something in the name of the one who said it brings redemption into the world" (McLemee, 2004). As interpreted by Rabbi Joseph Telushkin, the statement means that when a person fails to accredit a piece of information, he/she uses it for personal gain. When properly accredited, the information is being used for the purpose of expanding everyone's knowledge (McLemee, 2004).

This is one of the main arguments behind the ethical issue of plagiarism. Unlike copyright infringement, plagiarism includes more than directly copying a passage. The use of another person's idea without citation is also a form of plagiarism. Copyright law enforces economic interest, the violation of which can result in judicial punishment. Plagiarism enforces personal and ethical interest and will rarely go beyond the dean's office. One may not go to court for plagiarism, but can be punished severely at the higher education level (McLemee, 2004).

Audiovisual Intellectual Property and Piracy

In the past, one associated bootlegged films with poor sound quality, off-center images and the occasional silhouette of a fellow moviegoer coming in late. Today, movies still in theaters can be found and downloaded online. The quality is high and the cost is low. It is all a part of the relatively new wave of digital piracy that is making entertainment industry CEOs sweat. The potential loss of profit has demanded the involvement of the government, which has gone to great lengths to crack down on illegal downloading (Recording Industry Association of America, 2006).

The first online file-sharing program to receive significant attention from the Recording Industry Association of America (RIAA) was Napster in 1999

("Filesharing," 2005). Created by college dropout Shawn Fanning, it was a peer-to-peer program. Peer-to-peer file sharing services are especially fast and efficient for downloading audio and video files because they depend on the computing power of users, not the server. Multiple files can be downloaded from multiple locations without the large amount of traffic slowing the server down ("Peer-to-peer," 2007).

The legal battle that ensued between Napster and the RIAA resulted in Napster 2.0 and the current Napster To Go. Napster To Go offers over 3 million downloadable songs for a monthly rate ("Filesharing, 2005). The compromise was a victory for the RIAA. Grokster, a similar peer-to-peer program, was shut down after a Supreme Court decision in June. The case was reminiscent of *Sony Corporation of America v. Universal City Studios, Inc.,* in which the Supreme Court's decision ensured that VCRs, CD burners, iPods and all other technology capable of copyright infringement may be produced and sold by their respective companies without facing lawsuits. With the Grokster decision came not a negation of the former verdict but a new set of guidelines based on the idea of "inducement":

"[O]ne who distributes a device with the object of promoting its use to infringe copyright, as shown by clear expression or other affirmative steps taken to foster infringement, is liable for the resulting acts of infringement by third parties" [***MGM v. Grokster,*** *125 S. Ct. 2764 (U.S. Supreme Court, June 2005)*].

The recent Internet file-sharing cases have created a lot of grey area. For higher education institutions, this is an important issue because universities have been heavily targeted by the RIAA and the MPAA (Motion Picture Association of America). These organizations have found that a large percentage of illegal downloading takes place on college campuses. Schools with high-bandwidth networks can be especially popular targets. Lawsuits have been filed against hundreds of students for copyright infringement, and the pressure on colleges to police their own campuses is great (Brock and Young, 2006; Morris, 2006).

It is not hard to imagine that many university IT administrators are becoming frustrated and overwhelmed by the RIAA/MPAA's demands. The task of monitoring an entire campus network is no small one and is not necessarily associated with the normal responsibilities of university administration. There have even been complaints against the RIAA/MPAA and the overly extreme measures they've gone to, such as the prosecution of what in the past would have been deemed fair use (Read, 2006). Nonetheless, with the government behind them, these ultimatums must be honored to a reasonable degree, no matter how unclear "reasonable" may be. There are some basic steps, however, which many schools have taken with positive results.

Checklist: Steps to Avoid Liability for Illegal File Sharing

Step 1: Education. Many colleges have already introduced educational videos on copyright infringement, such as "Campus Downloading" from the RIAA. These videos have been made a part of freshman orientation (Read—"Critics," 2006). Other educational efforts include lectures and discussions on the subject. James Gibson of the University of Richmond is a law professor who went on a tour to various universities to talk with students about the ethical and legal sides of file sharing. He is a strong believer in education, saying, "What happens when a student goes home for Thanksgiving break? What happens when a student graduates? Unless they've internalized the reasons for copyright rules, there's no reason to think students will change their behavior" (Read—"Piracy," 2006).

Other educational measures that Gibson recommends include requiring students to pass a mandatory copyright law quiz, informing parents of the ramifications of Internet piracy, and reminding students regularly of these ramifications (Read—"Piracy," 2006). At the September 26, 2006 hearing on university efforts to combat Internet piracy before the Committee on Education and the Workforce, MPAA CEO Dan Glickman and RIAA President Cary Sherman mentioned these steps among others. They also emphasized the importance of instituting clear Internet policy in regard to downloading and file sharing. However, unlike Gibson, who believes in the education-only approach, Glickman and Sherman see such policy as effective only when strictly enforced with actual consequences (Glickman, 2006; Sherman, 2006).

Step 2: Technological Measures. The University of Florida and the University of California at Los Angeles have both developed software which recognizes and blocks the transfer of all files from unauthorized P2P programs. Students downloading such files are also warned that such activities are against university policy and, at UCLA, will have their Internet privileges suspended for a time. In both cases, only a fraction of these students become repeat offenders. The numbers are significantly lower among students starting at the universities with the software already in place (Read, 2004).

The benefit of installing such software for universities is a decrease in the number of complaints and subpoenas from the RIAA, MPAA and Congress. Both UCLA and U. of Florida have even been praised by the organizations for their efforts (Read, 2004). The downside of impartial blocking without regard to fair use remains an issue, but those who enjoy the legitimate benefits of P2P applications for scholarly purposes aren't necessarily out of luck. The RIAA and MPAA recognize these functions of P2P, although they maintain their stance that over 90% of non-pornographic use is against copyright law. With most universities still focusing on meeting anti-piracy standards, an efficient balance between both the enforcement of copyright law and the preservation of fair use doctrine is yet to be seen (Morris, 2006; Glickman, 2006).

Step 3: Legitimate Internet Services. Possibly the most important step for a university to take is offering students legal access to media files. With P2P services still available, it is hard to expect students to resist temptation when there is no alternative. Along with P2P blocking software, legitimate downloading programs are at the top of the RIAA/MPAA's list of demands of universities. Introducing a downloading service is recommended after piracy has been reduced through blocking and enforcement (Glickman, 2006). "Without first addressing the illicit P2P problem on campus, it is extremely difficult for legitimate services to take root" (Glickman, 2006).

The RIAA and the MPAA are happy about the increase in schools taking steps to prevent Internet piracy. As of October 2006, nearly 150 institutions offered legal downloading services and over 60 had installed blocking software (Read—"Entertainment," 2006). The most popular services have so far been Napster, Cdigx and Ruckus. The costs for students are little to nothing. ("Colleges," 2005). Ruckus, for example, is a free service for both students and the institution. "Ruckus pays for the music that we deliver out of our advertising proceeds," says Mike Bebel, president and CEO of Ruckus Network, Inc. (Bebel, 2006).

Music and movie downloading services are consumer entertainment products, which is one reason many institutions argue against an obligation to make them a standard part of their campuses. On the other hand, things like cable TV and the Internet are already commonplace in university dorm rooms. What are these online services but a new entertainment angle, offering universities an edge on the competition? David Donahue, associate dean for library and information services at Middlebury College, says, "I think we kid ourselves if we think we aren't providing 'entertainment services' already. The computer is the number one entertainment device for this age group. I don't think that it is a responsibility so much as a service enhancement" (Read and Young, 2006).

Step 4: Enforcement. Enforcement most often brings up the argument from universities that "we're not the music(/movie) industry's police" (Read—

"Entertainment," 2006). The question of responsibility is a difficult one. The RIAA and the MPAA consider Internet piracy to be no different than physical theft, and, based on the assumption that the average university would put a stop to on-campus distribution of stolen goods, the reaction against network distribution should be the same (Glickman, 2006).

An interesting new development has been the recent rise in closed network file sharing. P2P file sharing takes place over the public Internet. Because of the sheer number of users, it is impossible to catch every individual downloader, but the RIAA and the MPAA have been able to take action against many. A closed network entails an exchange of files without access to the Internet. Students can trade files among themselves using their campus Local Area Network (LAN). There is no chance of uncovering the illegal activity outside of the network. Of course, the number of users and the material to which they have access is limited. All the same, this was a point raised by the RIAA/MPAA in September to support their position (Glickman, 2006).

At the hearing in September, the RIAA/MPAA did not go as far as to suggest colleges be forced to enforce copyright law, but the topic has come up at Congress. Earlier in 2006, Congress discussed the possibility of ceasing federal funds for schools that fail to take certain steps against Internet piracy. The amendment was rejected, but one can see that the anti-piracy movement is not a temporary trend soon to fade away (Read—"Entertainment," 2006). As more schools comply with Congress and the RIAA/MPAA, other institutions will only be focused on more intensely. When it came to enforcement, the RIAA/MPAA recommended a "three strike" approach in September similar to other college disciplinary models already in use:

- First offense: Remove the offending user's computer from the network until the student complies with any obligations and understands the repercussions for further violations. Some schools require the student to talk to a University administrator before network access is restored.
- Second offense: Students lose network access for a certain period of time. Some schools are increasingly imposing monetary fines.
- Third offense: Students usually permanently lose all network access privileges and must report to the Dean of Students or Judicial Affairs for formal disciplinary proceedings. Some schools have suspended or even expelled students for third offenses (Glickman, 2006).

As of October 2006, the entertainment industry had notified 700 U.S. universities that the lawsuits against students would recommence in the near future.

The RIAA/MPAA planned to focus on students who continue to download illegally in spite of warnings and minor penalties. As in the past, universities will receive notice when their students are being sued, and those students will have the chance to settle their cases. The industry insists that every institution take action. While a legally binding requirement has yet to be created, universities choosing not to comply can at least expect to face many hours of aggravation (Read—"Entertainment," 2006). By July 2009, "Those in the know were widely reporting a figure just north of 30,000 cases—the RIAA never liked to provide exact numbers—but the music trade group stated in a recent court filing that the real number of people sued is only 18,000" (Anderson, 2009).

Impact of the Higher Education Opportunity Act

In what can only have been a lobbying triumph for the RIAA, the HEOA enshrines the main aims of the private download police. Under the act's "Peer-to-Peer (P2P) file sharing" provisions:

- Colleges and universities must remind their students annually that P2P file sharing could result in civil and criminal penalties; describe the potential penalties; present the school's policies, including disciplinary rules, with regard to P2P sharing activities.
- Schools also must certify to the U.S. Department of Education that they have developed plans to effectively battle unauthorized P2P activities among their student bodies; indicate what technology is being employed in their war on file sharing; so far as practical, offer their students legitimate alternatives to illegal file sharing.

Sources

Anderson, Nate. "Has RIAA Sued 18,000 people… or 35,000?" *Ars Technica,* July 8, 2009, http://arstechnica.com/tech-policy/news/2009/07/has-the-riaa-sued-18000-people-or-35000.ars.

Bebel, Mike. "Helping you legally download." *The Daily Princetonian,* December 15, 2006. Retrieved January 3, 2007 from http://www.dailyprincetonian.com/archives/2006/12/15/opinion/17024.shtml.

Bollag, Burton. "Don't Steal This Book." *The Chronicle of Higher Education,* April 2, 2004. Retrieved January 1, 2007 from http://chronicle.com/weekly/v50/i30/30a03801.htm.

Carlson, Scott, and Jeffrey R. Young. "Google Will Digitize and Search Millions of Books From 5 Top Research Libraries." *The Chronicle of Higher Education,* January 7, 2005. Retrieved January 2, 2007 from http://chronicle.com/weekly/v51/i18/18a03701.htm.

"Colleges with Legal Downloading Services (Sorted by Legal Service Used)." *The Chronicle of Higher Education,* January 28, 2005. Retrieved January 3, 2007 from http://chronicle.com/ weekly/v51/i21/5121downloadservice.htm.

Fischer, Karin. "Lengthy Fights Are Expected Over Measures on Accountability." *The Chronicle of Higher Education,* September 1, 2006. Retrieved January 1, 2007 from http://chronicle.com/ weekly/v53/i02/02a04202.htm.

Glickman, Dan. "Hearing on: The Internet and the College Campus: How the Entertainment Industry and Higher Education are Working to Combat Illegal Piracy." *Subcommittee on 21st Century Competitiveness, Committee on Education and the Workforce,* September 26, 2006. Retrieved January 2, 2007 from http://www.house.gov/ed_workforce/hearings/ 109th/21st/ piracy092606/glickman.htm.

Khanna, Garima. "CCT 260—*Intellectual Property*." *University of Toronto,* November 25, 2004. Retrieved January 1, 2007 from http://scholar.google.com/scholar?hl=en&lr=&q =cache:Yw1UaeAAQcoJ:home.utm.utoronto.ca/~gk/260essay1123.doc+RIAA+piracy+s tatistics.

"Filesharing—Napster—History." *M/Cyclopedia of New Media,* October 27, 2005. Retrieved January 2, 2007 from http://wiki.media-culture.org.au/index.php/Napster.

Foster, Andrea L. "Worried About Hackers? Buy Some Insurance." *The Chronicle of Higher Education,* October 13, 2006. Retrieved January 1, 2007 from http://chronicle.com/ weekly/v53/i08/08a04101.htm.

Gidjunis, Joseph. "Proposed Change in How Federal Government Collects Student Data Raises Privacy Concerns." *The Chronicle of Higher Education,* November 26, 2004. Retrieved December 31, 2006 from http://chronicle.com/weekly/v51/i14/14a02201.htm.

Glenn, David. "The Price of Plagiarism." *The Chronicle of Higher Education,* December 17, 2004. Retrieved January 2, 2007 from http://chronicle.com/weekly/v51/i17/ 17a01701.htm.

Lohmann, Fred von. "IAAL: What Peer-to-Peer Developers Need to Know about Copyright Law." *Electronic Frontier Foundation,* January, 2006. Retrieved January 2, 2007 from http://www.eff. org/IP/P2P/p2p_copyright_wp.php.

Kiernan, Vincent. "Show Your Hand, Not Your ID." *The Chronicle of Higher Education,* December 2, 2005. Retrieved January 1, 2007 from http://chronicle.com/weekly/v52/i15/ 15a02801.htm.

Lipka, Sara. "Officials Get Lecture on Privacy Laws." *The Chronicle of Higher Education,* March 24, 2006. Retrieved December 31, 2006 from http://chronicle.com/weekly/v52/ i29/29a04502.htm.

McLemee, Scott. "What Is Plagiarism?" *The Chronicle of Higher Education,* December 17, 2004. Retrieved January 1, 2007 from http://chronicle.com/weekly/v51/i17/ 17a00901.htm.

Monaghan, Peter. "Intellectual Property and the New Class Divisions." *The Chronicle of Higher Education,* January 28, 2005. Retrieved January 1, 2007 from http://chronicle. com/weekly/v51/i21/21a01402.htm.

Morris, Barry. "Preventing Piracy Not a Job for Academe." *The Chronicle of Higher Education,* November 24, 2006. Retrieved January 2, 2007 from http://chronicle.com/ weekly/v53/i14/ 14a05502.htm.

"Peer-to-peer." *Wikipedia,* January 1, 2007. Retrieved January 2, 2007 from http://en. wikipedia.org/wiki/Peer_to_peer.

Read, Brock. "Critics Say Recording-Industry Group's Antipiracy Video Distorts Facts." *The*

Chronicle of Higher Education, September 15, 2006. Retrieved January 2, 2007 from http:// chronicle.com/weekly/v53/i04/04a03801.htm.

Read, Brock. "Entertainment Officials Say Colleges Do Too Little to Fight Online Piracy." *The Chronicle of Higher Education,* October 13, 2006. Retrieved January 3, 2007 from http:// chronicle.com/weekly/v53/i08/08a04501.htm.

Read, Brock. "Lawmakers Laud Colleges for Efforts to Curb Illegal File Sharing." *The Chronicle of Higher Education,* October 15, 2004. Retrieved January 2, 2007 from http://chronicle.com/ weekly/v51/i08/08a03003.htm.

Read, Brock. "Piracy and Copyright: An Ethics Lesson." *The Chronicle of Higher Education,* May 19, 2006. Retrieved January 2, 2007 from http://chronicle.com/weekly/v52/i37/ 37a03301.htm.

Read, Brock, and Jeffrey R. Young. "Virtual Round Table: Campus Officials Discuss Online Music Services." *The Chronicle of Higher Education,* April 14, 2006. Retrieved January 2, 2007 from http://chronicle.com/weekly/v52/i32/32a03801.htm.

Recording Industry Association of America. Copyright 2003. Retrieved November 23, 2006 from http://www.riaa.com/default.asp.

Segal, Carolyn Foster. "Copy This." *The Chronicle of Higher Education,* September 15, 2006. Retrieved January 1, 2007 from http://chronicle.com/weekly/v53/i04/04b00501.htm.

Selingo, Jeffrey. "Education Dept. Gave Students' Records to FBI in Antiterrorist Operation." *The Chronicle of Higher Education,* September 8, 2006. Retrieved December 31, 2006 from http://chronicle.com/weekly/v53/i03/03a02301.htm.

Sherman, Cary. "Hearing on: The Internet and the College Campus: How the Entertainment Industry and Higher Education Are Working to Combat Illegal Piracy." *Subcommittee on 21st Century Competitiveness, Committee on Education and the Workforce,* September 26, 2006. Retrieved January 2, 2007 from http://www.house.gov/ed_workforce/hearings/ 109th/21st/ piracy092606/glickman.htm.

Smallwood, Scott. "The Fallout." *The Chronicle of Higher Education,* December 17, 2004. Retrieved January 2, 2007 from http://chronicle.com/weekly/v51/i17/17a01201.htm.

Stone, Elizabeth. "For Plagiarists, No Veil Over Past Mistakes." *The Chronicle of Higher Education,* June 17, 2005. Retrieved January 2, 2007 from http://chronicle.com/weekly/ v51/i41/ 41b00501.htm.

U.S. Department of Education. "Family Educational Rights and Privacy Act (FERPA)." *ED.gov*, February 17, 2005. Retrieved December 31, 2006 from http://www.ed.gov/ policy/gen/guid/fpco/ ferpa/ index.html.

Walters, Anne K. "Poll Finds Opposition to 'Unit Record' Plan." *The Chronicle of Higher Education,* July 21, 2006. Retrieved December 31, 2006 from http://chronicle.com/ weekly/v52/ i46/46a02102.htm.

Wasley, Paula. "*More Holes Than a Pound of Swiss Cheese*." *The Chronicle of Higher Education,* September 29, 2006. Retrieved January 1, 2007 from http://chronicle.com/ weekly/ v53/i06/06a03901.htm.

CHAPTER 10

International Students

Since the middle of the last century, students from around the globe have flocked to the United States, more than to any other nation, for their higher education. As with tourists and temporary workers, U.S. immigration policy prior to 9/11 was casual when it came to international students. Visa authorizations were issued on multi-copy forms, which foreigners took to U.S. embassies and consulates, where visas were issued with little or no fanfare. Armed with student visas, tens of thousands of aliens entered the U.S. annually, many to disappear into the general population. Their "host" colleges and universities had no obligation to report their failure to arrive as expected on campus.

As with so much else, the terrorist attacks of September 11, 2001, changed all that. Some of those who hijacked and drove airliners into the World Trade Center and the Pentagon held student visas. Some had actually studied at U.S. flight schools on those visas. In the aftermath of this worst attack on U.S. soil, the Immigration and Naturalization Service was split into a visa-processing service, the U.S. Citizenship and Immigration Service (USCIS) and, as an enforcement branch, the U.S. Immigration and Customs Enforcement (ICE) Agency. A new computer-based program is now the only way in which institutions of higher education can issue authorizations for student-visa applications.

Meanwhile, globalization has come to our campuses. Universities in England, Australia and elsewhere are competing—due to more relaxed visa standards, often very successfully—for significant shares of the students who once were an American monopoly.

Conversely, the U.S. is reaching out to the far corners of the globe, even to old enemies, for their best and brightest, as the following article illustrates:

Gazette Minute Interview

Joseph MacAde, Program Officer, Vietnam Education Foundation

Joe MacAde's 25 years of international experience include a six-year stint in Southeast Asia as a refugee-education program coordinator and, more recently, as the guiding hand behind accreditation efforts of a Korean-funded international university program on Long Island. His consulting work has taken him to China, Korea, Egypt, Qatar, Brazil, Australia and many European nations. GG's Jim Castagnera caught up with him at NAFSA's Annual Conference in Washington, D.C., two days before MacAde departed on a three-week visit to Hanoi, Ho Chi Minh City and Danang.

Will you briefly recount the history and mission of the Vietnam Education Foundation?

The South Vietnamese government borrowed quite a bit of money from the U.S. to keep the war going. Before the U.S. would agree to Vietnam fully joining the international community, this debt needed to be resolved. The idea of building up the science and technology capacity of the country by means of this debt originated with Senators John Kerry and John McCain. Our foundation sponsors Vietnamese doctoral students in the sciences. We push for placement in major universities, such as Harvard, Princeton and Yale. The new batch arriving for the fall, about 40 to 50, will bring the current total to about 270. Most are here for five-plus years under J-Visas. The Vietnamese government foots the bill.

The foundation's board includes the Secretaries of State, Treasury and Education, as well as several presidential appointees.

What does it mean to be the Program Officer for the foundation?

I handle the logistics involved in the fellowship program that I just described to you. I also run a Visiting Scholars Program. Academics come over here for short-term research and learning activities. We typically have eight to ten scholars placed with research universities for six months to a year each.

We've also recently begun to have Americans doing distance-learning courses for Vietnamese universities. This usually involves a visit by the American academic to the sponsoring university, which in turn gives the professor a letter of support.

On Saturday I leave for Vietnam to conduct three weeks of pre-departure orientation on American life and academic culture, the rules of the fellowship, and team building for the next 50 fellows.

What does the landscape of the higher education industry in Vietnam look like to you?

It's the typical profile of a third-world education system. Curriculum delivery is lecture based. Institutions lack facilities and other resources. Faculty are underpaid and overworked. No connection exists between research and the rest of the education enterprise. The system is centralized; all decisions must be run through the education ministry.

However, there is cause for optimism in a growing awareness of these problems. I detect an enthusiasm on the institutional level for changing things.

What opportunities, if any, are available to U.S. higher education providers in Vietnam?

There's a real interest in linkages at the institutional level. Such linkages, however, would likely be limited to science and engineering. And funding is always a big problem. Vietnamese higher education is resource-starved in every respect. But the economy is growing at the rate of eight percent annually, about the same rate as Ireland. And I find that more and more Vietnamese students are interested in studying abroad.

Do you find high interest among Vietnamese academics and doctoral students in working and studying in the United States?

Most definitely. Our foundation can only fund a small percentage. Vietnam has a much larger number who are technically qualified. The Ministry of Education and Training is creating a fund of its own to start up a parallel program to our own. Its ultimate goal is to turn out 20,000 Ph.D.s over an unspecified period of time. We're lending them technical assistance.

Source: The Greentree Gazette, *June 2008 (Reprinted with permission of* The Greentree Gazette: The Business Magazine for Higher Education.*)*

A Short Overview of International-Student Visas

The USCIS issues three general types of non-immigrant student visas:

1. The F-1 visa is issued to international (alien) students who typically intend to study in the United States for several years and earn a degree.
2. The J-1 visa is issued to international students who are exchange visitors to the United States, studying at an American university for a semester or two and then returning to their home institutions to complete their studies.

3. The M-1 visa is similar to the F-1 but is issued to international students studying at post-secondary trade schools.

All post-secondary schools that admit international students must track these students on the Student and Exchange Visitor Information System (SEVIS), a computer database accessible only to designated school officials and responsible officers. In the words of ICE, "Student and Exchange Visitor Program (SEVP) acts as the bridge for varied government organizations which have an interest in information on foreign students. SEVP uses web-based technology, the Student and Exchange Visitor Information System (SEVIS), to track and monitor schools and programs, students, exchange visitors and their dependents throughout the duration of approved participation within the U.S. education system.

"SEVP collects, maintains and provides the information so that only legitimate foreign students or exchange visitors gain entry to the United States. The result is an easily accessible information system that provides timely information to the Department of State, U.S. Customs and Border Protection, U.S. Citizenship and Immigration Services and U.S. Immigration and Customs Enforcement" (http://www.ice.gov/sevis/).

Under SEVIS, nonimmigrant aliens seeking to attend a U.S. college or university as a degree-seeking student must pass through a five-step process:

1. Apply to and be accepted by an SEVP-certified school.
    a. Be able to pay for the cost of schooling and living expenses while in the United States and furnish proof of sufficient funding to the school. Nonimmigrant students have limited work opportunities, so unless the school has promised an on-campus job, nonimmigrant students should not expect to work to pay expenses.
    b. Attend school full-time (except for Mexican or Canadian residents who live at home and commute to a United States school within 75 miles of the U.S. border).
2. When a school accepts a nonimmigrant applicant, it issues a Form I-20 for initial attendance. Prospective nonimmigrant students may apply to more than one SEVP-certified school but must choose one and use the Form I-20 from that school when applying for a visa.
3. After receiving the Form I-20, the prospective nonimmigrant student must pay the SEVIS I-901 fee at www.fmjfee.com.
4. The prospective nonimmigrant student must then obtain a student visa from an embassy or consulate abroad or, if from a visa exempt country such as Canada or Bermuda, apply for admittance at a U.S. POE.

5. After obtaining an F-1 or M-1 visa, the prospective student may apply for entry into the United States through a U.S. POE no more than 30 days prior to the program start date on the student's Form I-20.

Post-secondary schools covered by F-1 visas include:

1. Kindergarten through 12th grade (K–12) private schools
2. Public high schools (Nonimmigrant students are limited to a maximum of 12 months at a public high school.)
3. Colleges and universities to include 2-year community colleges
4. Fine arts schools and conservatories
5. Seminaries
6. Language training schools
7. Other schools that provide instruction in the liberal arts or the professions.

Schools coming under the M-1 visa are:

1. Community or junior colleges that offer technical or vocational instruction
2. Post-secondary vocational or business schools
3. Vocational or other nonacademic high schools

The visa applicant's proof of acceptance to one of these schools is the Form I-20, typically issued by the institution's admissions office via SEVIS. The Form I-20 is an official U.S. government form. A prospective nonimmigrant student must have a Form I-20 issued by an SEVP-certified school in order to become F-1 or M-1 student. Only an SEVP-certified school can issue a Form I-20 to students who have been accepted for enrollment. It acts as proof of acceptance and contains the information that is needed to pay the SEVIS I-901 fee, apply for a visa or change of status, and admission into the United States. The Form I-20 has the student's unique SEVIS identification (ID) number on the upper right hand side directly above the barcode. SEVIS ID numbers are an N followed by 9 digits.

If the student fails to report as anticipated on the issuing-institution's campus, the responsible institutional officer, such as the director of international programs or a member of the school's legal department, must cancel the I-20 on SEVIS, categorizing the applicant as a "No Show." The burden then falls on ICE to pursue the matter further if the agency so desires.

The International Student's Right to Work

The answer to whether or not an international student is permitted to work while studying in the U.S. is a qualified, and complicated, "yes." Some of the main circumstances under which such students may work are:

1. They may work on campus at the institutions they are attending, provided they have Social Security numbers.
2. After one academic year, F-1 students are allowed to apply for Optional Practical Training (OPT). OPT is available on a full- or part-time basis with third parties, including private corporations, provided the job relates to the course of study pursued by the student. Students typically reserve their period of OPT eligibility (one year full-time or two years part-time) for after graduation.
3. F-1 students also may work for third parties off campus if they can establish an economic hardship that did not exist at the time that they were issued visas to attend school in the United States.
4. After one academic year of university attendance in the United States, an F-1 student may be permitted to work for a third-party employer off campus under a university-sponsored program of Curricular Practical Training (CPT). Typically, a bona fide CPT program must be for college credit and be an integral part of the student's curricular requirements. Use of CPT typically does not prevent subsequent use of OPT.

The Social Security Administration requires that an F-1 visa holder applying for a Social Security number present the following four documents:

1. A valid passport;
2. A valid INS Form I-20, issued by the university he or she is attending;
3. A valid F-1 visa; and
4. An offer letter from the prospective employer (which usually will be the university the student is attending).

The administration is then required to provide the local office or sub-office of the U.S. ICE agency an opportunity to review and approve the application. This requirement sometimes can result in a lengthy delay in the issuance of the Social Security number, although most applications are successfully processed within a couple of weeks. Delays can sometimes be overcome by employer recourse to the office of the local congressional representative, which typically has a staffer charged with assisting constituents in such matters.

Should you wish to hire an F-1 student to work in your office, lab, or other facility, issues of which to be mindful include:

1. Number of hours they can work
2. Type of employment
3. Need to maintain F-1 status
4. Tax and social security implications
5. Reporting changes in employment and hours worked
6. Have a letter from each employer concerning the nature of the job and the work hours
7. Give the student a letter for social security purposes certifying that the job qualifies as on-campus employment and that the student is in F-1 status
8. Keep records on the student's employment in the school files; and
9. Terminate the student's SEVIS record if the student engages in any unauthorized employment or works hours in excess of those allowed

F-1 students can begin working as much as 30 days before the start of classes. They should have permission from the university before they begin work.

If an F-1 student finishes one program (such as a bachelor's degree) and starts another program at the same campus, he or she may continue on-campus employment as long as he or she plans to enroll for the next term.

The job has to be physically located on the school's campus or off-campus at the site of an educationally affiliated organization. Employment on-campus has to be for the school or for a company that contracts with the school to serve students directly. For example, if your school contracts with a food service company, F-1 students can work for the company at school facilities. However, they cannot work for the same company at any off-campus locations.

F-1 students cannot work for a company:

1. Contracting with the school for something other than student services, or
2. does not contract with the school, even if they are physically located on school property.

For example, they cannot work for a construction company even if the job site is on the campus. However, F-1 students can work for an educationally affiliated company, such as a school bookstore, even if it is not located on campus.

In the case of off-campus locations, educational affiliation means the location is associated with the school's established curriculum or related to contractually funded research projects at the post-graduate level.

Concerning Optional Practical Training after graduation, most international students seeking OPT employment opportunities with American corporations have hopes of remaining in the United States and in the employ of these American companies. The one-year OPT commitment enables the employer to ascertain the alien worker's suitability for long-term employment with the firm. In instances where the relationship has proved promising, the company's human resources department can sponsor the alien worker for an H-1B visa. The H-1B visa, if obtained, is good for three years with the possibility of a single renewal period of like length. From there, the alien employee typically will apply for permanent residency (i.e., a "green card").

International students holding F-1 visas must meet the following requirements to qualify for OPT:

1. The student can apply no sooner than one academic year after commencing his or her U.S. studies.
2. The student must apply before completing those studies.
3. The application is sent to the USCIS service center with jurisdiction over the university where the student is studying.
4. The applicant need not have a specific job offer in hand at the time of application, but must express intent to pursue a job opportunity related to his or her course of study.
5. The applicant must have maintained unbroken F-1 status while in the United States and must hold a valid passport and INS Form I-20.

Other International Student Visa Categories

The M-1 category, as noted above, includes students in vocational or other nonacademic programs, other than language training. Approval for the attendance of nonacademic students may be solicited by a community college or junior college that provides vocational or technical training and awards associate degrees; a vocational high school; a trade school; or a school of nonacademic training other than language training. Employment rules under this category are approximately the same as under the F-1 visa.

The J-1 (Exchange Visitor) visa is a different animal altogether. While USCIS oversees the F-1 and M-1 visa process, the U.S. Department of State deals directly with J-1 visas, which cover a wide range of nonimmigrant aliens, including visiting scholars and professors, as well as exchange students, who typically are in the U.S. for a semester or an academic year at most. Often these exchange students come to our institutions under one-for-one exchange agreements under which we reciprocate by sending our American students to study abroad at the sister institution.

The State Department's Exchange Visitor Program is carried out under the provisions of the Mutual Educational and Cultural Exchange Act of 1961, as amended. The purpose of the Act is to increase mutual understanding between the people of the United States and the people of other countries by means of educational and cultural exchanges. International educational and cultural exchanges are one of the most effective means of developing lasting and meaningful relationships. They provide an extremely valuable opportunity to experience the United States and the American way of life. Foreign nationals come to the United States to participate in a wide variety of educational and cultural exchange programs.

The Exchange Visitor Program is administered by the Office of Exchange Coordination and Designation in the Bureau of Educational and Cultural Affairs. The Internet website for information on the Exchange Visitor Program is http://exchanges.state.gov/education/jexchanges. At the conclusion of their program Exchange Visitor program participants are expected to return to their home countries to utilize the experience and skills they have acquired while in the United States.

In carrying out the responsibilities of the Exchange Visitor Program, the Department designates public and private entities to act as exchange sponsors. Designated sponsoring organizations facilitate the entry of foreign nationals into the United States as exchange visitors to complete the objectives of one of the exchange visitor program categories, which are:

- Au pair
- Camp Counselor
- Student, college/university
- Student, secondary
- Government Visitor
- International Visitor (reserved for U.S. Department of State use)
- Alien physician
- Professor
- Research Scholar
- Short-term Scholar

- Specialist
- Summer work/travel
- Teacher Trainee

http://travel.state.gov/visa/temp/types/types_1267.html

Curricular Practical Training

In addition to on-campus employment while studying and Optional Practical Training with third parties, typically following graduation, international students may qualify for curricular practical training related directly to their course of study at their institution. Deans, chairs and faculty are well-advised to be cognizant of CPT, since it is a highly versatile means of legally permitting your international students to work while pursuing their studies. CPT can be authorized by their institution without recourse to USCIS or ICE permission and is available for internships, co-op programs and independent study experiences with a wide range of third-party employers, with or without monetary compensation.

Checklist: Requirements of Curricular Practical Training in F-1 or J-1 Status

Definition: Curricular practical training (CPT) is employment pursuant to an internship requirement or internship elective which is an integral part of the established curriculum of your school, which will be counted towards completion of the student's degree. Co-operative programs and independent study experiences may also qualify.

Eligibility to engage in CPT: Your student must be a degree candidate who has been in lawful status for at least one academic year (albeit under some circumstances a student may be able to engage in CPT even at the very start of her/his educational experience at your institution). S/he must have been offered a specific training opportunity that must fall into one of the following categories:

- to satisfy an **internship requirement** expected of all students in your program and necessary for completion of her/his degree.
- to satisfy an **internship elective** which counts towards completion of her/his degree. The internship elective must be listed in your school's bulletin and must state in the official course description that it is specifically designed to allow students enrolled in the course to engage in off-campus internships.

- the internship may be done to engage in research necessary and integral to the completion of the doctoral dissertation.

Restrictions: US Citizenship and Immigration Services (USCIS) regulations do not place an absolute limit on the amount of CPT a student may undertake. However, if the student engages in one year or more of full-time CPT, s/he will lose her/his eligibility to engage in Optional Practical Training (see above).

CPT is always part-time during the academic year (maximum of 20 hrs/wk while classes are in session) unless the student is engaged in doctoral dissertation research. CPT may be full time during the vacation periods.

The student's SEVIS record must be updated by your institution's international student office and a SEVIS I-20 (for F-1s) or DS-2019 (for J-1s) must be reprinted and signed by both the student and the school's designated official or responsible officer, indicating the approved employment. The endorsement shold indicate the precise details of the authorized training, including the name and location of the employer, the specific dates of the training period, and whether it is full-time or part-time.

Procedure: Have your student submit the following documentation to your institution's international student office as early as 90 days but no less than 10 days before you wish her/him to begin employment. If the internship is tied to a specific course, your student must register for the course and must apply for curricular practical training during the normal registration period.

1. Current and all previously issued I-20s
2. Passport and I-94 card
3. Letter from the faculty member who will supervise the internship stating:
   a. the specific internship opportunity
   b. the specific degree requirement or elective course that it satisfies
   c. the minimum requirements to complete the internship
   d. a reasonable period of time needed to complete the internship (e.g., satisfying the requirements of a 1 semester, 3 credit course would normally be done in 1 semester or less)
   e. if CPT is for dissertation research, the student's adviser should provide a detailed letter stating the dissertation topic, what research will be carried out, and why it is necessary for the dissertation.
4. Letter offering internship employment from the employer including the following information:
   a. beginning and ending dates of employment
   b. how many hours s/he will work weekly

c. a description of the duties in sufficient detail to clearly show them as appropriate to meeting the requirements for your degree program
d. location where the employment will take place

The International Programs Office staff will:

1. Review your student's application for eligibility
2. If s/he is eligible, update her/his SEVIS record, print a SEVIS I-20 or DS-2019 form indicating the approved employment and give it to student. (The employer will need to see this authorization to put your student on the payroll.)

Special Considerations:

1. The student is still required to register for full-time course work, if authorized for curricular practical training during the academic year.
2. Curricular practical training that exceeds 20 hours per week constitutes full-time CPT. Students who engage in full-time CPT for twelve months or more prior to graduation will not be eligible for optional practical training (before or after completion of studies).

Undocumented Aliens Attending Our Institutions

All of the above sections deal with non-immigrant aliens who come to the U.S. annually in the tens of thousands to legally attend our institutions of higher learning on visas issued by the U.S. State Department following appropriate SEVIS authorization by the admitting institutions. Other students, illegal aliens, also attend our post-secondary schools. These are frequently the children of illegal parents, many of whom have been in the U.S. for decades. The U.S. Supreme Court ruled in two seminal cases that such children are entitled to a public K–12 education at the taxpayers' expense. ***Plyler v. Doe**, 457 U.S. 202, (U.S. Supreme Court, 1982)* (Texas statute which denies free education to alien children violates Equal Protection Clause) and ***Toll v. Moreno**, 458 U.S. 1, 102 S.Ct. 2977, 73 L.Ed.2d 563 (1982)* (University of Maryland's policy of denying treaty organization aliens the opportunity to pay reduced, in-state tuition constituted a violation of the Supremacy Clause).

In reaction to these decisions, the U.S. Congress passed statutes aimed at preventing these same students from advancing to public institutions of higher education. Meanwhile some seven states passed statutes of their own, permitting in-state tuition advantages for their illegal-alien residents. Out-of-state students, subject to much higher rates for attending the same state schools, have been challenging these statutes ever since. One example of such a challenge is ***Day v. Sebelius,*** *376 F.Supp.2d 1022 (U.S. District Court, D. Kansas, 2005).*

Facts. The Kansas legislature passed the instant statute in 2004. The court is aware of at least seven other states that have passed legislation to provide in-state tuition rates to illegal aliens: California, Illinois, New York, Oklahoma, Texas, Utah and Washington. The legislature of Maryland passed legislation to allow in-state tuition to illegal aliens, but the legislation was vetoed by the governor. At least two states have specifically passed statutes that do not allow illegal aliens to gain resident tuition status: Alaska and Mississippi. The legislature of Virginia passed legislation prohibiting illegal aliens from receiving resident tuition, but the legislation was vetoed by the governor. The court believed this was the first case to challenge the type of legislation passed by Kansas.

The plaintiffs' complaint consisted of seven claims for relief. The court shall spend some time analyzing the claims made by the plaintiffs due to arguments that have been made about the confusing nature of the claims.

In Count 1, which is entitled "Violation of 8 U.S.C. § 1621," plaintiffs contended that K.S.A. 76-731a violates 8 U.S.C. § 1621. According to the plaintiffs, § 1621 prohibits any state from offering any post-secondary educational benefit, including in-state tuition, to illegal aliens. The plaintiffs further allege that K.S.A. 76-731a does not meet the statutory loophole set forth in 8 U.S.C. § 1621(d), which allows states under certain circumstances to provide eligibility for illegal aliens to state benefits, because it does not contain the express statutory language required by federal law.

In Count 2, which is entitled "Violation of 8 U.S.C. § 1623," plaintiffs asserted that K.S.A. 76-731a violates 8 U.S.C. § 1623(a). According to the plaintiffs, § 1623 prohibits any state from providing any postsecondary education benefit, including in-state tuition, to an illegal alien unless a United States citizen is eligible for the same benefit. The plaintiffs further assert that § 1623 eliminated the application of 8 U.S.C. § 1621(d).

In Count 3, which is entitled "Violation of Regulations Governing Alien Students," plaintiffs contended that K.S.A. 76-731a violates the comprehensive regulatory scheme enacted by the federal government to govern the admission of nonimmigrant aliens to the United States for the purpose of enrolling them as students at post-secondary educational institutions. They specifically point to the Student and Exchange Visitor Information System (SEVIS), a comprehensive computerized system designed to track international students and exchange students. Plaintiffs contend that K.S.A. 76-731a frustrates this federal purpose by allowing aliens to illegally pose as students at Kansas institutions of higher education while remaining outside the SEVIS registration system.

In Count 4, which is entitled "Preemption," plaintiffs claimed that K.S.A. 76-731a is preempted by the federal regulation of immigration. Plaintiffs suggest that Congress clearly intended to "occupy the field" in the area of regulating the provision of public benefits to aliens without a lawful immigration status. They assert: "The power to regulate immigration is unquestionably an exclusively federal power, and any state statute that regulates immigration is unconstitutional and therefore proscribed.... States can neither add to nor take from conditions lawfully imposed upon the admission or residence of aliens in the United States.... [K.S.A. 76-731a] is preempted because it is impossible for a person who is an illegal alien or otherwise present in the United States to both receive postsecondary education under [K.S.A. 76-731a], and to comply with federal immigration law."

In Count 5, which is entitled "Creation of Residence Status Contrary to Federal Law," plaintiffs alleged that K.S.A. 76-731a creates residence status for illegal aliens contrary to federal law. Plaintiffs assert: "Congress has created a legal disability under federal law that renders illegal aliens incapable of claiming bona fide legal domicile in Kansas, notwithstanding the fact of physical presence or a subjective 'intent' to remain indefinitely in the jurisdiction." They further allege: "None of the members of the class of alien beneficiaries of [K.S.A. 76-731a] who are illegal aliens possesses federal authorization to remain in the United States for even the shortest period of time, and therefore cannot, as a matter of law acquire or possess the requisite intent to be a legal resident or domiciliary of Kansas. Kansas may not deem such non-citizens to possess such intent, nor alternatively waive such intent by exercise of its legislative powers." By doing so, plaintiffs argue that K.S.A. 76-731a violates the comprehensive scheme established by federal law for aliens.

In Count 6, which is entitled "Infringement Upon Exclusive Federal Powers," plaintiffs asserted that K.S.A. 76-731a impermissibly infringes on constitutional powers reserved to the federal government. They contend that the challenged Kansas law violates Congress' power over the regulation of interstate commerce and foreign affairs.

Finally, in Count 7, which is entitled "Violation of Equal Protection Clause of U.S. Constitution," plaintiffs contended that K.S.A. 76-731a violates the Equal Protection Clause of the United States Constitution. Plaintiffs assert that equal protection is denied them based upon the following argument: "Illegal aliens have been deemed by Defendants to be Kansas residents for the express purpose of affording such aliens state postsecondary education benefits to which they are not entitled under federal law. Defendants have further denied nonresident U.S. citizens Plaintiffs the identical postsecondary education benefits to which they are expressly entitled by federal law."

Holding. The district judge held:

1. interveners were not required to show standing;
2. governor did not meet *Ex parte Young* exception to Eleventh Amendment immunity;
3. students and parents lacked standing under federal statute prohibiting states from offering in-state tuition to illegal aliens;
4. no private right of action was created by statute limiting illegal aliens' eligibility for higher education benefits based on residence; and
5. students and parents lacked standing under Equal Protection Clause.

The net effect of this decision was to leave the underlying substantive issues for other battles on other days. These battles continue down to the present in a number of states, as the following recent article attests:

An Illegal Advantage

(National Review Online) This column was written by Peter Kirsanow.

May 10, 2006

Should it be cheaper for illegal immigrants to attend U.S. colleges than for U.S. citizens? Yes, according to lawmakers in California, Illinois, Kansas, New Mexico, New York, Oklahoma, Texas, Utah, and Washington.

Illegal immigrants residing in these states are eligible for in-state tuition rates at state colleges and universities. These rates afford a significant cost savings compared to the tuition rates charged to out-of-state students. On average, an out-of-state student pays three times as much in tuition costs as an in-state student to attend the same school. In some states this means an out-of-state student pays as much as $40,000 more over four years.

The primary rationale behind in-state tuition rates is that students whose parents have been paying taxes into the state treasury for the past 18 years—thereby providing revenue for that state's colleges—should receive a break over out-of-state students. But the rationale has scant applicability to students who are illegal immigrants. Most states require illegal immigrants to reside in the state for only 2–3 years before becoming eligible for in-state tuition rates.

In-state tuition for illegals is an increasingly popular concept among lawmakers. At least 20 additional states are considering legislation that would grant in-state tuition rates to illegal immigrants. Some U.S. senators are even considering extending in-state tuition for illegals to all fifty states. They're doing so in clear defiance of congressional intent to make such preferential treatment unlawful. Title 8 Section 1623 of the U.S. Code (part of the Illegal Immigration Reform Act of 1996) provides in pertinent part:

> Limitations on eligibility for preferential treatment of aliens not lawfully present on the basis of residence for higher education benefits
>
> a) Notwithstanding any other provision of law, an alien who is not lawfully present in the United States shall not be eligible on the basis of residence within a State (or political subdivision) for any postsecondary education benefit unless a citizen or national of the United States is eligible for such benefit without regard to whether the citizen or national is such a resident.

This Act isn't much of a deterrent. It's estimated that the majority of the 125,000 illegal immigrants attending the nation's colleges and universities are eligible for in-state tuition rates.

In-state tuition breaks may not be the only benefit granted to some illegal immigrants seeking to attend U.S. colleges and universities. Thomas Sowell, Roger Clegg, and Ed Blum have noted recently that illegal immigrants who are members of preferred minority groups are entitled to other benefits unavailable to the vast majority of American citizens.

At some schools, preferred-minority applicants are up to 100 times more likely to be admitted than similarly situated non-preferred (i.e., Asian or white) comparatives. Affirmative-action programs at some schools are structured in a way that, beyond a minimum level of qualification, preferred-minority applicants are virtually guaranteed admission. Consider the advantage to the illegal immigrant residing in, say, Illinois, who is also a preferred minority: If he applies to an Illinois state school with a typical affirmative-action program, he's dozens of times more likely to be admitted over a more qualified Asian or white U.S. citizen and will pay tens of thousands less for tuition than a U.S. citizen from outside the state. As the comedian Yakov Smirnoff—a legal immigrant—might say, "What a country!"

The preferences don't end at the undergrad level. Illegal immigrants from preferred-minority groups are also preferred in law-school admissions. In fact, the American Bar Association recently sought to compel law schools to grant preferences to certain minorities; schools that failed to do so could lose their ABA accreditation. No law school is excused—even if it's located in a state that has outlawed preferences (e.g., post-Prop. 209 California). Interpretation 211-1 of ABA Standard 211 makes the following breathtaking admonition: "The requirements of a constitutional provision or statute that purports to prohibit consideration of gender, race, ethnicity, or national origin in admissions or employment decisions is not a justification for a school's non-compliance with Standard 211 (mandating diversity)." In other words, "diversity" trumps the law, so schools better engage in preferences, or else.

In the next several months, high-school seniors will begin the college-application process in earnest. Many will soon discover that having a 4.0 GPA, 1500 SATs, and a dazzling extracurricular list means less than having the proper ethnicity. And being a U.S. citizen means nothing at all.

INDEX

EDUCATION MANAGEMENT EM:C3 Contexts, Constituents + Communities

M. Christopher Brown II, *General Editor*

The *Education Management: Contexts, Constituents, and Communities* ($EM:c^3$) series includes the best scholarship on the varied dynamics of educational leadership, management, and administration across the educational continuum. In order to disseminate ideas and strategies useful for schools, colleges, and the education community, each book investigates critical topics missing from the extant literature and engages one or more theoretical perspectives. This series bridges the gaps between the traditional management research, practical approaches to academic administration, and the fluid nature of organizational realities.

Additionally, the $EM:c^3$ series endeavors to provide meaningful guidance on continuing challenges to the effective and efficient management of educational contexts. Volumes in the series foreground important policy/praxis issues, developing professional trends, and the concerns of educational constituencies. The aim is to generate a corpus of scholarship that discusses the unique nature of education in the academic and social spaces of all school types (e.g., public, private, charter, parochial) and university types (e.g., public, private, historically black, tribal institutions, community colleges).

The $EM:c^3$ series offers thoughtful research presentations from leading experts in the fields of educational administration, higher education, organizational behavior, public administration, and related academic concentrations. Contributions represent research on the United States as well as other countries by comparison, address issues related to leadership at all levels of the educational system, and are written in a style accessible to scholars, educational practitioners and policymakers throughout the world.

For further information about the series and submitting manuscripts, please contact:

Dr. M. Christopher Brown II | *em_bookseries@yahoo.com*

To order other books in this series, please contact our Customer Service Department at:

(800) 770-LANG (within the U.S.)
(212) 647-7706 (outside the U.S.)
(212) 647-7707 FAX

Or browse online by series at www.peterlang.com

FSC
www.fsc.org
MIX
Papier | Fördert
gute Waldnutzung
FSC® C083411

Kolibri 360 GmbH
Ferdinand-Jühlke-Straße 7
99095 Erfurt, Deutschland
produktsicherheit@kolibri360.de